QUESNAY'S *TABLEAU ÉCONOMIQUE*

Franciscus Quesnay

in utriusque Medicinæ Magister, Academiæ Reg. Chirurg. Paris. Secretarius, et Scholæ Profess. Regius.

FRANÇOIS QUESNAY

QUESNAY'S
TABLEAU ÉCONOMIQUE

EDITED, WITH NEW MATERIAL,
TRANSLATIONS AND NOTES BY

MARGUERITE KUCZYNSKI
&
RONALD L. MEEK

LONDON: MACMILLAN
NEW YORK: AUGUSTUS M. KELLEY PUBLISHERS
FOR THE ROYAL ECONOMIC SOCIETY
AND THE AMERICAN ECONOMIC ASSOCIATION

English edition first published 1972 by
THE MACMILLAN PRESS LTD
London and Basingstoke
Associated companies in Toronto Dublin
Melbourne Johannesburg and Madras

and

AUGUSTUS M. KELLEY, PUBLISHERS
305 Allwood Road, Clifton, New Jersey 07012

Enlarged and revised with added material from the German edition
Tableau Économique, von François Quesnay
herausgegeben, eingeleitet und übersetzt
von Marguerite Kuczynski
Akademie-Verlag, Berlin, 1965

SBN 333 11173 7

ISBN 0 678 07007 5

Library of Congress catalog card no. 78–157694

Printed in Great Britain by
ROBERT MACLEHOSE AND CO LTD
The University Press, Glasgow

Contents

List of Abbreviations

A.D.H.   The continuation of the sixth part of Mirabeau's *L'Ami des Hommes*, entitled *Tableau Œconomique avec ses Explications*. The 12mo edition dated 1760 is used in the present volume.

B.E.A.   The edition of Quesnay's *Tableau Économique* published by the British Economic Association (London, 1894).

I.N.E.D.   The two-volume work entitled *François Quesnay et la Physiocratie* published by the Institut National d'Études Démographiques (Paris, 1958).

Meek   *The Economics of Physiocracy*, by Ronald L. Meek (London, 1962).

Oncken   *Oeuvres Économiques et Philosophiques de F. Quesnay*, edited by August Oncken (Paris, 1888).

P.R.   *Philosophie Rurale*, by Mirabeau (with the collaboration of Quesnay). The three-volume 12mo edition allegedly published '*à Amsterdam, chez les Libraires Associés*' and dated 1763 is used in the present volume.

I

The 1758-9 'Editions' of the
TABLEAU ÉCONOMIQUE

The 1758-9 'Editions' of the Tableau Économique

The story of the birth of Quesnay's *Tableau Économique* and its subsequent development has taken more than two centuries to unfold, and may not even yet have reached its conclusion. Discussion of the issues involved has been bedevilled, right from the beginning, by three factors in particular.

First, the *Tableau Économique* was basically a conceptual construct, or theoretical tool, rather than a specific 'picture' or 'table' whose origin can be precisely dated. The fundamental concept was first adumbrated in descriptive form,[1] and then in various diagrammatic forms ranging from the early 'zigzag' to the final *'formule'*. The contexts in which it appeared, the documents which appeared in association with it, the practical uses to which it was put, and the names of the authors putting it to these uses all varied greatly from time to time. This means that 'the' *Tableau Économique*, and the history of its different 'editions', are very difficult to pin down.

Second, the *Tableau Économique* had both a public history and a private history. By the time that the Physiocrats began to write the story of the development of their movement, at the end of the 1760s, the *Tableau Économique* was known to the majority of rank-and-file Physiocrats only in the forms which it had assumed in the sixth part of Mirabeau's *Friend of Mankind* (1760), in *Rural Philosophy* (1763), and in Quesnay's *Analysis* (1766), *First Economic Problem* (1766) and *Second Economic Problem* (1767). A privileged few, however, were aware of the fact that some time before these works appeared, at the end of the 1750s, Quesnay had produced, and distributed to a limited number of people, a small volume in which a diagrammatic formulation of the *Tableau Économique* had appeared in association with certain other documents. This volume gradually became known among the Physiocrats as the 'first edition' of the *Tableau Économique*, and the latter's history was traced from it. It was not until many years later, in the 1890s, that historians became aware of the fact that this so-called 'first edition' had actually been preceded by two earlier versions, the circulation of which had been extremely limited but which Quesnay himself had nevertheless referred to as the first and second editions. It has taken three-quarters of a century for modern historians to reconcile the private history of the *Tableau Économique*,

[1] Cf. Meek, p. 269.

thus suddenly revealed to them, with its public history as recorded by their Physiocratic predecessors.

Third, the problem of the origin and development of the *Tableau Économique* for some strange reason seems from the very beginning to have attracted historians who were accident-prone. It is really a quite extraordinary story: serious misapprehensions and confusions, passed on from generation to generation, about the dates of publication and contents of the different 'editions'; the incorrect identification of newly discovered documents; the disappearance for more than half a century after its discovery of a crucially important work of Quesnay's, and so on. Clearly there is a hoodoo on research in this field, which must necessarily inhibit any scholars who venture into it from claiming that their own conclusions are definitive.

With this in mind, let us begin the story where it was begun by Du Pont de Nemours in the well-known short history of the early days of the Physiocratic movement which he wrote for *Éphémérides* in 1769. The starting-point is that small volume of Quesnay's mentioned above, which was at this time beginning to become known to the Physiocrats as the 'first edition' of the *Tableau Économique*. It was, Du Pont said, 'a very fine edition in quarto, which was produced in the palace of Versailles'. It consisted, according to Du Pont's account, of a *tableau*, accompanied by an 'Explanation', and a set of 'general "Maxims" of economic government which were annexed to it under the title "Extract from the Royal Economic Maxims of M. de Sully"'. The 'Explanation' included 'an example of the method of calculating the sum total of a nation's wealth when one knows the *net product* of its territory and the state of its cultivation'. The 'Maxims', which were said to be twenty-four in number, revealed 'the conditions necessary to maintain the state of prosperity in a nation', and were accompanied by 'most interesting notes, written with the greatest nobility'. Copies of this edition, Du Pont said, were no longer to be found, 'except in the hands of the individuals to whom they were given'.[1]

So far as the date of publication of this so-called 'first edition' was concerned, Du Pont said that he did not know whether it should properly be 1758 or 1759. 'The author,' he wrote, 'who as is well known is M. Quesnay, has told us several times that this edition appeared in the month of December 1758 and that he is sure about the date. The *Friend of Mankind*, his first disciple, who was then intimately associated with him, assures us that it did

[1] Oncken, pp. 155–6. Du Pont's description of this 'edition' tallies with that of Forbonnais, *Principes et Observations Œconomiques* (1767) I 161–2. (The relevant passage is translated in Meek, p. 272, fn. 1.) Forbonnais added that the notes, of which there were a 'large number', were 'of greater length than the text'.

not appear until 1759, and not even at the beginning of that year, and that he too is sure about the date.'[1] It did not escape Du Pont's notice that this discrepancy was a somewhat curious one, since the episode was relatively recent and the two men most concerned were still alive and had both been directly consulted. But beyond delivering a philosophical aside about how difficult it was to write history, Du Pont himself did not pursue the matter further. Let us too leave it over, at any rate for the time being.

There is no doubt that Du Pont himself believed that the particular 'edition' which he was describing was actually the true 'first edition', and that he had no knowledge of the two earlier versions which, as we now know, had in fact preceded it.[2] There is also no doubt that he was assuming in his account that the majority of his readers would be unaware, if not of the existence of the 'edition', at any rate of its detailed contents. This 'edition', after all, had apparently been sent by Quesnay to only a small number of persons,[3] and such interest as may have existed for a time in this very scarce volume must soon have given way to a much wider and more intense interest in the lengthy developments and applications of the *Tableau Économique* which were published by Mirabeau in the sixth part of his *Friend of Mankind*, and by Mirabeau and Quesnay in their *Rural Philosophy*.

It was in fact by reference to later works such as these, rather than to the so-called 'first edition' described by Du Pont, that Quesnay's *Tableau Économique* was judged by contemporaries. For this 'edition', as we now know, was not reprinted, and although much of its textual content found its way into the later works, it underwent a radical transformation in the process. Even in the sixth part of *Friend of Mankind*, which appeared very soon after the so-called 'first edition', the separate identity of the original 'Explanation' and the notes to the 'Maxims' was completely lost, and a number of new attempts were made to use the technical apparatus of the *tableau* as a tool for the analysis of policy problems. In *Rural Philosophy* the 'zigzag' form of the *tableau* receded into the background, use being mainly made of a simplified '*précis*'; and in Quesnay's *Analysis* a new '*formule*' was developed which he also employed in his *First Economic Problem* and *Second Economic Problem*. The 'Maxims', it is true, were reprinted without very many alterations in the sixth part of *Friend of Mankind* and in *Rural Philosophy*, but no notes at all

[1] Oncken, p. 155.

[2] In this connection it is interesting to note that Du Pont refers to the sixth part of *L'Ami des Hommes* as containing 'the second explanation of the *Tableau Économique*' (Oncken, p. 157). Cf. also ibid., pp. 125–6 fn.

[3] This is implied in the statement by Du Pont quoted above, specifically stated by Forbonnais (loc. cit.), and confirmed by the fact that only one copy appears to be extant today.

were attached to them. The nearest that the Physiocrats came to a reversion to the so-called 'first edition' was in *Physiocratie* (1767), the famous collection of basic Physiocratic writings edited by Du Pont.[1] In this volume there was included a set of 'General Maxims of Economic Government', with extensive notes, which we now know to have been a revised version of the maxims and notes of the so-called 'first edition'. But even here the revisions were substantial. Du Pont presented the 'General Maxims' as a work in its own right, expunging almost all traces of its former connection with the *Tableau Économique* and making quite important changes in its form and content (including the addition of six new maxims).[2] The *Tableau Économique* as such was represented in *Physiocratie* only by Quesnay's *Analysis, First Economic Problem* and *Second Economic Problem.* And later editors of Physiocratic writings like Daire and Oncken followed much the same procedure when selecting the material to be included in their editions.

No doubt some of these later editors would have been only too happy to include in their collections the so-called 'first edition' described by Du Pont if a copy of it had been available to them. But no copy could at that time in fact be found; and Oncken, referring to this 'edition' in the collection of Quesnay's *Works* which he published in 1888, went so far as to say that 'in the earliest form in which it appeared, the *Tableau Économique* is lost to posterity'.[3] This fact did not worry Oncken unduly, however, since he assumed, correctly enough, that the first version of the *Tableau Économique* which had been *intended for the public* was not the so-called 'first edition' described by Du Pont at all, but rather the version included by Mirabeau in the sixth part of *Friend of Mankind.*[4] It should also be added here that at that time no evidence was available to scholars to suggest that the so-called 'first edition' might in actual fact have been preceded by earlier versions which could also lay claim to the title of 'edition'.

It was precisely this latter possibility, however, which was opened up in the late 1880s by the discovery, among the Mirabeau papers in the Archives Nationales at Paris, of a rich hoard of documents relating to the early days of Physiocracy,[5] including a number pertaining directly to the *Tableau Économique.* Among the latter were two vitally important letters from

---

[1] References to *Physiocratie* in the present volume are to the first part of that work allegedly published '*à Leyde, et . . . à Paris, chez Merlin*' and dated 1768. On the question of the actual date of publication of this edition, see the article by Luigi Einaudi in I.N.E.D., vol. I.

[2] See below, pp. 10–11.

[3] Oncken, p. 125 fn. Cf. ibid., p. 306 fn.   [4] Ibid., p. 125 fn.

[5] The manuscripts were catalogued by Weulersse in *Les Manuscrits Économiques de François Quesnay et du Marquis de Mirabeau aux Archives Nationales* (Paris, 1910).

Quesnay to Mirabeau, both undated.[1] In the first of these, Quesnay announced that he had 'tried to construct a fundamental *Tableau* of the economic order' which he was sending to Mirabeau for his perusal. In the second, he told Mirabeau (*inter alia*) that he would be sending him an enlarged and amended 'second edition' of this *Tableau,* which would start off with a revenue base of 600 livres instead of 400, and of which he was having three copies printed 'so as to get a better idea of things'. These letters afforded an obvious guideline in the new stage of the inquiry which had now been opened up, and prompted scholars to try to identify, among the Mirabeau papers, documents which corresponded to Quesnay's descriptions of the two versions – or 'editions', as he himself called them – of the 'fundamental *Tableau*' which he had sent to Mirabeau.

So far as the earlier of these two versions was concerned, only one document which fulfilled the requirement that the assumed revenue base should be 400 livres could be found in the papers. This was a manuscript document in Quesnay's handwriting, taking up three pages in all and written on a single sheet of paper folded in two, which consisted of one page containing a *tableau,* base 400, with explanatory comments, followed by two pages of notes headed 'Remarks on the Variations in the Distribution of the Annual Revenue of a Nation' and consisting essentially of twenty-two maxims. This document, after a certain interval of time, came to be generally accepted by commentators as a rough draft of the *true* 'first edition' of the *Tableau Économique,* i.e. the one sent by Quesnay to Mirabeau under cover of the earlier of the two letters mentioned in the last paragraph.

Is this document in fact a rough draft of the true 'first edition', *or is it the true 'first edition' itself?* The great majority of commentators have unreservedly accepted the first of these two hypotheses. The document, they have suggested, was merely a *'brouillon'*[2] or an *'épreuve manuscrite'*[3] of a printed version which has since been lost, and it was a copy of this printed version which Quesnay sent to Mirabeau under cover of the first of the two letters. But there is nothing in either of these letters which states, or which can be taken unambiguously to imply, that the first of the documents sent to Mirabeau was actually printed;[4] and the evidence as a whole seems to me to

---

[1] Published by Stephan Bauer in the *Economic Journal,* v (1895) 20–1. English translations will be found in Meek, pp. 108, 115–17.

[2] Weulersse, *Manuscrits Économiques,* p. 12.   [3] I.N.E.D., I 260, 308.

[4] The gently ironical tone of the particular context in which Quesnay speaks of his 'second edition' should be carefully noted here, as well as his statement that he is having three copies of it printed 'so as to get a better idea of things' (*'pour voir cela plus au clair'*). There is nothing here to imply that the earlier version of the *Tableau* had also been printed; indeed, if anything the implication would seem to be to the contrary.

be equally consistent with the second hypothesis. It does seem at least possible that the true 'first edition' which Quesnay sent to Mirabeau was not printed at all, but consisted simply of the manuscript document about which we are speaking, a copy of which Quesnay would no doubt have retained for his own use. How, on the first hypothesis, can one plausibly account for the presence of this document among Mirabeau's papers?[1]

Discussion of this problem, and of other questions relating to the true 'first edition,' was for many years complicated by a curious confusion between this very early 'edition' and the later and quite different one which Du Pont knew and described as the 'first edition'. The original source of this confusion, I believe, was Weulersse's influential account of the true 'first edition', in which, after describing the content of the manuscript document, he stated that it was produced in 'a very fine edition in quarto', of which only a small number of copies was run off.[2] The evidence which Weulersse produced to support this assertion, however, was simply the statement by Du Pont quoted on p. x above – a statement which could not possibly have referred to the *true* 'first edition'. By no stretch of the imagination could an 'edition' which Du Pont had described as consisting of a *tableau*, an 'Explanation' and a set of twenty-four maxims (with very extensive notes) under the title 'Extract from the Royal Economic Maxims of M. de Sully' be identified with an 'edition' consisting simply of a *tableau* and twenty-two maxims (without any notes) under the title 'Remarks on the Variations in the Distribution of the Annual Revenue of a Nation'.

The same confusion has also affected discussion of the date of publication of the true 'first edition'. Weulersse stated categorically that this was December 1758,[3] but the evidence which he cited to support this assertion consisted of a number of contemporary statements (collected together by Oncken)[4] which were clearly intended to relate not to the true 'first edition' at all but to the later 'very fine edition in quarto' described by Du Pont. Oddly enough, however, these contemporary statements were themselves in all probability mistaken; the errors cancel one another out; and the date of December 1758 is fairly certainly the correct one. A few words about this

[1] In my *Economics of Physiocracy*, pp. 271–2, I myself assumed without question that the 'first edition' was printed. I feel now that I should have been rather more agnostic on this point.

[2] Weulersse, *Le Mouvement Physiocratique en France de 1756 à 1770* (Paris, 1910) I 66 (last sentence, and fn. 6). Cf. the reference to a 'magnificent' edition in I.N.E.D., I 260.

[3] Weulersse, *Le Mouvement Physiocratique*, I 62 (second paragraph, and fn. 5). Cf. Weulersse's *Manuscrits Économiques*, p. 12, where the date of the first of the two letters from Quesnay to Mirabeau is given as 'December 1758 or the beginning of 1759'.

[4] Oncken, pp. 125–6 fn.

curious accident may be in order before we proceed from the true 'first edition' to the 'second edition'.

In a statement in *Éphémérides* in February 1768, the date of the appearance of the 'very fine edition in quarto' was given unequivocally as 1758.[1] Evidently this date was by then coming to be generally accepted as the correct one: in the previous year Baudeau, writing in the same journal about the same 'magnificent edition', had stated that it was produced in 'the months of November and December 1758';[2] and Du Pont himself, in a foreword to the 'General Maxims' in *Physiocratie*, had stated that these 'Maxims' and their notes had been printed for the first time, together with the *Tableau Économique*, in the month of December 1758.[3] In 1769, however, judging from his statement quoted on pp. x–xi above, Du Pont was beginning to have doubts about this date: Quesnay, he said, had told him several times that it was December 1758, but Mirabeau had claimed that it was actually some time fairly well on in 1759.

The most plausible explanation of this crucial discrepancy is that Quesnay and Mirabeau were thinking of two quite different 'editions'.[4] What *may* have happened is something like this. Quesnay, whenever his disciples asked him when the *Tableau Économique* had first appeared, always thought of the true 'first edition' which he had sent to Mirabeau under cover of his first letter, and answered 'December 1758'. Du Pont, Baudeau and others, knowing nothing of any 'editions' earlier than the 'very fine edition in quarto' which they accepted as the first, mistakenly ascribed this date of December 1758 to the latter. Du Pont, however, when he began writing his short history of the early days of the Physiocratic movement, came to feel that he ought properly to check up on this, and asked Mirabeau to confirm that the date of publication of the 'very fine edition in quarto' was in fact December

---

[1] Ibid.

[2] Ibid., p. 126 fn.

[3] *Physiocratie*, p. 104. What Du Pont says here and on the previous page of the introductory note seems to imply that all thirty of the 'Maximes Générales' which follow were included in the so-called 'first edition' allegedly published in December 1758. In actual fact the 'edition' to which Du Pont was referring included only twenty-four maxims, six new ones having been added in *Physiocratie* (very probably by Du Pont himself). In the slightly later statement quoted on p. x above, however, Du Pont gave the number of maxims in the so-called 'first edition' correctly as twenty-four. But in the remarkable chapters of his *Mémoires* which he wrote in 1792 when in hiding at Cormeilles (without access to his books and papers), he reverted to the notion that the 'first edition' had contained the thirty maxims of *Physiocratie*. See *L'Enfance et la Jeunesse de Du Pont de Nemours* (Paris, 1906) pp. 231–3. The account which Du Pont gives here of the printing of the 'first edition' is quite fascinating, although it would hardly be wise to place too much reliance on it.

[4] Cf. Schelle's explanation in *Revue d'Économie Politique*, XIX (Paris, 1905) 502.

1758. Mirabeau replied that it was actually 1759, and not even the beginning of that year. Subsequent commentators like Oncken, feeling no doubt that Quesnay, as the author of the work in question, was more likely to be right about its date of publication than Mirabeau, and being just as unaware as Du Pont of the existence of any earlier versions, accepted December 1758 as the date of publication of the 'first edition'.[1] Then, somewhat later, when the true 'first edition' came to light, this date of December 1758 was illogically ascribed to it by Weulersse and others – illogically, but probably correctly, since Weulersse's mistake in effect cancelled out the contemporary one.

In the story as we have so far developed it, the 'very fine edition in quarto' has been known to scholars only through Du Pont's description of it: no actual copy of the book has as yet physically manifested itself. Before we describe the odd way in which one in fact did so, in 1905, something must be said about the 'second edition' of the *Tableau Économique* which Quesnay seems to have produced fairly soon after the true 'first edition'. In relation to this 'second edition', counsel was for many years confused by the publication in 1894 by the British Economic Association (the forerunner of the Royal Economic Society) of a collection of documents from the Archives Nationales which was described by Bauer as 'the original edition of the Tableau',[2] by Schelle (in effect) as a proof of the 'second edition',[3] and in the British Economic Association's volume itself as the 'second printed edition'.[4] The implication of at any rate the two latter descriptions was that this collection in fact constituted that revised 'second edition' with a revenue base of 600 instead of 400 which had been announced in Quesnay's second letter to Mirabeau. The collection consists of (*a*) an engraved *tableau*, base 600, with a reference at the foot to an 'explanation on the following page'; (*b*) a printed 'Explanation of the *Tableau Économique*', with corrections in Quesnay's hand; (*c*) a printed *tableau*, base 600, with explanatory comments on either side; and (*d*) a printed set of twenty-three maxims, with a number of notes, under the title 'Extract from the Royal Economic Maxims of M. de Sully'.

It was perhaps natural enough, in the first flush of discovery of these important documents in the Archives, that this collection should have been identified with the 'second edition' referred to in Quesnay's letter to Mirabeau. But there are certain curious features of the collection taken as a whole which ought surely to have suggested even then that it was most unlikely

[1] Oncken, p. 126 fn.
[2] *Economic Journal*, v (1895) 16.
[3] Schelle, *Revue d'Économie Politique*, XIX (1905) 496–7, 501–2.
[4] B.E.A., p. vii.

that these four documents together should ever have constituted a single 'edition', whether the 'second' or any other. It was true that documents (*a*) and (*b*) were probably intended to be linked with one another, as was shown by the words 'see the explanation on the following page' at the foot of (*a*). It was also true that documents (*c*) and (*d*) were probably intended to be linked with one another, since the two folded sheets of which they consisted were lightly sewn together inside a third sheet which served as a cover. But the evidence was all against (*a*) and (*b*) having been intended to be linked with (*c*) and (*d*).[1] The most reasonable hypothesis – which eventually came to be accepted – was in fact that (*c*) and (*d*) together constituted the true 'second edition',[2] and that documents (*a*) and (*b*) were of a rather later date. But if this was so, for what purpose were documents (*a*) and (*b*) prepared?

This mystery was partially solved by Schelle's discovery, in 1905, of a copy of nothing less than that 'very fine edition in quarto' described by Du Pont in 1769. It then came to be realised that it was actually for this 'edition' – which had been called by Du Pont the 'first' but was now rechristened by Schelle the 'third' – that documents (*a*) and (*b*) in the British Economic Association's collection had been prepared, and that they did not form part of the true 'second edition' at all.[3] Unfortunately, however, Schelle's description of the 'third edition' in the article which he wrote about it[4] was grossly inadequate. All one could really gather from it was that this 'edition' apparently consisted of (i) an engraved *tableau*, base 600, probably identical with or at least similar to (*a*) in the British Economic Association's collection; (ii) an 'Explanation', probably identical with (*b*) in the British Economic Association's collection, but with the corrections made by Quesnay 'included in the text or put in a printed erratum'; and (iii) a set of maxims, similar in form to (*d*) in the British Economic Association's collection, but comprising twenty-four maxims instead of twenty-three and accompanied by 'considerably augmented' notes which were said to be very much the same as those to the 'General Maxims' of *Physiocratie*. The maxims of the 'third edition' were reproduced in full in Schelle's article (not always quite accurately, as now appears), but only a few paragraphs from the notes were included. Taking the article as a whole, its inaccuracies, vaguenesses and omissions were such as to make it of relatively limited use to scholars.

[1] See Meek, pp. 270–1, fn. 8.

[2] Another copy of this 'second edition', with a number of corrections in Quesnay's hand, is to be found in the Bibliothèque Nationale.

[3] Schelle himself, oddly enough, did not specifically draw the latter conclusion.

[4] *Revue d'Économique Politique*, XIX (1905) 490–521. See also Schelle's book *Le Docteur Quesnay, Chirurgien, Médecin de Madame de Pompadour et de Louis XV, Physiocrate* (Paris, 1907) chap. 4.

This would not have mattered so much, of course, if the copy of the 'third edition' which Schelle had discovered had been made available to scholars. But Schelle said nothing whatever in his article about how and where he came across it, or where it was now to be found; and various attempts made after his death to rediscover it were unsuccessful. This meant that later scholars wishing to trace the development of Quesnay's thought from the 'first edition' through to the 'third edition' were obliged to try to reconstruct the latter on the basis of Schelle's meagre description, and this sometimes led them into error. The appearance in 1958 of a new edition of Quesnay's works, published by the Institut National d'Études Démographiques, raised hopes in the hearts of some scholars, since the 'third edition' was therein referred to and described in terms which, it seemed, could hardly have been employed unless their authors had actually had access to a copy of the 'third edition' itself.[1] Upon inquiry, however, it was ascertained that these descriptions too were merely reconstructions, based not on the 'third edition' but on Schelle's article about it. And there the matter rested until 1965, when Mrs Kuczynski, having rediscovered the 'third edition' by means of a very brilliant piece of detective work, published it in a German edition in the G.D.R.[2]

Now that a copy of the 'third edition' has at last become available to scholars, as the result of Mrs Kuczynski's efforts, the documentation of the history of the *Tableau Économique* is probably just about as complete as it is ever likely to be.[3] So far as the 1758–9 'editions' are concerned, we can summarise their basic features as follows with a fair degree of confidence:

1. The 'first edition', which was probably produced by Quesnay round about December 1758, either consisted of, or was similar in form and content to, the manuscript document in the Archives Nationales which contains a *tableau* with a base of 400 followed by a set of twenty-two 'Remarks'. It may well have been printed, but no direct evidence of this exists and no printed copy has yet been discovered. There is no evidence that it was given to any-one except Mirabeau, so that 'edition' is clearly something of a courtesy title.

2. The 'second edition', which was probably produced two or three months later, consisted of documents (*c*) and (*d*) in the British Economic Association's collection, i.e. a *tableau* with a base of 600 followed by a set of

---

[1] I.N.E.D., i 261, 308; ii 668, 675 fn.

[2] *Tableau Économique, von François Quesnay* [*3. Ausgabe, 1759*], herausgegeben, eingeleitet und übersetzt von Marguerite Kuczynski (Akademie-Verlag, Berlin, 1965).

[3] Saying which, of course, a printed copy of the true 'first edition', together with a completely new 'edition' coming between the 'second' and the 'third', will forthwith be discovered!

twenty-three maxims under the title 'Extract from the Royal Economic Maxims of M. de Sully'. Quesnay stated that he was going to have three copies of this 'second edition' printed, and two printed copies have since been discovered. Once again there is no evidence that it was given to anyone except Mirabeau.

3. The 'third edition', which was probably produced somewhat later in 1759, consisted of a *tableau* with a base of 600 livres (identical with document (*a*) in the British Economic Association's collection), followed by an 'Explanation' (a revised version of document (*b*) in the British Economic Association's collection) and a set of twenty-four maxims, with very extensive notes, under the title 'Extract from the Royal Economic Maxims of M. de Sully'. It was produced in the form of 'a very fine edition in quarto'. Contemporary evidence suggests that more copies were printed of this 'third edition' than of the 'second edition', and that they were sent by Quesnay to certain selected individuals. They do not seem to have been sold to the public, however, and only one copy of the 'edition' has since been discovered.

The main purpose of the present volume is to make this 'third edition', known until 1965 only through Schelle's inadequate description and curtailed reproduction, available to English-speaking readers. The central item in the volume is therefore a facsimile reproduction of the copy of the 'third edition' rediscovered by Mrs Kuczynski, interleaved with an English translation of it and preceded by an introductory essay in which Mrs Kuczynski herself describes the fascinating process of its rediscovery.

But the present volume also has another purpose – to facilitate a textual comparison of the 'third edition' with the two 'editions' which preceded it and with certain related works which followed it. In the 'Notes' to the 'third edition', which are based quite largely upon those in Mrs Kuczynski's German edition, textual comparisons are made with the explanation of the *Tableau* published by Mirabeau in the sixth part of *Friend of Mankind*, with *Rural Philosophy*, with the 'General Maxims' of *Physiocratie* and with the maxims of the 'second edition'. In Appendix A will be found a facsimile of the *tableau* of the 'first edition', the French text of the 'Remarks', and an English translation of the whole document. In Appendix B will be found facsimiles of the two extant copies of the *tableau* of the 'second edition', a facsimile of the 'Maxims', and an English translation of the whole document.

A word of explanation is necessary in relation to the English translations, which are in the same style and use the same terminology as those in my *Economics of Physiocracy*. The point here is that the latter book already includes a translation of the 'Explanation' reproduced in the British Economic

Association's edition, of which the 'Explanation' of the 'third edition' is a revised version; and it also includes a translation of the 'General Maxims' of *Physiocratie*, in which a great deal of the actual text of the maxims and notes of the 'third edition' was in one way or another reproduced by Du Pont. In translating the 'third edition' for the present volume, therefore, it seemed more sensible to work forward from the former translation and backward from the latter, rather than to start the job all over again, and this is the procedure which has in fact been adopted. The translations of the 'first edition' and the 'second edition' which appear in the two appendices are also taken more or less directly from the translations of these documents in *Economics of Physiocracy*. I am extremely grateful to Messrs Allen and Unwin for permitting me to reproduce these translations, together with a few passages from my introduction and essays, in the present volume.[1]

The editors are also very grateful to the Eleutherian Mills Historical Library, Delaware, for allowing the reproduction of its copy of the 'third edition', and for other invaluable assistance; to the Akademie-Verlag, Berlin, for permission to reproduce certain material from Mrs Kuczynski's 1965 edition of the *Tableau Économique*; and to the Bibliothèque Nationale and Archives Nationales, Paris, for permission to reproduce a number of documents made available by them.

University of Leicester   RONALD L. MEEK

[1] See Meek, pp. 39–42, for a brief statement of the working rules adopted in making the translations.

Postscript

After this book had gone to press, I received a communication from Signor Vieri Becagli (Via Ricasoli 7, 50122 Florence, Italy) to the effect that he had just purchased from an antiquarian bookseller in Florence what appeared to be a copy of the 'third edition' of Quesnay's *Tableau Économique*. Sr Becagli was good enough to send me a xerox copy of his discovery, a study of which revealed that it was indeed another copy of the 'third edition', textually and typographically identical (excepting for a few misplaced letters) with the copy found by Mrs Kuczynski in the Eleutherian Mills Historical Library and reproduced in facsimile below in the present volume.

According to Sr Becagli's account, the booklet was originally bound together with others into a miscellany which was purchased in Rome many years ago by the Florence bookseller's father (now deceased) from another bookseller, unknown to the son. When Sr Becagli bought the booklet it had been separated from the other books by the Florence bookseller himself, and the latter had also destroyed the original binding of the miscellany (apparently a hard-paper one) because it appeared to be of no value and bore no *ex libris*. The bookseller assured Sr Becagli that the binding was datable, the relevant period being from the end of the eighteenth to the first twenty or thirty years of the nineteenth century. The booklet itself had no cover, beginning with the *tableau* glued to the other pages.

Sr Becagli had been able to trace two booklets which originally belonged to the same miscellany, namely Cajetani Fortes, *Sacri Consistorii Advocati Dissertatio de Jure Usucapiendi* (Rome, 1752); and Francesco Milizia, *Economia Pubblica* (Rome, 1798).

An article by Sr Becagli describing his discovery has now been published, under the title 'A proposito della prima edizione del "Tableau Économique"', in *Studi storici*, XII (1971), no 1, gennaio–marzo, pp. 171–81.

R. L. M.

2

The Search for the 'Third Edition' of the
TABLEAU ÉCONOMIQUE

2

The Search for the 'Third Edition' of the Tableau Économique*

Quesnay's original *Tableau Économique*[1] is known to have been a most elusive document, right from the time of its inception. This fact and the consequent theorising and surmising, often enough at cross-purposes, have been amply described by Professor Meek in the preceding essay.

To my way of thinking – and on this point I differ from Professor Meek – the *Tableau* in one important respect still *is* an elusive document, since a copy of a printed 'first edition' remains to be discovered. It seems to me to be rather *hors de caractère et hors de circonstance* to assume that Quesnay would have been satisfied with a 'mere' handwritten draft. It should be remembered that roughly at the same time Quesnay was having opuscules printed that were not only briefer than the *Tableau* draft[2] but were hardly as important in themselves as the *Tableau*, and certainly not as important in Quesnay's own estimation.[3] Furthermore, let us recall briefly the very haphazard succession of some of the incidents: the 'second edition', its existence hitherto utterly unsuspected, turns up (together with an earlier draft) 130 years after having left the printing press, the case for its final

---

* I am most grateful to the editors of the *Economic Review* (Tokyo), who have permitted me to make use, for this introductory essay, of my article 'Auf der Suche nach der "3. Ausgabe" des Tableau Économique von François Quesnay', which was published in their journal in July 1966.

[1] 'Original' is here taken to refer to the *Tableau* in the zigzag form used in the first three 'editions' and followed therein by remarks of varying length, the whole having been worked out and (anonymously) presented by Quesnay alone.

[2] *Aspect de la Psychologie* (1760) 4 pp. in-4to, reprinted in I.N.E.D., II 683–5; *Observations sur la Conservation de la Vue* (1760) 2 pp. in-4to, listed in I.N.E.D., I 308.

[3] Cf. his letter to Forbonnais, dated [14] Sep 1758 (I.N.E.D., I 298–300). Having explained the fundamental assumptions made, obviously for the construction of the *Tableau*, in order to arrive at 'the real knowledge of the process of circulation', Quesnay presents his departure from all previously used methods as 'a new course upon which no one has so far entered and which nevertheless constitutes the only road to follow in the search for the truth. . . . It is a beautiful piece of work which, up to the present, has not been made known to mankind.' (Translated from the original letter kindly put at my disposal by its owner, Mme Pierre Quesnay.)

differentiation from later materials being put forward as late as 1960;[1] the 'third edition' turns up, so to speak, in bits and pieces – unrecognised for what it was in 1889 and 1894, insufficiently identified in 1905, and made fully known as much as threescore years later. The very zigzag course of these discoveries of the 'zigzag' lets one hope that it may yet end with the link missing between the 1758 draft and the printed 'second edition' being found – that fortune may yet smile upon some searcher whose curiosity is persistent enough.

Perhaps I should explain that when I started some years ago on a German edition of the economic writings of Quesnay I included in my working programme the search for the lost 'editions'. Although I regarded this task as secondary in importance to the other matters that required attention, it was always present in my mind. Naturally, far more than to a totally unknown printed copy linked to the 1758 draft, it applied to the 'third edition', with its odd history of alternating losses and discoveries, (partial) publication and republication, crowned by its appearance in the latest bibliographical survey of Quesnay's work,[2] only to be followed by the news that it could no longer be found.[3] Under the circumstances, it did not seem too rash to assume that it might be found once more, and it was certainly tempting to devote thought and time to that end.

As is well known, neither in 1905 nor in any of his later writings did Schelle give any indication of the place where he had found what he called the 'third' or 'definitive' edition of the *Tableau*, nor did he publish any information about the circumstances which had led to its discovery. It would seem that he did not even speak about this matter to his colleagues in the academic world, for the President of the French Academy of Moral and Political Sciences, in a memorial address delivered after Schelle's death, made no express reference at all to what ought to have been considered as something of an event, and cut down to a dry little sentence his reference to this part of Schelle's work: 'To the celebrated Quesnay, he devoted a number of articles in the *Revue d'Économie Politique*.'[4] And in a much more detailed memorial address which Charles Rist delivered at a meeting of the same

[1] R. L. Meek, 'The Interpretation of the "Tableau Économique" ', *Economica* (Nov 1960) p. 322, fn. 3.

[2] I.N.E.D., 1 308. Leaving aside re-editions and translations of individual writings on matters medical, economic and mathematical, the bibliographer had carefully indicated one locus for all but five of the publications listed.

[3] Meek, loc. cit. Cf. also *Catalogue de la Bibliothèque du Professeur Gustave Schelle à l'Université d'Otaru* (Otaru, 1962) introduction, p. 2.

[4] E. de Seillière, *Allocution prononcée . . . à l'Occasion de la Mort de M. Gustave Schelle, le 2 juillet 1927*, published by the Académie des Sciences Morales et Politiques, Paris.

Academy,[1] he too made no mention of this particular discovery of Schelle's – quite deliberately, one may assume, since he was on the other hand at pains to pay his respects to Schelle for ferreting out an unknown *mémoire* by Gournay on the Lyons silk industry.[2] If Schelle had expected the official academic world to be transported with joy over his *Tableau* discovery, to the extent of being willing to overlook the fact that it was apparently supposed to take the report on faith without any opportunity for verification being given, he was to be disillusioned very soon, for the echo was practically nil. He was even to find that Georges Weulersse, the foremost authority on the Physiocrats, while mentioning the 'third edition' in two footnotes in his standard study of the movement,[3] preferred to quote the new maxim (added in the 'third edition' to the former set of twenty-three maxims) on the basis of the text published by Mirabeau in *Friend of Mankind*,[4] rather than on the basis of the newly discovered source.

Schelle's failure to comply with such elementary rules of scholarship seemed odd; indeed, considering the very impersonal nature of the material published it seemed inexplicable, and raised the question of whether there had been some extraneous influence. Omitting all reference to the where-abouts of the revised and enlarged 'Livret du Ménage',[5] Schelle had written: 'Fortune, which smiles upon the curious, has placed a copy of this edition in our hands',[6] and a little later he spoke, just as secretively, of 'the copy which we have before our eyes'.[7]

Now, had he not expressed himself rather similarly upon an earlier occasion – upon an occasion, moreover, when he was also dealing with materials of importance and quite unknown before he made use of them? When he wrote his study *Du Pont de Nemours et l'École Physiocratique* in 1888 he had indeed told the reader: 'In particular we have had, in our very hands, copies of more than three hundred letters which Turgot addressed to [Du Pont].'[8]

[1] 'Notice sur la Vie et les Travaux de M. Gustave Schelle (1845–1927)', in *Séances et Travaux de l'Académie des Sciences Morales et Politiques, Compte-rendus*, XCII (Paris, 1932) 162–89.

[2] Published in *Journal des Économistes* (Paris, Jan 1901) pp. 86–9.

[3] *Le Mouvement Physiocratique en France de 1756 à 1770* (Paris, 1910) I 69, fn. 4; 71, fn. 2.

[4] Ibid., I 71, fn. 1. It may also be pointed out that Weulersse did not list the 'third edition' in his exceedingly detailed bibliography.

[5] In actual fact, Quesnay had applied the term 'Little Book of Household Accounts' to the 'second edition' of the *Tableau*. Cf. the translation of his letter to Mirabeau in Meek, p. 117.

[6] 'Quesnay et le Tableau Économique', in *Revue d'Économie Politique*, XIX (Paris, 1905) 490.

[7] *Le Docteur Quesnay, Chirurgien, Médecin de Madame de Pompadour et de Louis XV, Physiocrate* (Paris, 1907) p. 261.   [8] Loc. cit., p. 5.

The similarity of the expressions used and of the pattern of reticence shown at times as widely apart as 1888 and 1907 – was this accidental, or did it stem from one and the same cause? Was the parallel too slender a straw in the wind to justify going the way it pointed? Surely if Schelle, who for a number of years was attached to the bibliophiles' journal *L'Intermédiaire des Chercheurs et Curieux*, had found that 'fortune . . . smiles upon the curious', he meant not only an unflagging curiosity, and a curiosity which would not disdain the smallest pointers, but also above all a readiness to re-examine a question despite the fact that it, or aspects germane to it, had to all appearances been settled long ago – about three-quarters of a century ago in our case, and upon good authority.[1] But with the passing of time changes might have been wrought: it was necessary to make sure, to reopen the question.

I re-read the biography written by Schelle in 1888, and I read it with rather different eyes. In particular, I noted the following points:

1. Du Pont's descendants had in their possession 'documents of exceptional value'.[2]

2. Most of Du Pont's descendants were living 'in America'.[3] The 'precious papers', then, were in all probability being conserved in that country. There was no indication of a definite locality, but seeing that the Du Ponts are not exactly unknown, that was hardly necessary.

3. Schelle had been given the opportunity of 'examining the most interesting' of the documents, among them the letters from Turgot already mentioned; but, as he explained, 'we have not been permitted to publish that correspondence . . . we were able to quote some passages from those letters and to borrow numerous bits of information from them'.[4]

4. No names were given of any of the descendants with whom Schelle had been in contact. He rendered his thanks in one instance to 'one of the great-grandsons of Du Pont de Nemours' – there have been quite a number of them – who had provided him with 'a wealth of details',[5]

---

[1] Soon after the publication of *Du Pont de Nemours et l'École Physiocratique*, Stephan Bauer, through Schelle as his intermediary, had raised the question whether the Du Pont family had in its possession any manuscripts by Quesnay left by their forbear among his papers (see Bauer, 'Zur Entstehung der Physiokratie auf Grund ungedruckter Schriften François Quesnays', in *Jahrbücher für Nationalökonomie und Statistik*, XXI (Jena, Aug 1890) 115, fn. 3). A few years later August Oncken, perhaps merely on the basis of Bauer's statement, expressed himself similarly in 'Entstehen und Werden der Physiokratischen Theorie', in *Vierteljahrsschrift für Staats- und Volkswirtschaft, Litteratur und Geschichte der Staatswissenschaften aller Länder*, V (Leipzig, 1896) 145.

[2] Loc. cit., p. 5.

[3] Ibid., chap. xvi (about Du Pont's descendants), pp. 391–8.

[4] Ibid., pp. 5–6.   [5] Ibid., p. 6, fn. 2.

and in another instance to 'the only daughter of Irénée still alive, for her graciously kind letters'.[1] The policy of leaving the family members protected by a degree of anonymity such as only they themselves could have insisted upon is even expressly stated: 'we wish to speak only of those who are dead'.[2]

5. There was no mention made of any printed writings of Quesnay's which Du Pont, the disciple, might in one way or another have acquired. On the other hand Schelle had quite obviously not only handled 'papers', but had also examined and listed a great many books and pamphlets in order to compile the extensive bibliography of Du Pont's own writings.[3]

Such were the gleanings from the account written in 1888.

Turning now to 1909, we find Schelle being allowed to say in his introduction to *La Vie de Turgot* that he had before his eyes the letters from Turgot to Du Pont used twenty years ago 'thanks to the affectionate goodwill of Colonel Du Pont de Nemours, U.S. Senator';[4] and at about the same time he is at long last permitted to begin preparations for the actual publication of a great many of these most important letters.[5]

This was indeed a change – with the reason for the change almost certainly to be found on the Du Pont side of the story.

Apart from general facts known to any student of the antecedents of American monopoly capitalism, I felt it might help to know what kind of persons had made up the generation of Du Ponts with whom Schelle had dealings in the 1880s and later. Had they had any personal interests which might have a bearing on these matters? And had these interests developed in a way such as would explain the change observed in Schelle's handling of the papers in the family's keeping?

There had been such an interest, and there had been such a development coinciding with my critical times: members of the Du Pont family had begun to edit some of the family papers which were of a biographical nature.

---

[1] Ibid., p. 395. (Not only is one left in the dark as to which one of three possible Irénées is meant, but *The National Cyclopaedia of American Biography* gives only the sons who have sprung from Du Pont marriages, and attaches no importance to the listing of daughters. Cf. p. xxiv, fn. 4.)

[2] *Du Pont de Nemours et l'École Physiocratique,* loc. cit.

[3] Ibid., pp. 399–432.   [4] Loc. cit., pp. 9–10.

[5] Cf. *Œuvres de Turgot et Documents le concernant, avec Biographie et Notes* (Paris, 1913–23). Having originally begun work on the edition with the nephew and heir of Turgot, Étienne Dubois de l'Estang (1851–1909), Schelle soon had to carry on by himself because death robbed him of his collaborator (ibid., préface, I (i)–ii).

In 1904, the 'great-grandson' to whom Schelle had rendered thanks in 1888,[1] H[enry]-A[lgernon] Du Pont de Nemours (1838–1925), affixed his signature to his preface to the memoirs written down by his forbear, the Physiocrat, for the latter's children in September 1792, at the very beginning of the *Convention* to which he stood in opposition. The great-grandson had these memoirs printed in 1906 in Paris 'for the family',[2] without allowing them to be circulated through commercial channels. In 1902 he had withdrawn from active business affairs, concerned mainly with railways, in order to pursue literary and historical interests.[3]

Another member of the family began working on the *Souvenirs de Madame V[ictor] M[arie] Du Pont de Nemours*, wife of the Physiocrat's eldest son. In 1908 she had them printed in Wilmington, Delaware, in an edition limited to fifty copies and as 'a strictly private publication' (according to the Library of Congress catalogue). But a surmise that it was she to whom Schelle had done homage for her 'graciously kind letters' and for the help she had extended to him, would not tally with the facts.[4]

Admittedly none of this was meant to go beyond the narrow confines of the family circle. But even so, the work it entailed was likely to foster a growing appreciation of the nature of historical research and of the demand, justifiably made by any serious historian, to draw – and to draw openly – upon the kind of sources which the Du Ponts were fortunate enough to have in their keeping; and it was also likely to weaken any unwarranted insistence on anonymity and splendid isolation.[5] And though the change was as yet small in the first years of the century, it was definitely there, and not only in the sense that the early *Mémoires* of Du Pont the Physiocrat and

[1] See above, p. xxviii.

[2] See *L'Enfance et la Jeunesse de Du Pont de Nemours racontées par lui-même*, préface, p. viii.

[3] See *The National Cyclopaedia of American Biography*, VI (New York, 1929) 457–8. A certain parallel with Schelle's life seems worth mentioning since it may have helped to cement the friendly relations between the two men. In 1903 Schelle retired from his post with the Ministry of Public Works (railways section) in order to devote himself entirely to work in the fields of history and economics (cf. Rist, loc. cit., pp. 167, 186).

[4] See above, p. xxix, fn. 1. That had been Sophie M. Du Pont, widow of Rear-Admiral S.-F. Du Pont.

[5] It may well be that any such insistence on anonymity was not unconnected with the years of fighting that very generation of Du Ponts had had to carry on for the rehabilitation of one of its members. Rear-Admiral Samuel-Francis Du Pont (1803–1865) had been held responsible for the failure of Union naval forces under his command to force the surrender of the port of Charleston, S.C., an important supply centre for the Confederacy during the American Civil War. In the absence of what he considered vitally important support from the territorials, he seems to have refused a second engagement for fear of unnecessary losses of human and material war potential. He had thereupon been released

the *Souvenirs* of one of his daughters-in-law no longer merely reposed in a family vault. Once started, the change deepened in the course of time,[1] and the Turgot edition profited immensely from it.

One might add that things had changed in yet another way: the relationship between H.-A. Du Pont de Nemours and Schelle was no longer, as it had naturally first been around 1888, one between a rich business magnate and a professional man, still obscure although already turned forty. Not only did they now meet more on the footing of two fellow-writers, but Schelle was to state proudly in his introduction to the first volume of his edition of Turgot's works: 'One day, it was granted to me to lay the hand of the former *Constituant*'s great-grandson in the hand of the great-great-nephew of Louis the XVI's minister.'[2]

But although Schelle is so much more explicit about these matters in *La Vie de Turgot*, and especially in the editorial additions to *Œuvres de Turgot*, there was even then no definite statement as to where the 'several hundred letters'[3] from Turgot were being kept – neither in the introduction to vol. 1, nor in the notes concerning individual letters, nor in the lengthy footnote giving particulars about the probable volume of the correspondence mentioned in Du Pont's *Mémoires*.[4] This is all the more striking since in the case of the other source materials edited or referred to, Schelle carefully informs the readers as to where they may be found.

Nevertheless, a bridge had been thrown between 1888 and 1909–13. Would it also connect 1888 and 1905? Had the change which led to H.-A.

---

from active service. As a public token of the exoneration won by the family, one of the squares in the fashionable centre of the country's capital was named after him in the early eighties (cf. *Du Pont de Nemours et l'École Physiocratique*, pp. 395–8). See W. B. Wood and J. E. Edmonds, *A History of the Civil War in the United States, 1861–1865* (New York, 1905) pp. 491–3.

[1] Up to the time of his death, H.-A. Du Pont de Nemours was to publish, via the normal book trade, a number of books and articles, partly on biographical, partly on military matters. One of his last books, *The Early Generations of the Du Ponts and Allied Families*, came out in New York in 1924.

[2] Loc. cit., pp. 9–10. Cf. also above, p. xxix, fn. 5.

[3] In 1888 Schelle had spoken of 'more than three hundred' which he described, as late as 1909, as running 'almost without a break in continuity from 1763 to 1781' (cf. *La Vie de Turgot*, loc. cit.). There is, in fact, no such letter explicitly dated 1763 in the Du Pont collection. But it looks as though Turgot had sought Du Pont's acquaintance while the latter was writing *De l'Exportation et de l'Importation des Grains*, and as though Turgot had read the manuscript (cf. *Œuvres de Turgot*, II 48, 405). And on the basis of other comments of Schelle's (ibid., pp. 45, 406) one feels that the letter assigned by him to 1764 in fact dates from the period just preceding 22 Dec 1763.

[4] Ibid., p. 405. Du Pont had spoken of 'about a thousand' which he said he had kept (*Mémoires*, p. 287).

Du Pont's signing the 1904 preface been effective enough for Schelle to be granted the right – circumscribed as yet, to judge from the evidence in his 1905 article – to publish the 'edition' of the *Tableau* which he had found? If such was the case, Schelle must have seen the 'third edition', perhaps as early as the 1880s, among the papers and books left by Quesnay's disciple.

Bauer had received 'No' for an answer when he raised the question whether the Du Pont heirs had in their possession any manuscripts by Quesnay. Would I be told 'No' if I inquired about a printed work by Quesnay? I decided to put my question and to address it to the present Pierre-Samuel. The answer was 'Yes'.[1]

Of course, none of this actually proves that the copy of the 'third edition' which is today part of the treasures in the Eleutherian Mills[2] Historical Library is identical with the copy which Schelle had had 'in his very hands' three- or fourscore years ago. But two of Quesnay's contemporaries who were well acquainted with his writings, the elder Mirabeau[3] and Forbonnais,[4] have told us that the 'third edition' was produced in a small number of copies only. It would be presumptuous to assume that I should have had the good fortune to find a second copy of this very small '*édition définitive*', and that Schelle's copy might therefore still turn up. I can only say that the hypothesis on which I went ahead worked, since it did lead to the finding of the only copy of the elusive volume as yet known to exist.

There is something to be added to my story.

A little more than two years before Du Pont had published, in November 1767, the selection of works by Quesnay known as *Physiocratie*, Quesnay had written in *Observations sur le Droit Naturel des Hommes Réunis en*

---

[1] It was given to me by the Eleutherian Mills Historical Library, a part of the Hagley-Mills Foundation Inc., which the Du Pont family had set up in 1952 (cf. *The Foundation Directory*, 2nd ed. (New York, 1964)). The administration of the literary treasures had thus become a matter of not quite so personal a nature as it had formerly been. It may even be that the presence of the 'third edition', bound as it is in another volume, became known only in connection with reorganisational work following upon the setting-up of the Library, and that I might have had 'No' for an answer if I had asked a dozen or so years earlier.

[2] Eleutherian Mills had been the name of the small powder works established about 1802 by Éleuthère-Irénée, the younger son of Du Pont the Physiocrat, and a godson of Turgot's. From it has grown the gigantic Du Pont Chemical trust.

[3] 'This summary explanation . . . [i.e. the 'third edition' – M.K.] existed in but few copies, and was little known, although valued by a small number of readers.' (Translated from Mirabeau's anonymously published *Précis de l'Ordre Légal* (Amsterdam, 1768), Note by the editor [Mirabeau himself – M.K.] pp. 3–4.)

[4] 'This celebrated *Tableau* appeared . . . in the form of a little booklet . . . sent to only a small number of persons.' (Translated from Forbonnais's *Principes et Observations Œconomiques* (Amsterdam, 1767) 1 (2) 161.)

Société: 'The basis of society is the means of men's subsistence and the wealth needed by the power that is to defend them.'[1] The primary factor, then, for Quesnay, was the economic basis.

The same view is clearly reflected in the very composition and content of the 'third edition'. To start with we have the graphical representation and, within that representation, first a pattern of production leading to a net surplus, and second a pattern of the distribution of that surplus ensuring its reproduction as part of the whole nation's subsistence. Roughly the same thing may be said of the 'Explanation' of the graphical representation which follows it. These conditions being assumed to exist, the working rules to be applied are then laid down in the 'Household Rules' or Maxims.

This is not the case in *Physiocratie*, where the maxims are given without being connected up with either graphical representation or 'Explanation', where all comments built on the numerical relations embodied therein are deleted, and where, above all, the superstructure is given precedence over the basis in the new introductory maxims I to IV.

Now considering that we have, in the case of Turgot's *Réflexions sur la Formation et la Distribution des Richesses*, direct and incontrovertible evidence of the lengths to which Du Pont, as editor, was ready to go (and to revert) in order to inject views of his own into writings entrusted to him;[2] considering, furthermore, that *Physiocratie* contains no statement that the copious and often far-reaching changes had been made with Quesnay's approval;[3] then the mere fact that the 'third edition', the most comprehensive of the *Tableau* 'editions' which we know to have been worked out by Quesnay alone, has now been made available to scholars does more than just fill a blank space in the bibliography of Quesnay's writings. It gives us Quesnay's very own revised and copiously annotated text, his very own, unamended way of linking things economic[4] and political into the 'fundamental *Tableau* of the economic order'.[5]

[1] *Journal de l'Agriculture, du Commerce et des Finances*, II (Sept 1765) 33. The text is at this point identical with that of 'Le Droit Naturel' in *Physiocratie*.

[2] Cf. my edition of the rediscovered *Tableau Économique* (Berlin, 1965) introduction, pp. xvii–xviii. As to the matter of the various versions of the *Mémoire sur les Municipalités* prepared by Du Pont and revised by Turgot, it bedevils us to this day.

[3] The Abbé Baudeau gave such an assurance, with reference to changes of far less importance, when he started, roughly about the time of the publication of *Physiocratie*, printing the instalments of his 'Explication du Tableau Économique à Mme de ***', in *Éphémérides du Citoyen* (Paris, 1767) vols. 11 and 12; (1768) vol. 3; (1770) vol. 2.

[4] Estimates of existing economic conditions as put forward in earlier writings, especially in 'Grains', furnish quite a number of elements from which the *Tableau* pattern stems. Pertinent connections are made below, in Part 4.

[5] Cf. above, p. xiii.

C

It is my pleasure and privilege to close this account with my thanks to the Akademie-Verlag, Berlin, for allowing use to be made, in this presentation of the *Tableau Économique* to the English reader, of my comparative notes which accompanied the 'third edition' republished in 1965.

MARGUERITE KUCZYNSKI

Berlin-Weissensee,
24 March 1969

3

The 'Third Edition' of the
TABLEAU ÉCONOMIQUE

Facsimile Reproduction and
English Translation

Ex Libris
Petri Du Pont, agriculturæ Regiæ
Societatis Suessionensia.
1764

TABLEAU ÉCONOMIQUE.

Objets à considérer, 1.° Trois sortes de dépenses ; 2.° leur source ; 3.° leurs avances ; 4.° leur distribution ; 5.° leurs effets ; 6.° leur reproduction ; 7.° leurs rapports entr'elles ; 8.° leurs rapports avec la population ; 9.° avec l'Agriculture ; 10.° avec l'industrie ; 11.° avec le commerce ; 12.° avec la masse des richesses d'une Nation.

DÉPENSES PRODUCTIVES relatives à l'Agriculture, &c.	DÉPENSES DU REVENU, l'Impôt prélevé, se partage aux Dépenses productives et aux Dépenses stériles.	DÉPENSES STÉRILES relatives à l'industrie, &c.
Avances annuelles pour produire un revenu de 600.tt sont 600.tt	*Revenu annuel de*	*Avances annuelles pour les Ouvrages des Dépenses stériles, sont 300.tt*
600. produisent net............	600.tt	
Productions		*Ouvrages, &c.*
300.tt reproduisent net.......	300.tt	300.tt
150. reproduisent net	150.	150.
75. reproduisent net..........	75.	75.
37.10.s reproduisent net.......	37..10.	37..10
18..15. reproduisent net........	18..15.	18..15
9...7...6.d reproduisent net......	9...7...6.d	9...7...6.d
4..13...9 reproduisent net......	4..13..9.	4..13...9
2..6..10. reproduisent net......	2..6..10.	2..6..10
1...3...5 reproduisent net........	1..3..5.	1...3...5
0..11...8 reproduisent net........	0..11...8.	0..11...8
0...5..10 reproduisent net.........	0..5..10.	0...5..10
0...2..11 reproduisent net.........	0...2..11.	0...2...11
0...1...5 reproduisent net.........	0...1..5	0....1...5
&c.		

REPRODUIT TOTAL .... 600.tt de revenu ; de plus, les frais annuels de 600.tt et les interets des avances primitives du Laboureur, de 300.tt que la terre restitue. Ainsi la reproduction est de 1500.tt compris le revenu de 600.tt qui est la base du calcul, abstraction faite de l'impôt prélevé, et des avances qu'exige sa reproduction annuelle, &c. Voyez l'Explication à la page suivante.

TABLEAU ÉCONOMIQUE[1]

Objects to be considered: (1) three kinds of expenditure; (2) their source; (3) their advances; (4) their distribution; (5) their effects; (6) their reproduction; (7) their relations with one another; (8) their relations with the population; (9) with agriculture; (10) with industry; (11) with trade; (12) with the total wealth of a nation.

PRODUCTIVE EXPENDITURE	EXPENDITURE OF THE REVENUE	STERILE EXPENDITURE
relative to agriculture, etc.	after deduction of taxes, is divided between productive expenditure and sterile expenditure	relative to industry, etc.
Annual advances required to produce a revenue of 600*l* are 600*l*	Annual revenue	Annual advances for the works of sterile expenditure are

600*l* produce net · · · · · · · · · · · · · · · ·600*l*   300*l*

Products *one-half goes here*   *one-half goes here*   Works, etc.

300*l* reproduce net · · · · · *one-half* · · · · ·300*l*   *one-half* · · · · · · · · ·300*l*

goes here   goes here

150 reproduce net · · · · · · · · ·150   *one-half, etc.* · · · · · · · · ·150
· · · · · · *one-half, etc.*

75 reproduce net · · · · · · · · · · ·75 ·75

37 · · 10[s] reproduce net · · · · · · · · · 37 · · 10 · · · · · · · · · · · · · 37 · · 10

18 · · 15 reproduce net · · · · · · · · · · 18 · · 15 · · · · · · · · · · · · · 18 · · 15

9 · · · 7 · · · 6[d] reproduce net · · · · · · · 9 · · · 7 · · · 6[d] · · · · · · 9 · · · 7 · · · 6[d]

4 · · 13 · · · 9 reproduce net · · · · · · · · 4 · · 13 · · · 9 · · · · · · · 4 · · 13 · · · 9

2 · · · 6 · · 10 reproduce net · · · · · · · · 2 · · · 6 · · 10 · · · · · · · 2 · · · 6 · · 10

1 · · · 3 · · · 5 reproduce net · · · · · · · · 1 · · · 3 · · · 5 · · · · · · · 1 · · · 3 · · · 5

0 · · 11 · · · 8 reproduce net · · · · · · · · 0 · · 11 · · · 8 · · · · · · · 0 · · 11 · · · 8

0 · · · 5 · · 10 reproduce net · · · · · · · · 0 · · · 5 · · 10 · · · · · · · 0 · · · 5 · · 10

0 · · · 2 · · 11 reproduce net · · · · · · · · 0 · · · 2 · · 11 · · · · · · · 0 · · · 2 · · 11

0 · · · 1 · · · 5 reproduce net · · · · · · · · 0 · · · 1 · · · 5 · · · · · · · 0 · · · 1 · · · 5

etc.

TOTAL REPRODUCED · · · · · · 600*l* of revenue; in addition, the annual costs of 600*l* and the interest on the original advances of the husbandman amounting to 300*l*, which the land restores. Thus the reproduction is 1500*l*, including the revenue of 600*l* which forms the base of the calculation, abstraction being made of the taxes deducted and of the advances which their annual reproduction entails, etc. See the Explanation on the following page.

EXPLICATION
DU TABLEAU ÉCONOMIQUE.

LES *Dépenses productives* font employées à l'agriculture, prairies, pâtures, forêts, mines, pêche, &c. pour per-pétuer les richeffes, en grains, boiffons, bois, beftiaux, matières premières des ouvrages de main-d'œuvre, &c.

Les *Dépenses stériles* se font en marchandifes de main-d'œuvre, logemens, vêtemens, intérêts d'argent, domes-tiques, frais de commerce, denrées étrangères, &c.

La vente du produit net que le Cultivateur a fait naître l'année précédente, par le moyen des *Avances annuelles* de 600 liv. employées à la culture par le Fermier, fournit au Propriétaire le payement d'un *revenu* de 600 livres.

Les *avances annuelles* de 300 liv. des dépenfes ftériles font employées pour les fonds & les frais du commerce, pour les achats de matière première d'ouvrage de main-d'œuvre, & pour la fubfiftance & autres befoins de l'ar-tifan, jufqu'à ce qu'il ait achevé & vendu fon ouvrage.

Les *600 liv. de revenu* font dépenfées par le Proprié-taire, moitié à la claffe des dépenfes productives en pain, vin, viande, &c. & l'autre moitié à la claffe des dépenfes ftériles en vêtemens, emmeublemens, uftenfiles, &c.

Ces dépenfes peuvent fe porter plus ou moins d'un côté ou de l'autre, felon que celui qui les fait fe livre plus ou moins au luxe de fubfiftance, ou au luxe de décoration. On a pris ici l'état moyen où les dépenfes reproductives renouvellent d'année en année le même revenu. Mais on

a

EXPLANATION

OF THE *TABLEAU ÉCONOMIQUE*[2]

Productive expenditure is employed in agriculture, grasslands, pastures, forests, mines, fishing, etc., in order to perpetuate wealth in the form of corn, drink, wood, livestock, raw materials for manufactured goods, etc.

Sterile expenditure is on manufactured commodities, house-room, clothing, interest on money, servants, commercial costs, foreign produce, etc.

The sale of the net product which the cultivator has generated in the previous year, by means of the *annual advances* of 600 livres employed in cultivation by the farmer, results in the payment to the proprietor of a *revenue* of 600 livres.

The *annual advances* of the sterile expenditure class, amounting to 300 livres, are employed for the capital and costs of trade, for the purchase of raw materials for manufactured goods, and for the subsistence and other needs of the artisan until he has completed and sold his work.

Of the *600 livres of revenue,* one-half is spent by the proprietor in purchasing bread, wine, meat, etc., from the productive expenditure class, and the other half in purchasing clothing, furnishings, utensils, etc., from the sterile expenditure class.

This expenditure may go more or less to one side or the other, according as the man who engages in it goes in more or less for luxury in the way of subsistence or for luxury in the way of ornamentation. We assume here a medium situation in which the reproductive expenditure renews the same revenue from year to year. But it is easy to estimate the changes which

peut juger facilement des changemens qui arriveroient dans la reproduction annuelle du revenu, selon que les dépenses stériles ou les dépenses productives l'emporteroient plus ou moins l'une sur l'autre : on peut, dis-je, en juger facilement par les changemens mêmes qui arriveroient dans l'ordre du tableau. Car supposé que le luxe de décoration augmentât d'un sixième chez le Propriétaire, d'un sixième chez l'Artisan, d'un sixième chez le Cultivateur, la reproduction du revenu de 600 liv. se réduiroit à 500 liv. Si au contraire l'augmentation de dépense étoit portée à ce degré du côté de la consommation, ou de l'exportation des denrées du cru, la reproduction du revenu de 600 liv. monteroit à 800 liv. ainsi progressivement. On voit par-là que l'excès du luxe de décoration peut très-promptement ruiner avec magnificence une Nation opulente.

Les 300 livres du revenu qui dans l'ordre du tableau ont passé aux dépenses productives, y rendent en argent des *avances,* lesquelles reproduisent net 300 liv. qui font partie de la reproduction du revenu du Propriétaire : Et par le reste de la distribution des sommes qui reviennent à cette même classe, le revenu total est reproduit annuellement. Ces 300 liv. dis-je, qui reviennent d'abord à la classe des dépenses productives par la vente des productions que le Propriétaire y achette, sont dépensées par le Fermier, moitié en consommation de productions fournies par cette même classe, & l'autre moitié en entretien de vêtemens, ustensiles, instrumens, &c. qu'il paye à la classe des dépenses stériles. Et elles renaissent avec le produit net.

Les 300 liv. du revenu du Propriétaire, qui ont passé à la classe des dépenses stériles, sont dépensées par l'artisan,

would take place in the annual reproduction of revenue, according as sterile expenditure or productive expenditure preponderated to a greater or lesser degree. It is easy to estimate them, I say, simply from the changes which would occur in the order of the *tableau*. Suppose, for example, that luxury in the way of ornamentation increased by one-sixth in the case of the proprietor, by one-sixth in the case of the artisan, and by one-sixth in the case of the cultivator. Then the revenue reproduced, which is now 600 livres, would be reduced to 400[3] livres. Suppose, on the other hand, that an increase of the same degree took place in expenditure on the consumption or export of raw produce. Then the revenue reproduced would increase from 600 to 800[4] livres, and so on in progression. Thus it can be seen that an opulent nation which indulges in excessive luxury in the way of ornamentation can very quickly be overwhelmed by its sumptuousness.

The 300 livres of revenue which according to the order of the *tableau* have passed into the hands of the class of productive expenditure, return to this class its *advances* in the form of money. These advances reproduce 300 livres net, which represents the reproduction of part of the proprietor's revenue; and it is by means of the remainder of the distribution of the sums of money which are returned to this same class that the total revenue is reproduced each year. These 300 livres, I say, which are returned at the beginning of the process to the productive expenditure class, by means of the sale of the products which the proprietor buys from it, are spent by the farmer, one-half in the consumption of products provided by this class itself, and the other half in keeping itself in clothing, utensils, implements, etc., for which it makes payment to the sterile expenditure class. And the 300 livres are regenerated with the net product.

The 300 livres of the proprietor's revenue which have passed into the hands of the sterile expenditure class are spent by the artisan, as to one-

moitié à la claſſe des dépenſes productives en achats de productions pour la ſubſiſtance, pour les matières premières des ouvrages, & pour le commerce extérieur; & l'autre moitié eſt partagée pour l'entretien, & pour la reſtitution des *avances*, à la claſſe même des dépenſes ſtériles. Cette circulation & cette diſtribution réciproque ſe continuent dans le même ordre par ſoudiviſions juſqu'au dernier denier des ſommes qui paſſent réciproquement d'une claſſe de dépenſes à l'autre claſſe de dépenſes.

La circulation porte 600 liv. à la claſſe des dépenſes ſtériles, ſur quoi il faut en retirer 300 livres pour les *avances annuelles*; il reſte 300 livres pour le ſalaire. Ce ſalaire eſt égal aux 300 liv. que cette claſſe reçoit de la claſſe des dépenſes productives, & les avances ſont égales aux 300 liv. du revenu qui paſſe à cette même claſſe de dépenſes ſtériles.

Les productions de l'autre claſſe ſont de 1200 livres, diſtraction faite de l'impôt, de la dixme, & de l'intérêt des avances du Laboureur, qui ſeront conſidérées à part, pour ne pas trop compliquer l'ordre des dépenſes. Dans la dépenſe des 1200 livres de productions, le Propriétaire du revenu en achette pour 300 liv. il en paſſe pour 300 liv. à la claſſe des dépenſes ſtériles, dont la moitié qui eſt de 150 liv. eſt conſommée pour la ſubſiſtance dans cette claſſe; l'autre moitié qui eſt de 150 liv. eſt enlevée pour le commerce extérieur qui ſe rapporte à cette même claſſe. Enfin il y en a pour 300 livres qui ſont conſommées dans la claſſe des dépenſes productives, par les hommes qui les font naître, & pour 300 liv. employées pour la nourriture & entretien des beſtiaux. Ainſi des 1200 livres de

half, in the purchase of products for his subsistence, for raw materials for his work, and for foreign trade, from the productive expenditure class; and the other half is distributed among the sterile expenditure class itself for its maintenance and for the restitution of its *advances*. This circulation and mutual distribution are continued in the same way by means of sub-divisions down to the last penny of the sums of money which mutually pass from the hands of one expenditure class into those of the other.

Circulation brings 600 livres to the sterile expenditure class, from which 300 livres have to be kept back for the *annual advances*, which leaves 300 livres for wages. These wages are equal to the 300 livres which this class receives from the productive expenditure class, and the advances are equal to the 300 livres of revenue which pass into the hands of this same sterile expenditure class.

The products of the other class amount to 1200 livres, abstracting from taxes, tithes, and interest on the husbandman's advances, which will be considered separately in order not to complicate the order of expenditure too much. The 1200 livres' worth of product are disposed of as follows: The proprietor of the revenue buys 300 livres' worth of them. 300 livres' worth passes into the hands of the sterile expenditure class, of which one-half, amounting to 150 livres, is consumed for subsistence within this class, and the other half, amounting to 150 livres, is taken for external trade, which is included in this same class.[5] Finally, 300 livres' worth are consumed within the productive expenditure class by the men who cause them to be generated; and 300 livres' worth are used for the feeding and maintenance of livestock. Thus of the 1200 livres' worth of product, 600

productions, cette claſſe en dépenſe 600 liv. & ſes *avances*
de 600 liv. lui ſont rendues en argent par les ventes qu'elle
fait au Propriétaire & à la claſſe des dépenſes ſtériles. Un
huitième du total de ces productions entre dans le commerce extérieur en exportation, ou en matières premières
& nourriture pour les ouvriers du pays qui vendent leurs
ouvrages aux autres Nations, où les ventes du Commer-
çant contrebalancent les achats des marchandiſes, & de la
matière d'or & d'argent que l'on tire de l'étranger.

Tel eſt l'ordre diſtributif de la conſommation des productions du cru entre les claſſes de citoyens, & telle eſt
l'idée que l'on doit ſe former de l'uſage & de l'étendue
du commerce extérieur d'une Nation agricole floriſſante.

Le débit réciproque d'une claſſe de dépenſe à l'autre
diſtribue le revenu de 600 livres de part & d'autre; ce
qui donne 300 livres de chaque côté, outre les avances
qui ſont conſervées. Le Propriétaire ſubſiſte par les 600
livres qu'il dépenſe. Les 300 livres diſtribuées a chaque
claſſe de dépenſes, ajoûtées aux produits de l'impôt, de
la dixme, &c. qui y ſont annexés, peuvent y nourrir un
homme dans l'une & dans l'autre: ainſi 600 liv. de revenu
& les dépendances peuvent faire ſubſiſter trois hommes
chefs de famille. Sur ce pied, 600 millions de revenu
peuvent faire ſubſiſter trois millions de familles eſtimées
à quatre perſonnes, de tout âge, par famille.

Les frais fournis par les *avances annuelles* de la claſſe
des dépenſes productives qui renaiſſent auſſi chaque année,
& dont environ la moitié eſt dépenſée pour la nourriture
des beſtiaux, & l'autre moitié en payement de ſalaire pour
les hommes occupés aux travaux de cette claſſe, ajoûtent

300

are consumed by this class, and its *advances* of 600 livres are returned to it in the form of money through the sales which it makes to the proprietor and to the sterile expenditure class. One-eighth of the total of this product enters into external trade, either as exports or as raw materials and subsistence for the country's workers who sell their goods to other nations. The sales of the merchant counterbalance the purchases of the commodities and bullion which are obtained from abroad.[6]

Such is the order of the distribution and consumption of raw produce as between the different classes of citizens; and such is the view which we ought to take of the use and extent of external trade in a flourishing agricultural nation.

Mutual sales from one expenditure class to the other distribute the revenue of 600 livres to both sides, giving 300 livres to each, in addition to the advances which are maintained intact. The proprietor subsists by means of the 600 livres which he spends. The 300 livres distributed to each expenditure class, together with the product[7] of the taxes, the tithes, etc., which is added to them, can support one man in each: thus 600 livres of revenue together with the appurtenant sums can enable three heads of families to subsist. On this basis 600 millions of revenue can enable three million families to subsist, estimated at four persons of all ages per family.

The costs provided for by the *annual advances* of the productive expenditure class, which are also regenerated each year, and of which one-half is spent on the feeding of livestock and the other half in paying wages to the men engaged in the work carried on by this class, add 300 millions of

300 millions de dépenfes qui peuvent, avec la part des autres produits qui y font annexés, faire fubfifter encore un million de chefs de familles.

Ainfi ces 900 millions qui, abftraction faite de l'impôt, de la dixme, & des intérêts des avances annuelles & des avances primitives du Laboureur, renaîtroient annuellement des biens-fonds, pourroient faire fubfifter feize millions de perfonnes de tout âge, conformément à cet ordre de circulation & de diftribution des revenus annuels.

Par circulation, on entend ici les achats de la première main, payés par le revenu qui fe partage à toutes les claffes d'hommes, diftraction faite du commerce, qui multiplie les ventes & les achats, fans multiplier les chofes, & qui n'eft qu'un furcroît de dépenfes ftériles.

Les *richeffes de la claffe des Dépenfes productives* d'une Nation où les Propriétaires des terres ont conftamment 600 millions de revenu, peuvent être évaluées ainfi.

Un revenu de 600 millions pour les Propriétaires fuppofe en outre 300 millions d'impôts; & 150 millions pour la dixme du produit annuel, total frais compris, qui fe lèvent fur les parties de culture décimables: Ce qui forme en total 1 milliard 50 millions, le revenu compris: De plus, la reproduction de 1 milliard 50 millions d'avances annuelles, & 110 millions d'intérêt pour ces avances à 10 pour 100: Le tout enfemble eft ... 2,210,000,000[l].

Dans un royaume où il y auroit beaucoup de vignes, de bois, de prés, &c. il n'y auroit qu'environ les deux tiers de ces 2 milliards 210 millions, qui s'obtiendroient par le travail de la charrue. Cette partie exigeroit, dans un bon Etat de grande culture exécutée par des chevaux,

expenditure to the total; and this, together with the share of the other products which are added to them, can enable another one million heads of families to subsist.

Thus these 900 millions, which, abstracting from taxes, tithes, and interest on the annual advances and original advances of the husbandman, would be annually regenerated from landed property, could enable 16 million people of all ages to subsist according to this order of circulation and distribution of the annual revenue.

By circulation is here meant the purchases at first hand, paid for by the revenue which is shared out among all classes of men, abstracting from trade, which multiplies sales and purchases without multiplying things, and which represents nothing but an addition to sterile expenditure.

The *wealth of the productive expenditure class,* in a nation where the proprietors of land regularly receive a revenue of 600 millions, can be worked out as follows:

A revenue of 600 millions for the proprietors presupposes an extra 300 millions for taxes; and 150 millions for tithes on the annual product, all charges included, which are levied on the tithable branches of cultivation. This makes a total of 1050 millions, including the revenue. Add to these the reproduction of 1050 millions of annual advances, and 110 millions[8] of interest on these advances at 10 per cent, and the grand total becomes

. . . . 2,210,000,000 livres.[9]

In a kingdom with many vineyards, forests, meadows, etc., only about two-thirds of these 2210 millions would be obtained by means of ploughing. Assuming a satisfactory state of affairs in which large-scale cultivation was being carried on with the aid of horses, this portion would require

D

l'emploi de trois cens trente-trois mille, trois cens trente-quatre charrues à 120 arpens de terre par charrue; trois cens trente-trois mille, trois cens trente-quatre hommes pour les conduire; & 40 millions d'arpens de terre.

Cette culture pourroit, avec 5 ou 6 milliards d'avances, s'étendre en France à plus de 60 millions d'arpens.

On ne parle pas ici de la petite culture exécutée avec des bœufs, où il faudroit plus d'un million de charrues, & environ 2,000,000 d'hommes pour exploiter 40 millions d'arpens de terre, qui ne rapporteroient que les deux cinquièmes du produit que donne la grande culture. Cette petite culture à laquelle les Cultivateurs font réduits, faute de richesses pour établir les avances primitives, s'exécute aux dépens des biens-fonds mêmes, employés en grande partie pour les frais, & par des dépenses annuelles excessives pour la subsistance de la multitude d'hommes occupés à ce genre de culture, qui absorbent presque tout le produit. Cette culture ingrate, qui décèle la pauvreté & la ruine des Nations où elle domine, n'a aucun rapport à l'ordre du Tableau, qui est réglé sur l'état de la moitié de l'emploi d'une charrue, où les avances annuelles peuvent, au moyen du fond des avances primitives, produire cent pour cent.

Les avances primitives bien complettes de l'établissement d'une charrue dans la grande culture, pour le premier fond des dépenses en bestiaux, instrumens, semence, & nourriture, entretien, salaire, &c. dans le cours du travail de deux ans, avant la première récolte, font estimées 10,000 liv. ainsi le total pour trois cens trente-trois mille, trois cens trente-quatre charrues, est 3,333,340,000[l].

the employment of 333,334 ploughs at 120 *arpents* of land per plough; 333,334 men to drive them; and 40 million *arpents* of land.

With advances amounting to five or six milliards, it would be possible for this type of cultivation to be extended in France to more than 60 million *arpents*.[10]

We are not speaking here of small-scale cultivation carried on with the aid of oxen, in which more than a million ploughs and about two million men would be required to work 40 million *arpents* of land, and which would bring in only two-fifths of the product yielded by large-scale cultivation. This small-scale cultivation, to which cultivators are reduced owing to their lack of the wealth necessary to make the original advances, and in which the land is largely employed merely to cover the costs, is carried on at the expense of landed property itself, and involves an excessive annual expenditure for the subsistence of the great numbers of men engaged in this type of cultivation, which absorbs almost the whole of the product. This thankless type of cultivation, which reveals the poverty and ruin of those nations in which it predominates, has no connection with the order of the *tableau*, which is worked out on the basis of half the employment of a plough of land,[11] where the annual advances are able, with the aid of the fund of original advances, to produce 100 per cent.

The full total of the original advances required for putting a plough of land under large-scale cultivation, for the first fund of expenditure on livestock, implements, seed, food, upkeep, wages, etc.,[12] in the course of two years' labour prior to the first harvest, is estimated at 10,000 livres. Thus the total for 333,334[13] ploughs is 3,333,340,000 livres. (*See the articles* FARM,[14] FARMERS,[15] CORN[16] *in the Encyclopedia.*)

Voyez dans l'Encyclopédie les art. Ferme, Fermiers, Grains.

L'intérêt de ces avances doit rendre au moins 10 pour 100, parce que les produits de l'agriculture sont exposés à des accidens ruineux qui, en dix ans, enlèvent au moins la valeur de la récolte d'une année. Ces avances exigent d'ailleurs beaucoup d'entretien & de renouvellemens; ainsi le total des intérêts des avances primitives de l'établissement des Laboureurs, est . . . . 333,322,000$^{liv.}$

Les prés, les vignes, les étangs, les bois, &c. demandent peu d'avances primitives de la part des Fermiers. La valeur de ces avances peut être réduite, en y comprenant les dépenses primitives des plantations & autres ouvrages exécutés aux dépens des Propriétaires, à 1,000,000,000^l.

Mais les vignes & le jardinage exigent beaucoup d'avances annuelles qui, rapportées en commun avec celles des autres parties, peuvent du fort au foible, être comprises dans le total des avances annuelles exposées ci-dessus.

La reproduction totale annuelle en produit net, en avances annuelles avec leurs intérêts, & en intérêts des avances primitives, évaluée conformément à l'ordre du tableau, est . . . . 2,543,322,000^l.

Le territoire de la France pourroit, avec des avances & du débit, produire autant & même beaucoup plus.

De cette somme de 2,543,322,000^l, il y a 525 millions, qui font la moitié de la reproduction des avances annuelles, employées à la nourriture des bestiaux: Il reste, (si tout l'impôt rentre dans la circulation, & s'il ne porte pas sur les avances des Laboureurs.) . . 2,018,322,000^l.

The interest on these advances ought to amount to 10 per cent at least, since the products of agriculture are subject to disastrous accidents which, over a period of ten years, destroy at least the value of one year's harvest. Moreover, these advances require a great deal of upkeep and renewal. Thus the total interest on the original advances required for setting up the husbandmen is . . . . .333,322,000 livres.[17]

Meadows, vineyards, ponds, forests, etc., do not require very great original advances on the part of the farmers. The value of these advances, including in them the original expenditure on plantations and other work[18] carried out at the expense of the proprietors, can be reduced to 1,000,000,000 livres.[19]

But vineyards and gardens require large annual advances which, taken together with those of the other branches, may on the average be included in the total of annual advances set out above.

The total annual reproduction of net product, of annual advances with the interest thereon, and of interest on the original advances, worked out in accordance with the order of the tableau, is . . . . 2,543,322,000 livres.[20]

The territory of France, given advances and markets, could produce as much as this and even a great deal more.[21]

Of this sum of 2,543,322,000 livres,[22] 525 millions constitutes that half of the reproduction of the annual advances which is employed in feeding livestock. There remains (if the whole of the taxes go back into circulation, and if they do not encroach upon the advances of the husbandmen) . . . . 2,018,322,000 livres.[23]

C'eſt, POUR LA DÉPENSE DES HOMMES, *du fort au foible,* 504,580,500[l] *pour chaque million de chef de famille, ou pour un chef de famille* 562 *liv. que les accidens réduiſent environ à* 530[l]. Sur ce pied un Etat eſt puiſſant en tribut & en reſſources ; & les hommes y ſubſiſtent dans l'aiſance.

Le fond des terres qui produit annuellement au profit des hommes, 2,018,322,000[l], dont 1,050,000,000[l] ſont en produit net, étant eſtimé ſur le pied du denier 30, eſt dans ce point de vûe une richeſſe de 33,455,000,000[l], auquel il faut ajoûter les 4,333,340,000[l] d'avances primitives ; le total eſt 36,788,340,000[l]. En y réuniſſant les 2,543,322,000[l] du produit annuel,

LE TOTAL, FRAIS COMPRIS, DES RICHESSES DE LA CLASSE DES DÉPENSES PRODUCTIVES SERA... 40,331,662,000[l].

On n'a pas eſtimé à part la valeur & le produit des beſtiaux, parce qu'on les a compris dans les avances des Fermiers, & dans le total des produits annuels.

Nous plaçons ici les terres, parce que, relativement à leur valeur vénale, on peut les regarder en quelque ſorte comme des richeſſes mobiliaires, en ce que leur prix eſt aſſujéti aux variations de l'état des autres richeſſes néceſſaires pour la culture. Car les terres ſe déteriorent, & les Propriétaires perdent ſur la valeur vénale de leurs biens-fonds, à proportion que les richeſſes de leurs Fermiers dépériſſent.

Les *richeſſes de la claſſe des Dépenſes ſtériles* ſont 1.° le fond des avances annuelles ſtériles . . . 525,000,000[liv.]

2.° Avances primitives de cette claſſe pour établiſſemens de manufactures, pour

inſtrumens

That makes, FOR MEN'S EXPENDITURE, *504,580,500 livres on the average for each million heads of families, or 562 livres for each individual head of family, which accidents reduce to about 530 livres.*[24] On this basis a state is strong in taxable capacity and resources, and its people live in easy circumstances.[25]

The stock of land which annually produces for the benefit of men 2,018,322,000 livres,[26] of which 1,050,000,000 take the form of net product, when evaluated at the rate of one in 30,[27] constitutes from this point of view wealth amounting to 33,455,000,000 livres, to which must be added the original advances of 4,333,340,000 livres, making a total of 36,788,340,000.[28] Adding to this the 2,543,322,000 livres of annual product,[29]

THE TOTAL, COSTS INCLUDED, OF
THE WEALTH OF THE PRODUCTIVE
EXPENDITURE CLASS WILL BE: . . . . 40,331,662,000 livres.[30]

The value and the product of livestock have not been separately calculated, since they have been included in the advances of the farmers and in the total of the annual product.[31]

We include the land here because, relatively to its market value, it can be considered in something the same way as movable property, since its price is dependent upon changes in the other items of wealth required for cultivation.[32] For land deteriorates, and the proprietors lose on the market value of their landed property, to the extent that the wealth of their farmers is wasted away.

The *wealth of the sterile expenditure class* consists of 1. The total of the annual sterile advances . . . . 525,000,000 livres.[33]

2. The original advances of this class for setting up manufactures, for tools,

inftrumens , machines , moulins, forges
ou autres ufances, &c. 2,000,000,000¹

3.º L'argent monnoyé ou le pécule
d'une Nation agricole opulente, eft à
peu près égal au produit net qu'elle
retire annuellement de fes biens-fonds
par l'entremife du commerce. Ainfi . . . 1,000,000,000*

* Ou environ 18,600,000 de marcs d'argent. On remarque que le pécule de l'Angleterre refte fixé à peu près à cette proportion, qui, dans l'état préfent de fes richeffes, fe foûtient environ à 26 millions fterlins, ou à 11 millions de marcs d'argent. Si cette Nation s'eft trouvée expofée par fes guerres à des befoins preffans, & à des emprunts exceffifs, ce n'étoit pas par le défaut de l'argent, c'étoit par les dépenfes qui excédoient les revenus de l'Etat : Quand l'argent fourniroit aux emprunts, les revenus n'en feroient pas moins furchargés par les dettes; & la Nation feroit ruinée, fi la fource même des revenus en fouffroit un dépériffement progreffif, qui diminuât la reproduction annuelle des richeffes. C'eft fous ce point de vûe qu'il faut envifager l'état des Nations ; parce que le pécule eft toûjours renaiffant dans une Nation où les richeffes fe renouvellent continuellement & fans dépériffement. Pendant environ un fiècle, c'eft-à-dire , depuis 1450 jufqu'a 1550, il y a eu en Europe une grande diminution dans la quantité de l'argent, comme on peut en juger par le prix des marchandifes en ce temps-là; mais cette moindre quantité de pécule étoit indifférente aux Nations ; parce que la valeur vénale de cette richeffe étoit la même par-tout, & que, par rapport au pécule, leur état étoit le même relativement à leurs revenus, qui étoient par-tout également mefurés par la valeur uniforme de l'argent. Dans ce cas, il vaut mieux, pour la commodité des hommes, que ce foit la valeur qui fupplée à la maffe, que fi la maffe fuppléoit à la valeur. On eft porté à croire que c'eft la découverte de l'Amérique qui a procuré en Europe une plus grande abondance d'or & d'argent ; cependant la valeur de l'argent avoit baiffé vis-à-vis les marchandifes, au degré où elle eft aujourd'hui, avant l'arrivée de l'or & de l'argent de l'Amérique en Europe. Mais toutes ces variétés générales ne changent rien à l'état du pécule de chaque Nation, y étant toûjours proportionné aux revenus des biens-fonds & aux gains du commerce extérieur. Dans le fiècle précédent, fous Louis XIV, le marc d'argent monnoyé valoit 28 liv. Ainfi 18,600,000 de marcs valoient alors environ 500 millions. C'étoit à peu près l'état du pécule de la France dans ce temps où le Royaume étoit beaucoup plus riche qu'il n'étoit fur la fin du règne de ce Monarque.

En 1716, la refonte générale des efpèces ne monta pas à 400 millions ; le marc d'argent monnoyé étoit à 43 liv. 12 fols ; ainfi la maffe des efpèces de cette refonte ne montoit pas à neuf millions de marcs ; c'étoit plus de moitié moins que dans les refontes générales de 1683 & 1693. Cette maffe de pécule n'aura pû augmenter par les fabrications annuelles d'efpèces, qu'autant que le revenu de la Nation aura augmenté : Quelque confidérable que foit le total de ces fabrications annuelles depuis cette refonte, il aura moins fervi à augmenter la maffe d'argent monnoyé, qu'à reparer ce qui en eft enlevé annuellement par la contrebande, par les diverfes branches de commerce paffif, & par d'autres emplois de l'argent chez l'étranger ; car depuis 44 ans, le total de ces tranfmiffions annuelles bien calculé, fe trouveroit fort confidérable. L'augmentation du numéraire qui eft fixée depuis long-temps à 54 livres, ne prouve pas que la quantité du pécule de la Nation ait beaucoup augmenté. Ces eftimations font peu conformes aux opinions du vulgaire, fur la quantité d'argent monnoyé d'une Nation ; le peuple croit que c'eft dans l'argent que confifte la richeffe d'un Etat : mais l'argent, comme toutes les autres productions, n'eft richeffe qu'à raifon

machines, mills, forges, and other works,[34]

etc. . . . .   2,000,000,000 livres.

3. The coined money or money stock
of an opulent agricultural nation is about
equal to the net product which it obtains
annually from its landed property through
the medium of trade. Thus it is[35] . . . . . 1,000,000,000 livres.*

* [36] Or about 18,600,000 marks of silver. It is to be noted that the money stock of England remains fixed at about this proportion, which in the present state of its wealth maintains it at approximately 26 millions sterling, or 11 million marks of silver. If this nation has found itself in urgent need through its wars, and has been obliged to contract excessive loans, this was not due to a lack of money, but to the fact that the state's expenditure exceeded its revenue. When money is provided for loans, the debts add no less of a burden to the revenue, and the nation is ruined, if the very source of the revenue is progressively wasted away, causing a reduction in the annual reproduction of wealth. It is from this point of view that the state of a nation should be considered; for the money stock is always renascent in a nation where wealth is being renewed continually and without abatement. For about a century, i.e. from 1450 to 1550, there was a great reduction in the quantity of money in Europe, as can be seen from the prices of commodities in those times. But this smaller quantity of money was a matter of indifference to the nations, because the market value of this form of wealth was the same everywhere, and because, in proportion to the money stock, their condition was the same relatively to their revenues, which were everywhere measured alike in terms of the uniform value of silver. In such a case it conduces more to men's convenience that it should be value which makes up for quantity rather than quantity which makes up for value. We are led to believe that it was the discovery of America which procured a greater abundance of gold and silver in Europe; yet the value of silver had fallen relatively to commodities, to the level at which it stands today, before the arrival of the American gold and silver in Europe. But all these general variations have no effect at all on the state of the money stock of each

nation, which is always proportionate to the revenue from its landed property and to the gains from its external trade. In the last century, under Louis XIV, the mark of coined silver was worth 28 livres. Thus 18,600,000 marks were then worth about 500 million livres. This was roughly the size of the money stock in France in those times, when the kingdom was much wealthier than it was towards the end of the reign of this monarch.

In 1716, the general recoinage of specie did not amount to 400 millions; the mark of coined silver was at 43 livres 12 sous; thus the total amount of specie involved in this recoinage did not amount to nine million marks; and this was more than one-half less than the amounts involved in the general recoinages of 1683 and 1693. This total money stock can have been increased as a result of the annual production of specie only to the extent that the nation's revenue has been increased. However great the total of this annual production may have been since this recoinage, it will have served less to increase the total stock of coined money than to make up for what has been abstracted from it annually as a result of smuggling, the various branches of passive trade, and other methods of employing money in foreign countries; for over a period of 44 years the total of these annual transfers, if properly calculated, would be found to be very considerable. The rise in the money unit, which has been fixed for a long time at 54 livres, does not prove that the quantity of the nation's money stock has greatly increased. These views are hardly consistent with the notions vulgarly held concerning the quantity of coined money in a nation. The people believe that it is in money that the wealth of a state consists. But money, like all other products, constitutes wealth only in proportion to its market value; and it is

4.º La valeur foncière de 4 millions de maifons ou logemens pour 4 millions de familles, chaque maifon eftimée du fort au foible 1500 liv. eft . . . . . . 6,000,000,000.

5.º La valeur de l'emmeublement & uftenfiles de 4 millions de maifons eftimées du fort au foible environ à une année du revenu ou du gain de 4 millions de chefs de familles, eft . . . . . 3,000,000,000.

6.º La valeur de l'argenterie, bijoux, pierreries, glaces, tableaux, livres & autres ouvrages de main-d'œuvre durables, qui s'achettent ou fe tranfmettent par fucceffion, peut être, dans une Nation riche, de . . . . 3,000,000,000.

7.º La valeur des vaiffeaux marchands & militaires, & leurs dépendances, fi la Nation eft maritime; de plus, l'artillerie, les inftrumens & autres ouvrages durables pour la guerre de terre. Les édifices, décorations & autres ouvrages durables publics: tous ces objets enfemble peuvent être évalués à... 2,000,000,000.

On ne parle pas des marchandifes de main-d'œuvre

de fa valeur vénale, & n'eft pas plus difficile à acquérir que toute autre marchandife, en le payant par d'autres richeffes. Sa quantité dans un Etat y eft bornée à fon ufage, qui y eft réglé par les ventes & les achats dans fes dépenfes annuelles; & les dépenfes annuelles y font réglées par les revenus. Une Nation ne doit donc avoir d'argent monnoyé qu'à raifon de fes revenus; une plus grande quantité lui feroit inutile; elle en échangeroit le fuperflu avec les autres Nations, pour d'autres richeffes qui lui feroient plus avantageufes, ou plus fatisfaifantes; car les poffeffeurs de l'argent, même les plus économes, font toûjours attentifs à en retirer quelque profit. Si on trouve à le prêter dans le pays à un haut intérêt, c'eft une preuve qu'il n'y eft tout au plus que dans la proportion que nous avons obfervée, puifqu'on en paye l'ufage ou le befoin à fi haut prix.

4. The capital value of four million houses or dwelling-places for four million families, each house being valued on the average at 1500 livres, comes to . . . . . 6,000,000,000 livres.

5. The value of the furnishings and utensils of four million houses, estimated on the average at about one year's revenue or gain of four million heads of families, comes to . . . . 3,000,000,000 livres.[37]

6. The value of silver plate, jewellery, precious stones, mirrors, pictures, books, and other durable manufactured products, which are purchased or inherited, may in a wealthy nation amount to . . . . 3,000,000,000 livres.[38]

7. The value of merchant and military shipping, and their appurtenances, in the case of a maritime nation; in addition, the artillery, weapons, and other durable products required for land warfare; the buildings, ornamental structures, and other durable public works: all these things taken together can be valued at . . . . . . 2,000,000,000 livres.[39]

We do not take account here of the manufactured commodities and

no harder to acquire, by paying over other kinds of wealth for it, than any other commodity. Its quantity in a state is limited by the uses to which it can be put; these are regulated by the sales and purchases which take place in its annual expenditure; and its annual expenditure is regulated by its revenue. Thus a nation's stock of coined money should be no more than proportionate to its revenue; a greater quantity would be of no use to it; it would exchange the surplus with other nations in order to obtain other items of wealth which would be of greater benefit to it or which would afford it more satisfaction; for those who possess money, even the most thrifty of them, are always concerned with getting some profit from it. If it is found that money is being lent at a high rate of interest in a country, this is proof that the quantity of money is at most only in the proportion we have described, since those who need it or want the use of it are paying such a high price for it.[40]

& denrées exportées ou importées , & renfermées dans les boutiques & magafins des Commerçans, deftinées à l'ufage ou confommation annuelle , parce qu'elles font comprifes & comptées dans l'état des productions & dépenfes annuelles, conformément à l'ordre expofé dans le Tableau.

LE TOTAL DES RICHESSES DE LA CLASSE DES DÉPENSES STÉRILES peut être environ . . . . 18,000,000,000[1]

TOTAL GÉNÉRAL . . . . 59,000,000,000.

Suppofez erreur de $\frac{1}{20}$.e de plus ou de moins, c'eft . . . . 55 à 60,000,000,000.

Nous parlons d'une Nation opulente qui poffede un territoire & des avances qui lui rendent annuellement & fans dépériffement 1 milliard 50 millions de produit net ; mais toutes ces richeffes entretenues fucceffivement par ce produit annuel , peuvent fe détruire ou perdre leur valeur, dans la décadence d'une Nation agricole , par le fimple dépériffement des avances pour les dépenfes productives , lequel peut faire de grands progrès en peu de temps par huit caufes principales.

1.° Mauvaife forme d'impofition, qui porteroit fur les avances des Cultivateurs, *Noli me tangere;* c'eft la devife de ces avances.

2.° Surcharges de l'impôt en dépenfes de perception.

3.° Excès de luxe de décoration.

4.° Excès de dépenfes litigieufes.

5.° Défaut de commerce extérieur des productions des biens-fonds.

produce which are exported and imported, and which are stored in the shops and warehouses of the merchants and destined for annual use or consumption, since they are included and taken account of in the figures of annual product and expenditure, in conformity with the order set out in the *tableau*.

THE TOTAL OF THE WEALTH OF

THE STERILE EXPENDITURE CLASS

may amount to about[41] . . . . 18,000,000,000 livres.[42]

GRAND TOTAL . . . . 59,000,000,000 livres.[43]

That is, assuming a possible error of

one-twentieth either way . . . . . 55 to 60,000,000,000 livres.[44]

We are speaking here of an opulent nation with a territory and advances which yield it annually and without any abatement a net product of 1050 millions. But all these items of wealth, which are successively maintained by this annual product, may be destroyed or lose their value if an agricultural nation falls into a state of decline, simply through the wasting away of the advances required for productive expenditure. This wasting away can make considerable headway in a short time for eight principal reasons:

1. A bad system of tax-assessment, which encroaches upon the cultivators' advances. *Noli me tangere* – that is the motto for these advances.

2. An extra burden of taxation due to the costs of collection.

3. An excess of luxury in the way of ornamentation.

4. Excessive expenditure on litigation.

5. A lack of external trade in the products of landed property.

6.º Défaut de liberté dans le commerce intérieur des denrées du crû, & dans la culture.

7.º Vexations personnelles des habitans de la campagne.

8.º Défaut du retour du produit net annuel à la claffe des dépenfes productives.

E R R A T A. corrigé

Page ij, ligne 9, *400 liv.* lifez *500 liv.* ligne 13, *800 liv.* lifez *700 liv.*

EXTRAIT

6. A lack of freedom of internal trade in raw produce, and in cultivation.

7. The personal harassment of the inhabitants of the countryside.

8. Failure of the annual net product to return to the productive expenditure class.

ERRATA[45]

Page ij, line 9: For '400 livres' read '500 livres'.
line 13: For '800 livres' read '700 livres'.

EXTRAIT

DES

ÉCONOMIES ROYALES DE M. DE SULLY.

ON voit dans le Tableau précédent que dans l'ordre de la circulation régulière de 600 millions de revenu annuel, ces 600 millions s'obtiennent au moyen de 900 millions d'avances annuelles * & se diftribuent annuel-

---

* Il faut ajoûter l'impôt aux 600 millions de revenu : s'il eft de 300 millions, & la dixme de 150 millions, le produit net doit être de 1,050 millions. Mais les avances annuelles, qui le font naître, & les avances primitives pour former d'abord l'établiffement des Laboureurs, feront enfemble d'environ quatre milliards : Ainfi il faut remarquer que les terres les plus fertiles feroient nulles fans les richeffes néceffaires pour fubvenir aux dépenfes de la culture, & que la dégradation de l'agriculture dans un royaume ne doit pas être imputée à la pareffe des hommes, mais à leur indigence.

L'impôt bien ordonné, c'eft-à-dire l'impôt qui ne dégénere pas en *fpoliation*, par une mauvaife forme d'impofition, doit être regardé comme une partie du revenu détachée du produit net des biens-fonds d'une Nation agricole ; car autrement il n'auroit aucune règle proportionnelle avec lui-même, ni avec le revenu, ni avec l'état des fujets contribuables ; il pourroit infenfiblement tout ruiner avant que le Miniftère s'en aperçût.

L'impofition du tribut ne doit donc porter que fur le revenu, c'eft-à-dire, fur le produit net annuel des biens-fonds, & non fur les avances des Laboureurs, ni fur les hommes de travail, ni fur la vente des marchandifes ; car dans ces derniers cas il eft deftructif. Sur les avances des Laboureurs ce ne feroit pas un impôt, mais une fpoliation qui éteindroit la reproduction, détérioreroit les terres, ruineroit les Fermiers, les Propriétaires, & l'État : Sur le falaire des hommes de travail & fur la vente des marchan-difes, il eft arbitraire, & les frais de perception

furpafferoient l'impot, retomberoient fans règle fur les revenus de la Nation & fur les revenus de l'Etat. Il faut diftinguer ici l'impofition d'avec l'impot ; l'impofition feroit le triple de l'impot, & s'étendroit fur l'impot même ; car dans toutes les dépenfes de l'Etat, les taxes impofées fur les marchandifes, feroient payées par l'impot. Ainfi cet impot feroit trompeur & ruineux.

L'impofition fur les hommes de travail qui vivent de leur falaire, n'eft rigoureufement parlant, qu'une impofition fur le travail, qui eft payée par ceux qui employent les Ouvriers : de même qu'une impofition fur les chevaux qui laboursent la terre, ne feroit réellement qu'une impofition fur les dépenfes mêmes de la culture. Ainfi l'impofition fur les hommes, & non fur le revenu, porteroit fur les frais mêmes de l'induftrie & de l'agriculture, & retomberoit doublement en perte fur le revenu des biens-fonds, & conduiroit rapidemment à la deftruction de l'impôt. On doit penfer de cet impôt comme des taxes fur les marchandifes, qui tomberoient auffi en pure perte fur le revenu, fur l'impot & fur les dépenfes de la culture, & exigeroient des frais immenfes qu'il feroit impoffible d'éviter dans un grand Etat.

Cependant ce genre d'impofition eft forcément la reffource des petits Etats maritimes, qui fubfiftent par un commerce de trafic néceffairement affujéti à l'impôt ; ou des grands Etats, lorfque l'agriculture eft tombée dans un tel dépériffement que le revenu du territoire ne pourroit plus fubvenir au payement de l'impôt. Mais dans le dernier cas, cette ref-

A

EXTRACT

FROM

THE ROYAL ECONOMIC MAXIMS OF M. DE SULLY[46]

From the preceding *tableau* it can be seen that in the order of the regular circulation of 600 millions of annual revenue, these 600 millions are obtained by means of 900 millions of annual advances,* and are distributed

* It is necessary to add taxes to the 600 millions of revenue. If these taxes amount to 300 millions, and tithes to 150 millions, the net product will be 1050 millions. But the annual advances which generate it, and the original advances required in the beginning to set the husbandmen up in their enterprises, will total about four milliards.[47] Thus it should be noted that the most fertile land would be worthless without the wealth necessary to meet the expenses of cultivation, and that the deterioration of a kingdom's agriculture ought to be attributed not to men's idleness but to their poverty.[48]

A properly organised tax, i.e. a tax which does not degenerate into *spoliation* by reason of a bad form of assessment, should be regarded as a portion of revenue taken out of the net product of the landed property of an agricultural nation; for otherwise it would not be subject to any rule keeping it in proportion with itself, nor with the revenue, nor with the situation of tax-paying subjects, and it could imperceptibly ruin everything before the administration became aware of it.[49]

Thus the contribution should be assessed only on the revenue, i.e. on the annual net product of landed property, and not on the advances of husbandmen, or on labourers, or on the sale of commodities, for in the latter cases it is destructive. On the advances of husbandmen it would represent not taxation but spoliation, which would wipe out reproduction, cause the land to deteriorate, and ruin the farmers, the proprietors, and the state. On the wages of labourers and the sale of commodities it is arbitrary, and the costs of collection would exceed the tax and be thrown back in an unregulated way on the revenue of the nation and on the revenue of the

state. We have to distinguish here between taxes assessed and taxes received; taxes assessed would be three times taxes received, and would encroach upon taxes received themselves; for in all state expenditure taxes assessed on commodities would be paid for out of taxes received. Thus such taxes would be delusive and ruinous.[50]

The assessment of taxes on labourers who live off their wages is strictly speaking nothing more than an assessment on their labour, which is paid by those who employ the workers, in the same way that an assessment on the horses which plough the land would really be nothing more than an assessment on the expenses of cultivation themselves. Thus an assessment on men rather than on the revenue would be borne by industrial and agricultural costs themselves, and it would be thrown back on the revenue of landed property in a way which involved a double loss, and would rapidly lead to the wiping out of tax receipts. This tax should be regarded in the same way as taxes on commodities, which would also be borne to no purpose by the revenue, by the tax receipts, and by the expenses of cultivation, and would entail charges which it would be impossible to avoid in a large state.[51]

Recourse to assessments of this kind, however, must necessarily be had by small maritime states which get their living by means of re-export trade, the latter being inevitably subjected to taxation; or by large states where agriculture has fallen into such a state of decline that the territory's revenue could not provide for the payment of the taxes. But in the latter case this expedient means

2

lement à quatre millions de chefs de familles. Il y a un million de Propriétaires, dont la dépenſe eſt eſtimée, du fort au foible, à 600 liv. pour chacun [*a*], & trois millions de chefs de famille occupés aux travaux ou emplois lucratifs, qui chacun, du fort au foible, retirent 300 liv. pour leur dépenſe [*b*].

ſource eſt une ſurcharge qui réduit le peuple à une épargne forcée ſur la conſommation, qui arrête le travail, qui éteint la reproduction, & qui acheve de ruiner les Sujets, & le Souverain.

On a ſouvent parlé de l'établiſſement de l'impôt payé en nature par la récolte en forme de Dixme : ce genre d'impoſition ſeroit à la vérité proportionnel au produit total de la récolte, les frais compris ; mais il n'auroit aucun rapport avec le produit net ; plus la terre eſt médiocre, & plus la récolte eſt foible, plus il eſt onéreux & injuſte.

L'impôt doit donc être pris immédiatement ſur le produit net des biens-fonds ; car de quelque maniere qu'il ſoit impoſé dans un royaume qui tire ſes richeſſes de ſon territoire, il eſt toûjours payé par les biens-fonds : Ainſi la forme d'impoſition la plus ſimple, la plus réglée, la plus profitable à l'Etat, & la moins onéreuſe aux contribuables, eſt celle qui eſt établie proportionnellement & immédiatement à la ſource des richeſſes continuellement renaiſſantes. Il s'agit ici de l'impôt ordinaire, & non des ſubventions paſſageres, exigées par les beſoins preſſans de l'Etat, pour leſquels le gouvernement ſeroit forcé de recourir à des reſſources ſubſidiaires, ſans préjudicier à la culture.

[*a*] Les 600 millions de revenu peuvent être partagés à un plus petit nombre de propriétaires : Dans ce cas, moins il y auroit de propriétaires, plus la dépenſe de leur revenu ſurpaſſeroit la conſommation que chacun d'eux pourroit faire perſonnellement ; mais ils feroient des libéralités, ou raſſembleroient d'autres hommes pour conſommer avec eux ce que leur revenu fourniroit pour leurs dépenſes : ainſi ces dépenſes ſe trouveroient diſtribuées à peu près, comme s'il y avoit un plus grand nombre de propriétaires bornés chacun à une moindre dépenſe. On doit penſer de même de l'inégalité des gains ou des profits des hommes des autres

claſſes, où les avances, les intérêts & les profits des Entrepreneurs d'agriculture, de commerce, de manufactures, &c. ſe tranſmettent aux Ouvriers, & qui par une diſtribution ſucceſſive & réciproque, fourniſſent par gradation, & tour à tour, des gains ou des ſalaires à tous les hommes qui exercent des profeſſions lucratives, d'où il arrive que la dépenſe même des riches n'eſt qu'une tranſmiſſion diſtributive de dépenſes, qui s'étend à tous les autres citoyens ſelon l'ordre de leur ſalaire.

[*b*] L'impôt de 300 millions eſt compté en dehors des 600 millions de revenu ; ainſi tout ce qui en rentre dans la circulation, s'il n'eſt pas ſpoliatif, eſt regagné par les ſujets, & eſt un ſurcroît au revenu de 600 millions, qui leur eſt diſtribué. Si tout l'impôt eſt dépenſé dans le pays, il formera avec le revenu & le produit de la dixme de 150 millions, 1,050,000,000. Les intérêts des avances primitives & annuelles des Laboureurs, ſeront alors environ de 443,300,000, & la reproduction annuelle de la moitié des frais employés en ſalaires d'hommes, (car on ne parle pas ici des frais pour la nourriture des animaux de travail, &c.) fournira 525 millions. Le total eſt 2,018,300,000, pour la dépenſe de 16 millions de perſonnes de tout âge, dont près de moitié eſt en bas âge, & de peu de dépenſe. Ainſi dans cette ſuppoſition, le peuple eſt dans l'aiſance ; car la dépenſe de 16 millions de perſonnes de tout âge, ne ſeroit qu'à peu près égale à celle de onze millions de perſonnes hors de bas âge ; il y auroit donc, l'impôt compris, environ deux cens millions à dépenſer pour un million d'hommes. Mais il n'y a qu'une riche culture qui puiſſe élever le Souverain & la Nation à ce degré permanent de puiſſance & de proſpérité. Ce calcul ſuppoſe un établiſſement d'agriculture où les avances annuelles rendent cent pour cent de produit net ; car ſi elles rendoient moitié ou trois quarts moins

annually to four million heads of families. There are one million proprietors, whose average expenditure is estimated at 600 livres each [a], and three million heads of families engaged in remunerative work or employment, each of whom draws on the average 300 livres for his expenditure [b].[52]

an added burden which reduces the people to forced economies in consumption, causes labour to be checked, wipes out reproduction, and finishes by ruining subject and sovereign.[53]

People have often talked about establishing a tax payable in kind from the harvest in the form of a tithe. This kind of assessment would certainly be proportionate to the total product of the harvest, costs included; but it would not bear any relation to the net product. The more inferior the land, and the poorer the harvest, the more burdensome and unjust it is.[54]

Thus taxes should be laid directly on the net product of landed property; for in whatever manner they may be assessed in a kingdom which draws its wealth from its territory, they are always paid by landed property. Thus the form of assessment which is the most simple, the most regular, the most profitable to the state, and the least burdensome to the tax-payers, is that which is made proportionate to and laid directly on the source of continually regenerated wealth. It is a question here of normal taxes and not of transitory subventions necessitated by the urgent needs of the state, for which the Government would be forced to have recourse to additional expedients, without injury to cultivation.[55]

[a] The 600 millions of revenue may be divided among a smaller number of proprietors. In that case, the fewer proprietors there were, the more would the expenditure of their revenue exceed the amount which each of them would personally be able to consume. But then they would indulge in liberality, or gather together other men to consume with them what their revenue provided for their expenditure, so that this expenditure would turn out to be distributed in almost the same way as if there had been a greater number of proprietors limited to a smaller individual expenditure. We should regard in the same way inequalities in the gains or profits of men in the other classes, where the advances, the

interest and the profits of entrepreneurs in agriculture, commerce, manufacture, etc., are passed on to the workmen, and provide, by means of a mutual distribution which proceeds round by round in successive steps, profits or wages for all men who carry on remunerative occupations. Thus it comes about that the expenditure of wealth is only a distribution and transference of expenditure, which is spread out among all the other citizens in accordance with the kind of reward they receive.[56]

[b] The taxes of 300 millions are taken into account apart from the 600 millions of revenue. Thus all of the tax which comes back into circulation, if it is not spoliatory, is regained by the subjects, and represents an addition to the revenue of 600 millions which is distributed to them. If the whole of the tax is spent within the country, then together with the revenue and the product of the tithes of 150 millions it will make up 1,050,000,000. The interest on the original and annual advances of the husbandmen will then be about 443,300,000,[57] and the annual reproduction of the one-half of the costs which is devoted to paying men's wages (for we are not speaking here of the costs of feeding the working animals, etc.) will provide 525 millions. The total is 2,018,300,000[58] for the expenditure of 16 million persons of all ages, about half of whom are children whose expenses are small. Thus in the assumed circumstances people live well, for the expenses of 16 million persons of all ages would be equal to those of only about 11 million adults, so that each million men would have about 200 millions (taxes included) to spend. But it is only a wealthy state of cultivation which can raise the sovereign and the nation permanently to this height of power and prosperity. This calculation assumes a state of affairs in agriculture in which the annual advances yield a net product of 100 per cent; for if they yielded one-half or three-quarters less than this,

Mais dans cette diſtribution on ſuppoſe,

1.° Que la totalité des 600 millions de revenu entre dans la circulation annuelle & la parcourt dans toute ſon étendue, qu'il ne ſe forme point de fortunes pécuniaires, ou du moins qu'il y ait compenſation entre celles qui ſe forment, & celles qui reviennent dans la circulation * ; car autrement ces fortunes pécuniaires arrêteroient le cours d'une partie de ce revenu annuel de la Nation, & retiendroient le pécule ou la finance du royaume, au préjudice de la rentrée des avances, de la rétribution du ſalaire des artiſans, de la reproduction du revenu, & de l'impôt.

2.° Qu'une partie de la ſomme des revenus ne paſſe pas chez l'étranger, ſans retour en argent & en marchandiſes.

3.° Que la Nation ne ſouffre pas de perte dans ſon commerce réciproque avec l'étranger, quand même ce commerce ſeroit fort profitable aux Commerçans, en gagnant ſur leurs concitoyens dans la vente des marchandiſes qu'ils rapportent ; car alors l'accroiſſement de fortune de ces Commerçans eſt un retranchement dans la circulation des revenus, qui eſt préjudiciable à la diſtribution & à la reproduction.

par erreur de gouvernement, il y auroit de grands frais, peu de revenu, & une population qui ne feroit preſque qu'en menu peuple, occupé dans les campagnes, ſans profit pour l'Etat, à une mauvaiſe culture, qui le feroit ſubſiſter miſérablement.

* On ne doit pas entendre ſimplement par les fortunes qui rentrent dans la circulation, les fortunes qui ſe détruiſent, mais auſſi les fortunes ſtériles ou oiſives, qui deviennent actives, & qui ſont employées, par exemple, à former les avances des grandes entrepriſes d'agriculture, de commerce, & de manufactures profitables, ou à acquérir des biens-fonds dont les revenus rentrent annuellement dans la circulation : C'eſt même par ces fortunes actives bien établies, qu'un Etat a de la conſiſtance, qu'il a de grandes richeſſes aſſurées pour faire renaître annuellement de grandes richeſſes, pour entretenir une population dans l'aiſance, & pour aſſurer la proſpérité de l'Etat & la puiſſance du Souverain. Mais on ne doit pas penſer de même des fortunes pécuniaires qui tirent des intérêts de l'argent, & qui ne ſont pas établis ſur des fonds productifs, ni celles qui ſont employées à des acquiſitions de Charges inutiles, de Priviléges, &c. & qui ſont des fortunes rongeantes, & onéreuſes à la Nation.

But in this distribution it is assumed:

1. [59] That the whole of the 600 millions of revenue enters into the annual circulation, and runs through it to the full extent of its course; and that it is never formed into monetary fortunes, or at least that those which are formed are counterbalanced by those which come back into circulation;* for otherwise these monetary fortunes would check the flow of a part of this annual revenue of the nation, and hold back the money stock or finance of the kingdom, to the detriment of the return of the advances, the payment of the artisans' wages, the reproduction of the revenue, and the taxes.

2. [60] That no part of the sum of the revenues passes into the hands of foreign countries without return in money and commodities.

3. [61] That the nation does not suffer any loss in its mutual trade with foreign countries, even if this trade is very profitable to the merchants through the gains they make out of their fellow-citizens on the sale of the commodities they import; for then the increase in the fortunes of these merchants represents a deduction from the circulation of the revenue, which is detrimental to distribution and reproduction.

owing to a mistaken government policy, costs would be high, there would be little revenue, and the population would consist almost entirely of lower-class people working in the countryside, without any profit to the state, at a poor type of cultivation which obliged them to live in wretchedness.[62]

* By the fortunes which come back into circulation we should understand not simply those fortunes which are destroyed, but also those sterile or idle fortunes which become active, and which are employed, for example, to form the advances of large enterprises in agriculture, trade, and profitable manufactures, or to acquire landed property whose revenue comes back into circulation each year. Indeed, it is by virtue of these active fortunes, when they are properly used in business, that a state possesses stability, and that it is secure in its possession of great wealth which is used each year to regenerate great wealth, to maintain its population in comfort, and to ensure the prosperity of the state and the power of the sovereign. But we should not regard in the same way the monetary fortunes which are drawn from interest on money and which are not charged on productive funds, nor those which are employed in the acquisition of useless offices, privileges, etc., and are burdensome fortunes which undermine the nation.[63]

4.° Qu'on ne soit pas trompé par un avantage apparent du commerce réciproque avec l'étranger, en jugeant simplement par la balance des sommes en argent, sans examiner le plus ou le moins de profit qui résulte des marchandises mêmes que l'on a vendues & de celles que l'on a achetées : car souvent la perte est pour la Nation qui reçoit un surplus en argent, & cette perte se tourne au préjudice de la distribution & de la reproduction des revenus. Dans le commerce réciproque des denrées du crû que l'on achette de l'étranger, & des marchandises de main-d'œuvre qu'on lui vend, le desavantage est ordinairement du côté de ces dernières marchandises, parce qu'on retire beaucoup plus de profit de la vente des denrées du crû.

5.° Que les Propriétaires & ceux qui exercent les professions lucratives, ne soient pas portés, par quelqu'inquiétude qui ne seroit pas prévûe par le Gouvernement, à se livrer à des épargnes stériles, qui retrancheroient de la circulation & de la distribution une portion de leurs revenus ou de leurs gains.

6.° Que l'administration des finances, soit dans la perception des impôts, soit dans les dépenses du Gouvernement, n'occasionne pas de fortunes pécuniaires, qui dérobent une partie des revenus à la circulation, à la distribution, & à la reproduction.

7.° Que l'impôt ne soit pas destructif ou disproportionné à la masse du revenu de la Nation ; que son augmentation suive l'augmentation du revenu ; qu'il soit établi immédiatement sur le produit net des biens-fonds, & non sur les denrées, où il multiplieroit les frais de perception,

&

4. [64] That people are not taken in by a seeming advantage in mutual trade with foreign countries, through judging it simply with reference to the balance of the sums of money involved and not examining the greater or lesser profit which results from the particular commodities which are sold and purchased; for the loss often falls on the nation which receives a surplus in money, and this loss operates to the detriment of the distribution and reproduction of the revenue. In the mutual trade of the raw produce which is purchased from abroad and the manufactured commodities which are sold abroad, the disadvantage usually lies on the side of the latter commodities, because much more profit is yielded by the sale of raw produce.

5. [65] That the proprietors and those engaged in remunerative occupations are not led by any anxiety, unforeseen by the Government, to give themselves over to sterile saving, which would deduct from circulation and distribution a portion of their revenues or gains.

6. [66] That the administration of finance, whether in the collection of taxes or in the expenditure of the Government, does not bring about the formation of monetary fortunes, which steal a portion of the revenue away from circulation, distribution, and reproduction.

7. [67] That taxes are not destructive or disproportionate to the mass of the nation's revenue; that their increase follows the increase of the revenue; and that they are laid directly on the net product of landed property, and not on produce, where they would increase the costs of

& préjudicieroit au Commerce : Qu'il ne se prenne pas non plus sur les avances des Fermiers des biens-fonds ; car les avances de l'agriculture d'un royaume doivent être envisagées comme un immeuble qui doit être conservé précieusement pour la production de l'impôt & du revenu de la Nation, autrement l'impôt dégénère en spoliation, & cause un dépérissement qui ruine promptement un Etat [a].

[a] L'établissement simple de l'imposition à la source des revenus, c'est-à-dire, sur le produit net des terres qui fournit le revenu des Propriétaires, devient fort difficile dans un Royaume où, faute d'avances, l'agriculture est tombée en ruine ; ou du moins dans une telle dégradation, qu'elle ne peut se prêter à aucun cadastre fixe & proportionné aux qualités des terres qui sont mal cultivées, & dont le produit est borné à l'état de la culture ; car l'amélioration de la culture, qui pourroit résulter d'une meilleure administration, rendroit aussitôt le cadastre très-irrégulier.

D'ailleurs tout le produit net d'une culture ruinée seroit à peine suffisant pour payer l'impôt ; ainsi il ne peut pas alors être établi totalement sur le revenu des Propriétaires : Mais doit-on alors recourir à des impositions ruineuses ? Est-ce donc dans une Nation agricole la seule ressource d'un Etat où l'agriculture est ruinée, ou réduite par la pauvreté des Cultivateurs, presque toute en petite culture ? Si l'agriculture y étoit en vigueur, elle pourroit seule fournir amplement à l'impôt, & il ne seroit pas onéreux comme les taxes multipliées & surchargées de frais de perception : Mais on les croit de plus en plus inévitables, à mesure que le dépérissement augmente.

Cependant il faut au moins commencer par supprimer au plus tôt les impositions arbitraires établies sur les Fermiers, sans quoi ce genre d'imposition ruineuse acheveroit de détruire entierement les revenus du Royaume. L'imposition sur les biens-fonds la plus difficile à régler, est celle qui s'établit sur la petite culture, où il n'y a pas de fermage qui puisse servir de mesure, où c'est le propriétaire même qui fournit les avances, & où le produit net est très-foible & fort incertain. Cette culture qui s'exé-cute par des Métayers dans les Pays où l'impôt a détruit les Fermiers, & qui est la derniere ressource de l'agriculture ruinée, exige beaucoup de ménagement ; car un impôt un peu onéreux enleve ses avances, & l'anéantit entierement. Il faut donc bien distinguer les terres réduites à cette petite culture, & qui, à proportion du produit, sont labourées à grands frais & souvent sans aucun profit, d'avec la grande culture exécutée par de riches Fermiers, lesquels assurent aux Propriétaires un revenu déterminé qui peut servir de regle exacte pour une imposition proportionnelle, qui doit être payée par le Propriétaire, & non par le Fermier, si ce n'est à compte sur le fermage qu'il doit au Propriétaire : alors les Propriétaires, fixés invariablement à cette regle par le Gouvernement, pour toutes les terres affermées, seroient attentifs, pour la sureté de leur revenu & de l'impôt, à n'affermer leurs terres qu'à de riches Fermiers ; cette précaution assureroit les succès de l'agriculture, & les Fermiers n'ayant plus d'inquiétude sur l'imposition pendant le cours de leurs baux, se multiplieroient ; la petite culture disparoîtroit successivement ; les revenus des Propriétaires, & l'impôt s'accroîtroient à proportion, par l'augmentation des produits des biens-fonds cultivés par de riches Laboureurs.

Une Nation florissante, cependant chargée de subsides établis sur divers objets, & bornée à un territoire qui n'est pas fort étendu, a sû affermir sa puissance & assurer sa prospérité, en exemptant la charrue de toute imposition. Les Propriétaires chargés eux-mêmes de l'impôt, souffrent dans les temps de guerre des subventions passageres, qui pendant ces temps orageux peuvent restraindre leurs dépenses ; mais les travaux de la culture des terres n'en sont point ralentis,

B

collection, and operate to the detriment of trade. That they are also not taken from the advances of the farmers of landed property; for the advances of a kingdom's agriculture ought to be regarded as if they were fixed property which should be preserved with great care in order to ensure the production of the taxes and the revenue of the nation. Otherwise taxation degenerates into spoliation, and brings about a state of decline which very soon ruins the state [a].

[a] [68] The simple establishment of an assessment on the source of revenue, i.e. on the net product of the land which provides the revenue of the proprietors, becomes very difficult in a kingdom where for want of advances agriculture has fallen into decay, or at least into such a deteriorated state that no cadastral survey would yield results which were permanent and properly adjusted to the qualities of the land, which is badly cultivated and whose product is limited by the state of cultivation; for the improvement of cultivation which better administration could bring about would immediately render the survey very unreliable.[69]

Moreover, the whole net product of a ruined agriculture would scarcely be sufficient to pay the taxes; thus they cannot then be laid entirely on the revenue of the proprietors. But should recourse therefore be had to ruinous assessments? Is this, in an agricultural nation, the only expedient open to a state in which agriculture is ruined, or almost completely reduced to small-scale cultivation through the poverty of the cultivators? If agriculture were in full vigour there, it alone could amply provide for the taxes, and they would not be burdensome as taxes are when they are increased and surcharged with costs of collection. But they are believed to be more and more inevitable in the proportion that the decline increases.[70]

Nevertheless, we must at least begin by doing away as soon as possible with the arbitrary assessments laid on the farmers, for unless we did so this ruinous kind of assessment would end by completely destroying the kingdom's revenue. The assessment on landed property which is the most difficult to regulate is that which is laid on small-scale cultivation, where there is no rent to serve as a measure, where it is the proprietor himself who provides the advances, and where the net product is very small and uncertain. This type of cultivation,

which is carried on by *métayers* in areas where taxation has destroyed the farmers, and which is the last resort of ruined agriculture, has to be treated very carefully, for a small tax burden robs it of its advances and completely wipes it out. Thus we should be careful to distinguish land which is reduced to this small-scale cultivation, and which relatively to its product is worked at high cost and often without any profit, with large-scale cultivation carried on by rich farmers, who guarantee the proprietors a fixed revenue which can serve as an exact rule for a proportional assessment, which should be paid by the proprietor, and not by the farmer, if it is not taken account of in the rent which he owes to the proprietor. The proprietors, with this invariable rule fixed for them by the Government, in respect of all land let out on lease, would then take good care, in order to safeguard their revenue and the taxes, to let their land only to rich farmers; and this policy would ensure the success of agriculture. The farmers, no longer subject to anxiety about an assessment during the term of their leases, would increase in numbers; small-scale cultivation would disappear in one case after the other; and the revenue of the proprietors and the taxes would be proportionately increased owing to the increase in the produce of the landed property cultivated by rich husbandmen.[71]

There is a flourishing nation which, burdened as it is with subsidies laid on different objects and confined to a territory which is not very extensive, has nevertheless been able to consolidate its power and ensure its prosperity by exempting agriculture from all assessments. The proprietors, upon whom the taxes are laid, bear the burden of temporary subsidies during war-time, which may restrict their expenditure in this stormy period; but the work of cultivating the land is never

8.º Que les avances des Fermiers ſoient ſuffiſantes pour que les dépenſes de la culture reproduiſent au moins cent pour cent ; car ſi les avances ne ſont pas ſuffiſantes, les dépenſes de la culture ſont plus grandes à proportion, & donnent moins de produit net [a].

& le débit, & la valeur vénale des biens-fonds ſont toûjours aſſurés par la liberté du commerce extérieur des denrées du crû ; l'agriculture & la multiplication des beſtiaux ne ſouffrent aucune dégradation pendant les guerres les plus longues & les plus diſpendieuſes : les Propriétaires retrouvent à la paix leurs terres bien cultivées & bien entretenues, & leurs grands revenus bien maintenus & bien aſſurés. Il eſt aiſé par-là d'appercevoir la différence qu'il y a entre un impôt exhorbitant & un impôt ſpoliatif ; car par la forme de l'impoſition, un impôt peut être ſpoliatif ſans être exhorbitant, ou peut être exhorbitant ſans être ſpoliatif. Cette Nation, inépuiſable par ſes richeſſes toujours renaiſſantes, ſoutient avec des forces militaires ſur terre & ſur mer, des guerres opiniâtres par des revenus aſſurés qui ſe renouvellent annuellement ſans dépériſſement & qui réparent ſes forces.

[a] Autrefois dans tel Royaume les avances ne produiſoient du fort au foible, l'impôt ſur le Laboureur compris, qu'environ vingt pour cent, qui ſe diſtribuoient à la dixme, à l'impôt, au Propriétaire : Diſtraction faite des repriſes annuelles du Laboureur : Ainſi *déficit* de quatre cinquièmes ſur le produit net des avances, avec la perte ſur l'emploi & le revenu des terres qui ſuppléoient elles-mêmes aux frais d'une pauvre culture, & qu'on laiſſoit en friche alternativement pendant pluſieurs années pour les réparer, & les remettre en état de produire un peu de récolte : Alors la plus grande partie des habitans étoit dans la miſère, & ſans profit pour l'Etat : Car *tel eſt le produit net des avances au-delà des dépenſes, tel eſt auſſi le produit net du travail des hommes qui le font naître : Et tel eſt le produit net des biens-fonds, tel eſt le produit net pour le revenu, pour l'impôt & pour la ſubſiſtance des différentes claſſes d'hommes d'une Nation.* Ainſi plus les avances ſont inſuffiſantes, moins les hommes, les terres ſont profitables à l'Etat. Les Colons qui ſubſiſtent miſérablement d'une culture ingrate, ne ſervent qu'à entretenir in-fructueuſement la population d'une pauvre Nation.

L'impôt dans ce Royaume étoit preſque tout établi arbitrairement ſur les Fermiers, ſur les Ouvriers & ſur les marchandiſes ; ainſi il portoit directement & indirectement ſur les avances des dépenſes de la culture, ce qui chargeoit les biens - fonds d'environ 200 millions pour l'impôt ordinaire, & autant pour la régie, les frais de perception, &c. Et les produits du ſol ne rendoient plus à la Nation, dans les derniers temps, à en juger par le dépouillement de la taxe d'un dixième ſur les fonds productifs, & par l'examen des produits des terres, qu'environ 400 millions de revenu, y compris la dixme & les autres revenus eccléſiaſtiques : Triſte produit d'un grand & excellent territoire, & d'une grande & laborieuſe population ! L'exportation des grains étoit défendue ; la production étoit bornée à la conſommation de la Nation ; la moitié des terres reſtoient en friches, on défendoit d'y planter des vignes ; le commerce intérieur des grains étoit livré à une police arbitraire, le débit étoit continuellement interrompu entre les Provinces ; & la valeur vénale des denrées toûjours incertaine.

Les avances des dépenſes productives étoient enlevées ſucceſſivement par l'impot, au préjudice de la reproduction qui diminuoit d'année en année ; les enfans des Laboureurs abandonnoient les campagnes ; le ſur-faix de l'impot ſur le prix naturel des denrées & du ſalaire des Ouvriers, ajoutoit un tiers en ſus au prix des marchandiſes & des frais de ſalaire dans la dépenſe du revenu de 400 millions ; ce qui réduiſoit en valeur réelle à 268 millions, & portoit le même préjudice au commerce extérieur & à l'emploi de l'impot qui rentroit dans la circulation. Dans la dépenſe de l'impot de 200 millions, l'Etat payoit pour ſa part 65 millions de l'impoſition établie ſur les denrées & ſur le ſalaire des hommes ; ce qui réduiſoit en valeur réelle l'impôt de 200 millions, qui entroit au Tréſor, à 145 millions. En rapportant toute cette réduction à

8. [72] That the advances of the farmers are sufficient to enable the expenses of cultivation to reproduce at least 100 per cent; for if the advances are not sufficient, the expenses of cultivation are proportionately higher and yield less net product [a].

slowed down, and the market for landed property and its market value are always assured by freedom of external trade in raw produce. Agriculture and livestock breeding do not suffer any decline during the longest and most costly wars; and when peace comes the proprietors find that their land has been well cultivated and well kept up, and their high revenue well maintained and well safeguarded. From this it is easy to see the difference which exists between an excessive tax and a spoliatory one; for according to the way in which it is assessed, a tax may be spoliatory without being excessive, or excessive without being spoliatory. This nation, inexhaustible by reason of its ever renascent wealth, maintains military forces on land and sea and sustains severe wars by means of assured revenues which are annually renewed without any decline and which restore its strength.[73]

[a] [74] In former times, in a kingdom of this kind, the advances produced on the average, taxes on the husbandman included, only about 20 per cent, which was distributed between tithes, taxes, and the proprietor, after deducting the annual returns of the husbandman. Thus there was a *deficit* of four-fifths in the net product of the advances, in addition to the loss of revenue involved in the employment of the land which was used to make up for the costs of a poor type of cultivation, and which was allowed to lie fallow in rotation for several years in order to restore it and put it once again in a position to produce a meagre harvest. At that time the majority of the inhabitants lived in poverty, and their activities brought no profit to the state. For *as the net product of advances over and above expenses is, so is also the net product of the labour of the men who generate it; and as the net product of landed property is, so is the net product available for revenue, taxation, and the subsistence of the different classes of men in a nation.* Thus the more insufficient the advances are, the less profitable the men and the land are to the state. Husbandmen who make a wretched living from a thankless type of culti-

vation serve only to maintain profitlessly the population of a poor nation.[75]

In this kingdom taxes were almost all laid arbitrarily on farmers, workers, and commodities. Thus they bore directly and indirectly upon the advances of the expenditure involved in cultivation, which charged landed property with about 200 millions for the ordinary taxes, and as much again for administration, costs of collection, etc. And in recent years, judging from the total of the tax of one-tenth on productive property and from an examination of the products of the land, the produce of the soil did not yield to the nation more than about 400 millions of revenue, including the tithes and other ecclesiastical revenues – a deplorable product for a large and splendid territory and a large and hard-working population! The export of corn was forbidden; production was limited to the nation's consumption; half the land lay fallow; the planting of vineyards was forbidden; internal trade in corn was subjected to an arbitrary system of regulation; the sale of corn from province to province was continually hindered; and the market value of produce was always uncertain.[76]

The advances of productive expenditure were successively eaten away by taxation, to the detriment of reproduction which diminished year by year; the children of the husbandmen abandoned the countryside; the additional burden of taxes on the natural price of produce and the worker's wages added one-third to the price of commodities and the wage-costs upon which the revenue of 400 millions was spent, which meant that in real terms its value was reduced to 268 millions; and it did the same damage to foreign trade and to the employment of the taxes which came back into circulation. In the expenditure of the taxes of 200 millions, the state for its part paid 65 millions of the assessment laid on produce and men's wages, which reduced to 145 millions[77] the real value of the taxes of 200 millions which accrued to the Treasury. When we bring back into the picture the whole of that reduction to 100

9.º Que les enfans des Fermiers s'établissent dans les campagnes pour y perpétuer les Laboureurs : car si quelques vexations leur font ab andonner les campagnes, & les

100 millions d'impôt fourni pour la masse de l'imposition, qui ajoûtoit en pure perte un faux prix à la vraie valeur vénale des denrées, on aperçoit que cet impôt de 100 millions, se payant à lui-même 65 millions, étoit presque annullé par l'imposition.

Cet impôt illusoire & destructif, donnoit une fausse idée des revenus & des richesses du Royaume. On comptoit d'une part 400 millions de revenu pour les Propriétaires, sans s'apercevoir que ce revenu & tout l'impôt, réduits à leur valeur réelle, ne formoient ensemble qu'environ 400 millions ; & on comptoit d'une autre 400 millions d'imposition, ce qui sembloit former un revenu total de 800 millions ; mais à travers cette confusion, on démêle clairement que le revenu de 400 millions, & l'imposition totale de 400 millions, qui en apparence forment ensemble un produit réel de 800 millions, se réduisoit à environ 400 millions de produit net ; & que le surplus, qui étoit 400 millions, ne consistant qu'en faux impôts & en faux frais, n'étoit qu'un surcroît de dépenses stériles & onéreuses, qui détruisoit radicalement chaque année environ 135 millions de produit réel ¶ qui tomboit en déchet sur les avances des Fermiers, sur le produit net des biens-fonds, sur les ouvrages de main-d'œuvre, & sur l'impôt ; sans y comprendre le dépérissement progressif qu'entraînoit la spoliation causée par la partie de l'impôt arbitraire établie sur les Fermiers, & qui joint au défaut de débit, faisoit tomber les terres en petite culture, & en friches. C'étoit à ce degré de décadence, où les dépenses de la culture ne produisoient plus, l'impôt compris, que 25 pour cent, encore étoit-ce par

le bénéfice de la grande culture qui existoit encore pour un quart dans le Royaume. Voyez dans l'*Encyclopédie*, article *GRAINS*, où l'on voit qu'une Nation perd annuellement les quatre cinquièmes du produit de sa culture. On ne suivra pas ici la marche rapide des progrès de cette décadence, elle est facile à entrevoir dans sa cause, & aussi facile à arrêter, ou en prévoir les funestes effets, avant qu'ils anéantissent un Etat.

Tous ces desordres & tous ces abus ont été reconnus ; & la gloire de les réparer étoit réservée à un Ministere plus éclairé : Mais les besoins de l'Etat & les circonstances ne se prêtent pas toûjours aux vûes que l'on se propose pour les réformes que peut exiger une bonne administration dans l'économie politique, quoique très-essentielles & très-pressantes pour la sûreté d'un Etat.

Le commerce réciproque avec l'étranger rapporte des marchandises qui sont payées par les revenus de la Nation en argent ou en échange ; ainsi, dans le détail des revenus d'un Royaume, il n'en faut pas faire un objet à part qui formeroit un double emploi. Il faut penser de même des loyers de maisons & des rentes d'intérêts d'argent ; car ce sont, pour ceux qui les payent, des dépenses qui se tirent d'une autre source, excepté les rentes placées sur les terres, qui sont assignées sur un fond productif ; mais ces rentes sont comprises dans le produit du revenu des terres : Ainsi ce sont les terres & les avances des Fermiers pour la culture, qui sont la source des revenus des Nations agricoles.

¶ *Formez le Tableau économique sur le pied de 400 millions de produit net, & de 400 millions d'imposition onéreuse, ce qui forme au total 800 millions, dont 200, qui sont la moitié du produit net, passent à la classe des dépenses productives, & 600 à celle des dépenses stériles ; les distributions entre les deux classes étant posées, les reproduits de la classe des dépenses produc-* ves ne monteront qu'à 665 millions au lieu de 800. Les avances annuelles de la culture, qui, les reprises du Laboureur à part, ne donnoient alors de produit net qu'environ 20 pour cent, doivent être supposées d'environ 1200 millions, partie en pure perte, pour 400 millions de produit net. Plus l'imposition destructive augmenteroit, plus l'impôt diminueroit & plus la dégradation s'accroitroit.

9. [78] That the children of farmers are settled in the countryside, so that there are always husbandmen there. For if they are harassed into abandoning the countryside and withdrawing to the towns, they take

millions of the total tax revenue yielded by the assessment, which falsely and to no purpose inflated the true market value of the produce, we see that this tax of 100 millions, which paid 65 millions to itself, was almost wiped out as a result of the method of assessment.[79]

This delusive and destructive tax gave a false idea of the kingdom's revenue and wealth. On the one hand, the revenue of the proprietors was reckoned as 400 millions, without it being realised that this revenue and the whole of the taxes, reduced to their real value, together made up only about 400 millions. On the other hand, the assessments were reckoned as 400 millions, which appeared to make up a total revenue of 800 millions. But upon disentangling this confusion we see clearly that the revenue of 400 millions and the total assessment of 400 millions, which seem at first sight to make up together a real product of 800 millions, were reduced to about 400 millions of net product, and that the surplus of 400 millions, consisting only of false taxes and unnecessary expenses, represented nothing but an additional burden of sterile expenses, which each year completely destroyed about 135 millions of real product,¶ and caused a falling-off in the advances of the farmers, the net product of landed property, manufactured goods, and taxes. And this takes no account of the progressive decline produced by the spoliation brought about by the portion of the taxes which was arbitrarily laid on the farmers, which when combined with the lack of sales led to land being cultivated on a small-scale basis and allowed to lie fallow. Such was the extent of the decline that the expenses of cultivation did not produce more than 25 per cent, taxes included, and even this was owing to the gains from the large-scale cultivation which still existed over a quarter of the kingdom. See the article *CORN* in the *Encyclopedia*, where a nation is described which loses every year four-fifths of the product of its cultivation. We shall not follow out here the course of this rapid process of decline: it is easy to catch sight of its cause, and it is also easy to stop it, or to foresee its deplorable effects before they reduce a state to nothing.[80]

All these irregularities and abuses have been recognised; and the glory of redressing them was reserved for a more enlightened Minister. But the needs of the state and particular circumstances do not always harmonise with the views put forward concerning the reforms which good administration in political economy may require, even though they are very necessary and very urgent from the point of view of the security of the state.[81]

Mutual trade with foreign countries brings in commodities which are paid for by the nation's revenue in money or in bartered goods. Thus we do not have to put this down as a separate item in the detailed account of a kingdom's revenue, since that would constitute double-counting. House-rent and income derived from interest on money must be regarded in the same way; for from the point of view of those who pay them, these constitute expenditure which is drawn from another source, with the exception of income charged on land, where the liability is placed on a productive fund; but this income is included in the product of the revenue of the land. Thus it is the land and the advances made by the farmers for purposes of cultivation which constitute the source of the revenue of agricultural nations.[82]

¶ [83] Draw up the *Tableau Économique* on the basis of 400 millions of net product and 400 millions of burdensome assessments, which makes a total of 800 millions, of which 200, constituting one-half of the net product, pass into the hands of the productive expenditure class, and 600 into those of the sterile expenditure class. When the distributions between the two classes are drawn in, the reproduction of the productive expenditure class will amount to only 665 millions instead of 800. The annual advances of cultivation, which, the returns of the husbandman apart, will then yield a net product of only about 20 per cent, must be assumed to be about 1200 millions, part of which is to no purpose, in order to give 400 millions of net product. The more that destructive assessments grow, the more the tax receipts will diminish and the more the decline will increase.

8

déterminent à se retirer dans les villes, ils y portent les richesses de leurs peres, qui étoient employées à la culture. Ce sont moins les hommes que les richesses qu'il faut attirer dans les campagnes ; car plus on employe de richesses à la culture des grains, moins elle occupe d'hommes, plus elle prospere, & plus elle donne de profit net. Telle est la grande culture des riches Fermiers, en comparaison de la petite culture des pauvrais Métayers qui labourent avec des bœufs ou avec des vaches [a].

10.º Que l'on évite la désertion des habitans qui emportent leurs richesses hors du Royaume.

11.º Que l'on n'empêche point le commerce extérieur des denrées du crû ; *car tel est le débit, telle est la reproduction* [b].

[a] Dans la grande culture, un homme seul conduit une charrue tirée par des chevaux, qui fait autant de travail que trois charrues tirées par des bœufs, & conduites par six hommes : Dans ce dernier cas, faute d'avances primitives pour l'établissement d'une grande culture, la dépense annuelle est excessive par proportion au produit net, qui est presque nul, & on y employe dix ou douze fois plus de terre. Les Propriétaires manquans de Fermiers en état de subvenir à la dépense d'une bonne culture, les avances se font aux dépens de la terre, & tout en pure perte ; le produit des prés est consommé, pendant l'hiver, par les bœufs de labour, & on leur laisse une partie de la terre pour leur pâturage pendant l'été : le produit net de la récolte approche si fort de la non-valeur, que la moindre imposition fait renoncer à ces restes de la culture ; ce qui arrive même en bien des endroits tout simplement par la pauvreté des habitans. On dit qu'il y a une Nation pauvre qui est réduite à cette petite culture dans les trois quarts de son territoire, & qu'il y a d'ailleurs plus d'un tiers des terres cultivables qui sont en non-valeur. Mais le Gouvernement est occupé à arrêter les progrès de cette dégradation & à pourvoir aux moyens de la réparer.

[b] Si on arrête le commerce extérieur des grains & des autres productions du crû, on borne l'agriculture à l'état de la population, au lieu d'étendre la population par l'agriculture : La vente des productions du crû à l'étranger augmente le revenu des biens-fonds ; cette augmentation de revenu augmente la dépense des Propriétaires ; cette augmentation de dépense attire les hommes dans le Royaume ; cette augmentation de population augmente la consommation des productions du crû ; cette augmentation de consommation & la vente à l'étranger accélerent de part & d'autre les progrès de l'agriculture, de la population & des revenus.

Par la liberté & la facilité du commerce extérieur d'exportation & d'importation, les grains ont constamment un prix plus égal : car le prix le plus égal, est celui qui a cours entre les Nations commerçantes. Ce commerce aplanit en tout temps l'inégalité annuelle des récoltes des Nations, en apportant tour à tour chez celles qui sont dans la pénurie, le superflu de celles qui sont dans l'abondance, & remet partout & toûjours les productions & le prix à peu près au même niveau. C'est pourquoi les Nations commerçantes qui n'ont pas de terres à ensemencer, ont leur pain aussi assuré que celles

there their fathers' wealth which used to be employed in cultivation. It is not so much men as wealth which must be attracted to the countryside; for the more wealth is employed in the cultivation of corn, the fewer men it requires, the more it prospers, and the more net profit it yields. Such is the large-scale cultivation carried on by rich farmers, in comparison with the small-scale cultivation carried on by poor *métayers* who plough with the aid of oxen or cows [a].

10. [84] That the desertion of inhabitants who take their wealth out of the kingdom is avoided.

11. [85] That no barriers at all are raised to external trade in raw produce; *for as the market is, so is the reproduction* [b].

[a] [86] In large-scale cultivation one man alone drives a plough drawn by horses, which does as much work as three ploughs drawn by oxen and driven by six men. In the latter case, because of a lack of the original advances required for the introduction of large-scale cultivation, the annual expenses are excessive in relation to the net product, which is almost zero, and ten or twelve times more land is employed. When the proprietors lack farmers in a position to meet the expenses of proper cultivation, the advances are made at the expense of the land, all to no purpose; the produce of the meadows is consumed during the winter by the labouring oxen, and a part of the land is left aside for their pasturage during the summer; and the net product of the harvest is so nearly valueless that the smallest tax makes it necessary to give up these remnants of cultivation, which in fact happens in many places simply by reason of the poverty of the inhabitants. It is said that there is a poor nation which is reduced to this small-scale cultivation over three-quarters of its territory, and that in addition more than a third of the cultivable land is going to waste. But the Government is engaged in stopping the course of this decline and in providing the means for setting things right again.[87]

[b] [88] If external trade in corn and other raw produce is stopped, agriculture is limited by the state of the population, instead of the population being increased through agriculture. The sale of raw produce abroad increases the revenue from landed property; this increase in revenue increases the proprietors' expenditure; this increase in expenditure attracts men into the kingdom; this increase in population increases the consumption of raw produce; this increase in consumption and the sales abroad both accelerate the advance of agriculture, population, and revenue.

As a result of a free and unobstructed export and import trade, corn always commands a more equal price, for the most equal price is that which is current among trading nations. This trade all the time smooths out the annual inequalities in nations' harvests, by supplying in turn those which are suffering from a scarcity with the surplus of those which have plenty, and always and everywhere brings products and prices back to almost the same level. That is why trading nations which have no land to till are just as sure of their bread as those which cultivate large territories. The slightest price advantage in a country attracts the commodity to it, and equality is continually re-established.

1 2.° Qu'on ne faſſe point baiſſer le prix des denrées & des marchandiſes dans le Royaume ; car le commerce réci-proque avec l'Etranger deviendroit déſavantageux à la Nation [*a*]. *TELLE EST LA VALEUR VENALE, TEL EST LE REVENU. Abondance & non-valeur n'eſt pas richeſſe. Diſette & cherté eſt miſère. Abondance & cherté eſt opulence* [*b*].

qui cultivent de grands territoires. Le moindre avantage ſur le prix dans un pays, y attire la mar-chandiſe, & l'égalité ſe rétablit continuellement.

Or il eſt démontré qu'indépendamment du débit à l'étranger, & d'un plus haut prix, la ſeule égalité conſtante du prix augmente de plus d'un ſixième le revenu des terres ; qu'elle accroît & aſſure les avances de la culture ; qu'elle évite les chertés exceſſives qui diminuent la population ; & qu'elle empêche les non-valeurs qui font languir l'agriculture : Au lieu que l'in-terdiction du commerce extérieur eſt cauſe que l'on manque ſouvent du néceſſaire ; que la culture qui eſt trop meſurée aux beſoins de la Nation, fait varier les prix autant que les bonnes & les mauvaiſes années font varier les récoltes ; que cette culture limitée laiſſe une grande partie des terres en non-valeur & ſans revenu ; que l'incertitude du débit inquiète les Fermiers, arrête les dépenſes de la culture, fait baiſſer le prix du fermage ; que ce dépériſſement s'ac-croît de plus en plus, à meſure que la Nation ſouffre d'une précaution inſidieuſe, qui enfin la ruine entièrement.

Si, pour ne pas manquer de grains, on s'ima-ginoit d'en défendre la vente à l'étranger, & d'empêcher auſſi les Commerçans de remplir des greniers dans les années abondantes, qui doivent ſuppléer aux mauvaiſes années, d'em-pêcher, dis-je, de multiplier ces magaſins libres, où la concurrence des Commerçans préſerve du monopole, procure aux Laboureurs du débit dans l'abondance, & ſoûtient l'abondance dans la ſté-rilité ; il faudroit conclurre des principes d'une adminiſtration ſi craintive & ſi étrangère à une Nation agricole, qui ne peut s'enrichir que par le débit de ſes productions, qu'on devroit auſſi reſtraindre, autant qu'on le pourroit, la conſom-mation du blé dans le pays, en y réduiſant

la nourriture du menu peuple aux pommes de terre, au blé noir, au gland, &c. & qu'il faudroit, par une prévoyance ſi déplacée & ſi ruineuſe, empêcher le tranſport des blés des Pro-vinces où il abonde, dans celles qui ſont dans la diſette, & dans celles qui ſont dégarnies par des permiſſions particulières ou furtives. Quels abus, quels monopoles cette police arbitraire & deſtructive n'occaſionneroit-elle pas dans un Royaume ! Que deviendroient la culture des terres, les revenus, l'impôt, le ſalaire des hom-mes, & les forces de la Nation !

[*a*] Si, par exemple, on achette de l'étranger telle quantité de marchandiſes pour la valeur d'un ſetier de blé du prix de 20 livres, il en faudroit deux ſetiers pour payer la même quan-tité de cette marchandiſe, ſi le Gouvernement faiſoit baiſſer le prix du blé à 10 livres.

[*b*] On doit diſtinguer dans un Etat les biens qui ont une valeur uſuelle & qui n'ont pas de valeur vénale, d'avec les richeſſes qui ont une valeur uſuelle & une valeur vénale ; par exemple, les Sauvages de la Louiſiane jouiſſoient de beau-coup de biens, tels ſont l'eau, le bois, le gibier, les fruits de la terre, &c. qui n'étoient pas des richeſſes, parce qu'ils n'avoient pas de valeur vénale : Mais depuis que quelques bran-ches de commerce ſe ſont établies entre eux & les François, les Anglois, les Eſpagnols, &c. une partie de ces biens a acquis une valeur vénale & eſt devenue richeſſe. Ainſi l'adminiſ-tration d'un Royaume doit tendre à procurer tout enſemble à la Nation, la plus grande abondance poſſible de productions, & la plus grande valeur vénale poſſible ; parce qu'avec de grandes richeſſes, elle ſe procure par le com-merce toutes autres ſortes de richeſſes, & de l'or & de l'argent dans la proportion convenable à l'état de ſes richeſſes.

C

12. [89] That the prices of produce and commodities in the kingdom are never made to fall; for then mutual foreign trade would become disadvantageous to the nation [a]. AS THE MARKET VALUE IS, SO IS THE REVENUE. *Abundance plus valuelessness does not equal wealth. Scarcity plus dearness equals poverty. Abundance plus dearness equals opulence* [b].

It has been shown that, independently of foreign sales and an increase in price, the constant equality of prices alone increases the revenue from the land by more than one-sixth;[90] that it increases and safeguards the advances necessary for cultivation; that it avoids excessively high prices which reduce the population; and that it prevents agriculture from wasting away through its produce becoming valueless. The prohibition of external trade, on the other hand, is the reason why necessaries are often lacking; why agriculture which is too closely proportioned to the needs of the nation causes prices to vary to the extent that good and bad years cause harvests to vary; why this limited agriculture leaves a large part of the land going to waste without yielding any revenue; why the uncertainty of the market causes anxiety to the farmers, halts expenditure on cultivation, and lowers the level of rent; and why this decline increases more and more, to the extent that the nation suffers from an insidious measure which ends by ruining it completely.

Suppose that for the purpose of avoiding any lack of corn we imagined that the sale of it abroad was forbidden, and also that merchants were prevented from filling up the warehouses in abundant years in order to make up for bad years; that it was forbidden, I say, to expand these free stores, where competition between merchants wards off monopoly, enables husbandmen to sell their produce in abundant years, and maintains abundance in sterile years. We should have to conclude, on the basis of these timorous administrative principles, so alien to an agricultural nation which can enrich itself only through the sale of its produce, that we should also restrict as much as possible the consumption of corn in the country, by reducing the food of its lower classes to potatoes, buckwheat, acorns, etc.; and that we should adopt so improper and ruinous a measure as to prevent the transport of corn from provinces where it is abundant to those which are suffering from scarcity and those whose supplies are depleted as a result of the issue of exclusive or secret licences. What abuses, what monpolies, this arbitrary and destructive policy would bring about in a kingdom! What would become of the cultivation of the land, the revenue, the taxes, men's wages, and the strength of the nation![91]

[a] [92] If, for example, we buy from abroad a certain quantity of commodities for the value of one *setier* of corn priced at 20 livres, two *setiers* of it would be necessary to pay for the same quantity of this commodity if the Government forced the price of corn down to 10 livres.[93]

[b] [94] A distinction should be made in a state between goods which have use value but which have no market value, and wealth, which has both use value and market value. For example, the savages of Louisiana used to enjoy many goods, such as water, wood, game, and the fruits of the earth, which did not constitute wealth because they had no market value. But after a number of branches of trade were opened up between them and the French, the English, the Spaniards, etc., a part of these goods has acquired market value and has become wealth. Thus the administration of a kingdom ought to aim at procuring for the nation at one and the same time the greatest possible abundance of products and the greatest possible market value, because with the aid of great wealth it procures for itself through trade all other kinds of wealth, and gold and silver in the proportions appropriate to the state of its wealth.[95]

13.° Que l'on ne croie pas que le bon marché des denrées foit profitable au menu peuple ; car le bas prix des denrées fait baiffer leur falaire, diminue leur aifance, leur procure moins de travail ou d'occupations lucratives, & diminue le revenu de la Nation (*a*).

14.° Qu'on ne diminue pas l'aifance du bas peuple ; car il ne pourroit pas affez contribuer à la confommation des denrées qui ne peuvent être confommées que dans le pays, & la reproduction & le revenu de la Nation diminueroient (*b*).

15.° Qu'on favorife la multiplication des beftiaux ; car

(*a*) La cherté du blé, par exemple, pourvû qu'elle foit conftante dans un Royaume agricole, eft plus avantageufe au menu peuple que le bas prix : Le falaire de la journée du manouvrier s'établit fur le prix du blé, & eft le vingtième du prix du fetier. Sur ce pied, fi le prix du blé étoit conftamment à 20 livres, le manouvrier gagneroit dans le cours de l'année environ 260 liv. il en dépenferoit en blé pour lui & fa famille 200 livres, & il lui refteroit 60 liv. pour les autres befoins ; fi au contraire le fetier de blé ne valoit que 10 livres, il ne gagneroit que 130 liv. il en dépenferoit 100 liv. en blé, & il ne lui refteroit, pour les autres befoins, que 30 liv. auffi voit-on que les Provinces où le blé eft cher font beaucoup plus peuplées que celles où il eft à bas prix.

Le même avantage fe trouve pour toutes les autres claffes d'hommes, pour le gain des Cultivateurs, pour le revenu des Propriétaires, pour l'impôt, pour la profpérité de l'Etat : car alors le produit des terres dédommage largement du furcroît des frais de falaires & de nourriture ; il eft aifé de s'en convaincre par le calcul des dépenfes & des accroiffemens des produits.

(*b*) Pour autorifer les vexations fur les habitans de la campagne, les exacteurs ont avancé pour maxime, *qu'il faut que les Payfans foient pauvres pour les empêcher d'être pareffeux:* Les bourgeois dédaigneux ont adopté volontiers cette

maxime barbare, parce qu'ils font moins attentifs à d'autres maximes plus décifives, qui font que l'*homme qui ne peut rien conferver ne travaille précifément que pour gagner de quoi fe nourrir* ; & *qu'en général tout homme qui peut conferver eft laborieux*, parce que tout homme eft avide de richeffes. Une autre caufe de la pareffe du Payfan opprimé eft le trop bas prix du falaire, & le peu d'emploi dans les pays où la gêne du commerce des productions a fait tomber les denrées en non-valeur, & où d'autres caufes ont ruiné l'agriculture. Les vexations, le bas prix des denrées, & un gain infuffifant pour les exciter au travail, les rendent pareffeux, braconniers, vagabons & pillards. La pauvreté forcée n'eft donc pas le moyen de rendre les Payfans laborieux : Il n'y a que la propriété & la jouiffance affurées de leur gain qui puiffent leur donner du courage & de l'activité.

Les Miniftres dirigés par des fentimens d'humanité, par une éducation fupérieure, & par des vûes plus étendues, rejettent avec indignation les maximes odieufes & deftructives qui ne tendent qu'à la dévaftation des campagnes ; car ils n'ignorent pas que ce font les richeffes des habitans de la campagne qui font naître les richeffes de la Nation. *PAUVRES PAYSANS, PAUVRE ROYAUME,*

13. [96] That people do not believe that cheapness of produce is profitable to the lower classes; for a low price of produce causes a fall in their wages, reduces their well-being, makes less work or remunerative occupations available for them, and reduces the nation's revenue (a).

14. [97] That the well-being of the lower orders is not reduced; for then they would not be able to contribute sufficiently to the consumption of the produce which can be consumed only within the country, and the reproduction and revenue of the nation would be reduced (b).

15. [98] That the breeding of livestock is encouraged; for it is livestock

(a) [99] A high price of corn, for example, provided that it is constant, is more advantageous to the lower classes in an agricultural kingdom than a low price. The daily wage of a labourer is fixed on the basis of the price of corn, and amounts to a twentieth of the price of one *setier*. On this basis, if the price of corn were constantly at 20 livres, the labourer would earn about 260 livres in the course of the year. He would spend 200 livres of this on corn for himself and his family, and would have 60 livres left over for other needs. If on the other hand a *setier* of corn were worth only 10 livres, he would earn only 130 livres. He would spend 100 livres of this on corn, and would have only 30 livres left over for other needs. It is for this reason that we observe that provinces where corn is dear are much more populous than those where it is at a low price.

The same benefit is received in the case of all other classes of men, in the case of the gains of the cultivators, the revenue of the proprietors, the taxes, and the prosperity of the state. For in these cases the product of the land amply compensates for the addition to the cost of wages and food. It is easy to convince oneself of this by making a calculation of the expenses and the increase in produce.[100]

(b) [101] In order to justify the harassment of the inhabitants of the countryside, the extortioners have put forward as a maxim *that it is necessary that the peasants should be poor, so as to prevent them from being idle.* The contemptuous bourgeois have readily adopted this cruel maxim because they pay less heed to other more peremptory maxims, namely that *the man who is unable to save anything does only just as much work as is necessary to earn him his food; and that in general all men who can save are industrious, because all men are greedy for wealth.* Another cause of the idleness of the oppressed peasant is that wages and employment are at too low a level in countries where restrictions on trade have rendered produce valueless, and where other causes have ruined agriculture. Harassment, a low price of produce, and a gain which is insufficient to stimulate them to work, render them idle men, poachers, vagabonds, and robbers. Thus enforced poverty is not the way to render the peasants industrious: it is only a guarantee of the ownership and enjoyment of their gains which can put heart into them and make them diligent.

Ministers who are guided by feelings of humanity, by superior education, and by more far-seeing views, indignantly reject hateful and destructive maxims which lead only to the devastation of the countryside. For they are not unaware of the fact that it is the wealth of the inhabitants of the countryside which gives birth to the wealth of the nation. POOR PEASANTS, POOR KINGDOM.[102]

ce font eux qui fourniffent aux terres les engrais qui procurent les riches moiffons (c).

(a) Cet avantage s'obtient par le débit, par l'emploi & l'ufage des laines dans le Royaume, par la grande confommation de la viande, du laitage, du beurre, du fromage, &c. fur-tout par le menu peuple qui eft le plus nombreux: car ce n'eft qu'à raifon de cette confommation que les beftiaux ont du débit & qu'on les multiplie : & c'eft encore cette confommation qui procure d'abondantes récoltes par la multiplication même des beftiaux. Cette abondance de récolte & de beftiaux, éloigne toute inquiétude de famine dans un Royaume fi fertile en fubfiftance. La nourriture que les beftiaux y fourniffent aux hommes, y diminue la confommation du blé; & la Nation peut en vendre une plus grande quantité à l'étranger, & accroître continuellement fes richeffes par le commerce d'une production fi précieufe. L'aifance du menu peuple contribue donc par-là effentiellement à la profpérité d'un Etat.

Le profit fur les beftiaux fe confond avec le profit fur la culture à l'égard du revenu du Propriétaire; parce que le prix du loyer d'une ferme s'établit à raifon du produit qu'elle peut donner par la culture & par la nourriture des beftiaux dans les pays où les avances des Fermiers ne font pas expofées à être enlevées par un impot arbitraire. Mais lorfque l'impot eft établi fur le Fermier, le revenu de la terre tombe dans le dépériffement, parce que les Fermiers n'ofent faire les avances des achats des beftiaux, dans la crainte qu'ils ne leur attirent une impofition ruineufe; alors faute d'une quantité fuffifante de beftiaux, pour fournir les engrais à la terre, la culture dépérit, les frais des travaux en terres maigres abforbent le produit net, & détruifent le revenu.

Le profit des beftiaux contribue tellement au produit des biens-fonds, que l'un fe mefure par l'autre, & que ces deux parties ne doivent pas être féparées dans l'évaluation des produits de la culture calculée par le revenu du Propriétaire : Car c'eft plus par le moyen des beftiaux qu'on obtient le produit net qui fournit le revenu & l'impot, que par le travail des hommes, qui feul rendroit à peine les frais de leur fubfiftance. Mais il faut de grandes avances pour les achats des beftiaux ; c'eft pourquoi le Gouvernement

doit plus attirer les richeffes à la campagne que les hommes. On n'y manquera pas d'hommes s'il y a des richeffes; mais fans richeffes tout y dépérit; les terres tombent en non-valeur, & le Royaume eft fans reffource & fans forces.

Il faut donc qu'il y ait une entière fûreté pour l'emploi des richeffes à la culture, une pleine liberté de commerce des productions. Ce ne font pas les richeffes qui font naître les richeffes qui doivent être chargées de l'impot: D'ailleurs les Fermiers & leurs familles doivent être exempts de toutes charges perfonnelles, auxquelles des habitans riches & néceffaires dans leur emploi, ne doivent pas être affujétis, de crainte qu'ils n'emportent dans les villes les richeffes qu'ils employent à l'agriculture, pour y jouir des prérogatives qu'un Gouvernement peu éclairé y accorderoit par préférence au mercénaire citadin. Les bourgeois aifés, fur-tout les Marchands détailleurs qui ne gagnent que fur le public, & dont le trop grand nombre dans les villes eft onéreux à la Nation; ces bourgeois, dis-je, trouveroient pour leurs enfans dans l'agriculture protégée & honorée, des établiffemens plus folides & moins ferviles que dans les villes; leurs richeffes ramenées à la campagne fertiliferoient les terres, multiplieroient les richeffes, & affureroient la profpérité & la puiffance de l'Etat.

Il y a une remarque à faire fur les Nobles qui cultivent leurs biens à la campagne; il y en a beaucoup qui n'ont pas en propriété un terrein fuffifant pour l'emploi de leurs charrues ou de leurs facultés, & il y a alors de la perte fur leurs dépenfes & fur leurs emplois. Seroit-ce déparer la Nobleffe que de leur permettre d'affermer des terres pour étendre leur culture & leurs occupations au profit de l'Etat; fur-tout dans un pays où la charge de l'impôt (devenue deshonnête) ne feroit plus établie ni fur les perfonnes, ni fur les Cultivateurs? Eft-il indécent à un Duc & Pair de louer un hôtel dans une ville? Le payement d'un fermage, n'affujétit à aucune dépendance envers qui que ce foit, pas plus que le payement d'un habit, d'une rente, d'un loyer, &c. Mais de plus on doit remarquer dans l'agriculture, que le poffeffeur de la terre, & le poffeffeur des

which provides the land with the manure which procures abundant crops (c).[103]

(a) [104] This advantage is brought about through the sale, employment, and use of wool in the kingdom, through the high consumption of meat, milk foods, butter, cheese, etc., above all by the lower classes, who are the most numerous. For it is only in proportion to this consumption that markets for livestock can be found and that people breed them; and it is this consumption, moreover, which procures abundant harvests, as a result of the breeding of the livestock itself. This abundance of harvests and livestock removes all anxiety about famine in a kingdom which is so productive of subsistence goods. The food which livestock provides for men in such a kingdom reduces their consumption of corn, so that the nation can sell a great quantity of it abroad and continually increase its wealth by means of its trade in so valuable a product. In this way, therefore, the comfortable circumstances of the lower classes necessarily contribute to the prosperity of the state.

The profit from livestock is confused with the profit from cultivation so far as the proprietor's revenue is concerned, since the rent payable for the lease of a farm is fixed in proportion to the product which it can yield through cultivation and through the raising of livestock, in countries where the farmers' advances are not exposed to the danger of being wiped out by arbitrary taxes. But when taxes are laid on the farmer, the revenue from the land falls into a decline, because farmers do not dare to make advances for the purchase of livestock, fearing that this will draw a ruinous tax down upon them. Thus for want of a sufficient number of livestock to provide manure for the land, cultivation declines, and the costs of working poor land swallow up the net product and wipe out the revenue.

The profit from livestock contributes to the product of landed property to such a degree that the one is measured by the other, and these two parts should not be separated when reckoning the value of the products of cultivation, calculated by reference to the proprietor's revenue.[105] For then the net product which provides the revenue and the taxes is procured more by means of the livestock than by means of the labour of men, whose returns if they worked alone would barely cover the cost of their subsistence. But large advances are necessary for the purchase of livestock: that is why the Government ought to be more concerned with attracting wealth to the countryside than with attracting men. Men will not be lacking if there is wealth there; but without wealth there is a general decline, the land becomes valueless, and the kingdom is left without resources and power.

Thus there must be complete security for the employment of wealth in cultivation, and full freedom of trade in produce. The wealth which gives birth to wealth ought not to be burdened with taxes. The farmers and their families, moreover, ought to be exempted from all personal contributions, to which wealthy inhabitants in essential occupations should not be subjected, in case they carry off into the towns the wealth which they employ in agriculture, in order to enjoy there the privileges which an unenlightened Government, with its preference for town-dwelling hirelings, would grant them. The comfortably placed bourgeois, above all the retail traders who make money only at the expense of the public and whose over-abundance in the towns is burdensome to the nation – these bourgeois, I say, would find in an agriculture which was protected and honoured sounder and less servile businesses in which to settle their children than those which are to be found in the towns. Their wealth, when brought back to the countryside, would render the land fertile, increase wealth, and ensure the prosperity and power of the state.

There is one point which should be made about the noblemen who cultivate their property in the countryside. There are many of them who do not own a sufficient quantity of land for the employment of their ploughs or their abilities, so that they are subjected to a loss on their expenditure and their activities. Would it take away from the dignity of the nobility to allow them to rent land for the purpose of extending their cultivation and activities to the benefit of the state, especially in a country where the burden of taxes (having become improper) was no longer laid either on persons or on cultivators? Is it unseemly for a duke and peer to rent a mansion in a town? The payment of rent for a farm does not involve any dependence upon anyone, any more than does the payment made for a coat, an annuity, or the rent of a house. Further, it should be noted that in agriculture the possessor of the land and the possessor of the advances necessary for cultivation

16.° Que l'on ne provoque point le luxe de décoration, parce qu'il ne fe foûtient qu'au préjudice du luxe de fubfiftance, qui entretient le débit & le bon prix des denrées du crû, & la reproduction des revenus de la Nation [*a*].

17.° Que le Gouvernement économique ne s'occupe qu'à favorifer les dépenfes productives & le commerce extérieur des denrées du crû, & qu'il laiffe aller d'elles-mêmes les dépenfes ftériles [*b*].

avances de la culture font tous deux également Propriétaires ; & qu'à cet égard la dignité eft égale de part & d'autre. Les Nobles, en étendant leurs entreprifes de culture, contribueroient par cet emploi à la profpérité de l'Etat, & ils y trouveroient des reffources pour foutenir leurs dépenfes & celles de leurs enfans dans l'état militaire. De tout temps la Nobleffe & l'Agriculture ont été réunies : Dans les Nations libres le fermage des terres, délivré des impofitions arbitraires & perfonnelles, eft fort indifférent en lui-même ; les redevances attachées aux biens, & auxquelles les Nobles mêmes font affujétis, ont-elles jamais déparé la Nobleffe, ni l'Agriculture ?

[*a*] On peut voir par la diftribution marquée dans le Tableau, que fi la dépenfe de la Nation fe portoit plus du côté des dépenfes ftériles que du côté des dépenfes productives, le revenu diminueroit à proportion, que le progrès de cette diminution augmenteroit fucceffivement dans le même ordre d'année en année. De-là vient que les grandes dépenfes en luxe de décoration & de fafte font ruineufes. Si au contraire la dépenfe de la Nation fe porte du côté des dépenfes productives, le revenu augmentera & les progrès de cette augmentation s'accroîtront de même fucceffivement : il n'eft donc pas vrai que les genres de dépenfes foient indifférens.

Ce que nous venons de remarquer à l'égard des grandes dépenfes de confommation des denrées du crû, doit fe rapporter aux Nations agricoles : Mais on doit penfer autrement à l'égard des petites Nations commerçantes qui n'ont pas de territoire ; car elles doivent épargner en tout genre de dépenfes, pour conferver & accroître

le fond des richeffes néceffaires à leur commerce ; & pour commercer à moins de frais que les autres Nations, afin de pouvoir s'affurer les avantages de la concurrence dans les achats & dans les ventes chez l'étranger. Ces petites Nations commerçantes doivent être regardées comme les agens du commerce des grands Etats ; parce qu'il eft plus avantageux à ceux-ci de commercer par leur entremife, que de fe charger eux-mêmes de différentes parties de commerce qu'ils exerceroient avec plus de dépenfes, & dont ils retireroient moins de profit, qu'en fe procurant chez eux une grande concurrence de Commerçans étrangers ; car elles évitent par-là le monopole des Commerçans du pays.

[*b*] Les travaux des marchandifes de main-d'œuvre & d'induftrie pour l'ufage de la Nation, ne font qu'un objet difpendieux, & non une fource de revenu. Ils ne peuvent procurer de profit net dans la vente à l'étranger, que dans les pays où la main-d'œuvre eft à bon marché par le bas prix des denrées qui fervent à la fubfiftance des Ouvriers ; condition fort defavantageufe au produit des biens-fonds ; auffi ne doit-elle pas exifter dans les Etats qui ont la liberté & la facilité d'un commerce extérieur qui foutient le débit & le prix des denrées du crû, & qui heureufement détruit le petit produit net qu'on pourroit retirer d'un commerce extérieur de marchandifes de main-d'œuvre, où le gain feroit établi fur la perte qui réfulteroit du bas prix des productions des biens-fonds. On ne confond pas ici le produit net ou le revenu pour la Nation, avec le gain des Commerçans & Entrepreneurs de manufactures ; ce gain doit être mis au rang des frais par rapport

18.°

16. [106] That no encouragement at all is given to luxury in the way of ornamentation; for this is maintained only to the detriment of luxury in the way of subsistence, which sustains the market for raw produce, its proper price, and the reproduction of the nation's revenue [a].

17. [107] That the Government's economic policy is concerned only with encouraging productive expenditure and external trade in raw produce, and that it refrains from interfering with sterile expenditure [b].

are both equally proprietors, and that on this account there is equal dignity on each side. The noblemen, by extending their agricultural enterprises, would contribute through this activity to the prosperity of the state, and they would find there the means to maintain their expenditure and that of their children in the military profession. At all times the nobility and agriculture have been linked together. In free nations, the rent of land, relieved of arbitrary and personal taxes, is in itself a matter of complete indifference. Have the dues attached to property, to which noblemen themselves are subject, ever degraded either the nobility or agriculture?[108]

[a] [109] It can be seen from the distribution delineated in the *tableau* that if the nation's expenditure went more to the sterile expenditure side than to the productive expenditure side, the revenue would fall proportionately, and that this fall would increase in the same progression from year to year successively. It follows that a high level of expenditure on luxury in the way of ornamentation and conspicuous consumption is ruinous. If on the other hand the nation's expenditure goes to the productive expenditure side the revenue will rise, and this rise will in the same way increase successively from year to year. Thus it is not true that the type of expenditure is a matter of indifference.

What we have just said with reference to a high level of expenditure on the consumption of raw produce properly applies to agricultural nations. But we should consider the small trading nations which have no territory in a different light; for they are obliged to be sparing in all types of expenditure in order to conserve and increase the fund of wealth which is necessary for their trade, and in order to carry on their trade at less cost than other nations, with the aim of being able to secure for themselves the benefits of competition in sales and purchases abroad. These small trading nations should be regarded as the commercial agents of the large states, because it is more advantageous to the latter to trade through them than to burden themselves with different branches of trade which they would carry on at greater expense and from which they would draw less profit than if they brought about a high degree of competition of foreign merchants within their borders. For in this way they keep clear of the monopoly of the country's merchants.[110]

[b] [111] The work involved in making manufactured and industrial commodities for the nation's use is simply something which costs money and not a source of revenue. It cannot yield any net profit through sale abroad, except in countries where manufacturing labour is cheap because of the low price of the produce which serves for the subsistence of the workers, a condition which is very disadvantageous so far as the product of landed property is concerned. Also, such a condition should not be found in states with a free and unobstructed external trade which maintains the sales and prices of raw produce, and which happily does away with the small net product which could be obtained from an external trade in manufactured commodities, the gain from which would be based on the loss which would result from the low prices of the products of landed property. Here the net product or revenue accruing to the nation is not confused with the gains of the merchants and manufacturing entrepreneurs; these gains, from the point of view of the nation, ought to be ranked as costs.

18.º Qu'on n'espère de ressources pour les besoins extraordinaires de l'Etat, que de la prospérité de la Nation & non du crédit des Financiers : car *les fortunes pécuniaires sont des richesses clandestines qui ne connoissent ni Roi ni patrie.*

à la Nation ; il ne suffiroit pas, par exemple, d'avoir de riches Laboureurs, si le territoire qu'ils cultiveroient ne produisoit que pour eux.

Il y a des Royaumes pauvres où la plufpart des Manufactures de luxe trop multipliées, sont soutenus par des priviléges exclusifs, en mettant la Nation à contribution par des prohibitions qui lui interdisent l'usage d'autres marchandises de main-d'œuvre. Il n'en est pas de même de l'agriculture & du commerce des productions des biens-fonds, où la concurrence la plus active multiplie les richesses des Nations qui possedent de grands territoires.

Nous ne parlons pas ici du commerce de trafic qui est le lot des petits Etats maritimes : un grand Etat ne doit pas quitter la charrue pour devenir Voiturier. On n'oubliera jamais qu'un Ministre du dernier siecle, ébloui du Commerce des Hollandois & de l'éclat des Manufactures de luxe, a jeté sa patrie dans un tel delire, que l'on ne parloit plus que commerce & argent, sans penser au véritable emploi de l'argent, ni au véritable commerce du Pays.

Ce Ministre si estimable par ses bonnes intentions, mais trop attaché à ses idées, voulut faire naître les richesses du travail des doigts, au préjudice de la source même des richesses, & dérangea toute la constitution économique d'une Nation agricole. Le commerce extérieur des grains fut arrêté pour faire vivre le fabricant à bas prix ; le débit du blé dans l'intérieur du Royaume fut livré à une police arbitraire qui interrompoit le commerce entre les Provinces. Les protecteurs de l'industrie, les Magistrats des villes, pour se procurer des blés à bas prix, ruinoient, par un mauvais calcul, leurs villes & leurs provinces, en dégradant insensiblement la culture de leurs terres : tout tendoit à la destruction des revenus des biens-fonds, des manufactures, du commerce & de l'industrie, qui dans une Nation agricole ne peuvent se soutenir que par les produits du sol ; car ce sont ces produits qui fourniffent au commerce l'exportation du superflu, & qui payent les revenus aux Propriétaires, & le salaire des hommes employés aux travaux lucratifs. Diverses causes d'émigrations des hommes & des richesses hâterent les progrès de cette destruction.

Les hommes & l'argent furent détournés de l'agriculture, & employés aux manufactures de soie, de coton, de laines étrangeres, au préjudice des manufactures de laines du pays & de la multiplication des troupeaux. On provoqua le luxe de décoration qui fit des progrès très-rapides ; l'administration des Provinces, pressée par les besoins de l'Etat, ne laissoit plus de sureté dans les campagnes pour l'emploi visible des richesses nécessaires à la reproduction annuelle des richesses ; on laissa tomber une grande partie des terres en petite culture, en friches & en non-valeur : Les revenus des Propriétaires des biens-fonds furent sacrifiés en pure perte à un commerce mercantil qui ne pouvoit contribuer à l'impot. L'agriculture dégradée & accablée ne pouvoit plus y subvenir, on l'étendit de plus en plus sur les hommes, sur les alimens, sur le commerce des denrées du crû ; il se multiplia en dépenses & en déprédations dans la perception ; & il devint l'objet d'un systeme de finance, qui enrichit la capitale des dépouilles des Provinces : Le trafic de l'argent à intérêt forma un genre principal de revenus fondés en argent & tirés de l'argent ; ce qui n'étoit, par rapport à la Nation, qu'un produit imaginaire, qui échappoit à l'impot & rongeoit l'Etat. Ces revenus établis sur l'argent, & l'aspect de l'opulence soutenu par la magnificence d'un luxe ruineux, en imposoient au vulgaire, & diminuoient de plus en plus la reproduction des richesses réelles, & le pécule de la Nation. Hé malheureusement les causes de ce desordre général ont été trop long-temps ignorées ! *Inde mali labes.* Mais aujourd'hui le Gouvernement est attaché à des principes plus lumineux ; il connoit les ressources du Royaume, & les moyens d'y ramener l'abondance.

D

18. [112] That means to meet the extraordinary needs of the state are expected to be found only in the prosperity of the nation and not in the credit of financiers; for *monetary fortunes are a clandestine form of wealth which knows neither king nor country.*

It would not be sufficient, for example, to have rich husbandmen, if the territory which they cultivated were to produce for them alone.

There are poor kingdoms where the greater part of the over-abundant luxury manufactures are kept going by means of exclusive privileges, laying the nation under contribution through prohibitions forbidding it to use other manufactured commodities. This is not the case with agriculture and trade in the products of landed property, where the most energetic competition results in the expansion of the wealth of nations with large territories.

I do not speak here of re-export trade, to which small maritime states are fated. A large state should not abandon the plough in order to become a carrier. It will never be forgotten that a Minister of the last century, dazzled by the trade of the Dutch and the glitter of luxury manufactures, brought his country to such a state of frenzy that no one talked about anything but trade and money, without reflecting on the true employment of money or on a country's true trade.

This Minister, whose good intentions were so worthy of esteem but who was too much a prisoner of his ideas, tried to bring about the generation of wealth from the work of men's hands, to the detriment of the very source of wealth, and put the whole economic constitution of an agricultural nation out of gear. External trade in corn was stopped in order to bring about a low cost of living for the manufacturer; and the sale of corn inside the kingdom was subjected to an arbitrary system of regulation which cut off trade between provinces. The protectors of industry, the justices in the towns, in order to procure corn at a low price, ruined their towns and provinces through poor calculation by causing a gradual decline in the cultivation of their land. Everything tended to bring about the destruction of the revenue of landed property, manufactures, trade, and industry, which, in an agricultural nation, can be maintained only through the produce of the soil. For it is this produce which provides trade with a surplus for export, and which pays revenue to the proprietors and wages to the men engaged in remunerative activities. Different causes bringing about the emigration of men and wealth quickened the pace of this course of destruction.

Men and money were diverted from agriculture and employed in manufactures of silk, cotton, and foreign wool, to the detriment of the manufacture of home-produced wool and the expansion of flocks and herds. Luxury in the way of ornamentation was encouraged, and made very rapid progress. The administration of the provinces, harassed by the needs of the state, no longer offered any security in the countryside for the ready employment of the wealth necessary for the annual reproduction of wealth, and a large part of the land was allowed to become reduced to small-scale cultivation, to be left lying fallow, and to become valueless. The revenue of the proprietors of landed property was uselessly sacrificed to a mercantile trade which could make no contribution to taxes. Agriculture, depressed and overburdened as it was, could no longer provide for them, and their coverage was extended more and more to include men, food, and trade in raw produce; they were increased through misappropriation and the expenses of collection; and a system of finance grew up around them which enriched the capital with the spoils of the provinces. Traffic in money lent out at interest created a very important kind of revenue based on money and drawn from money, which from the point of view of the nation was only an imaginary product, eluding taxation and gnawing away at the state. This revenue based on money, and the appearance of opulence, maintained by the splendour of ruinous luxury, imposed upon the vulgar, and reduced further and further the reproduction of real wealth and the money stock of the nation. Unhappily, alas, the causes of this general disorder remained unknown for too long a time: *inde mali labes.* But today the Government has accepted more enlightened principles; it knows where the resources of the kingdom are to be found, and the means of restoring abundance to it.[113]

14

-19.° Que l'Etat évite les emprunts qui forment des rentes financières, qui chargent l'Etat de dettes dévorantes, & qui occafionnent un commerce ou trafic de finance, par l'entremife des papiers commerçables, où l'efcompte augmente de plus en plus les fortunes pécuniaires ftériles, qui féparent la finance de l'agriculture, & qui la privent des richeffes néceffaires pour l'amélioration des biens-fonds & pour la culture des terres.

20.° Qu'une Nation qui a un grand territoire à cultiver & la facilité d'exercer un grand commerce des denrées du crû, n'étende pas trop l'emploi de l'argent & des hommes aux manufactures & au commerce de luxe, au préjudice des travaux & des dépenfes de l'agriculture [a]; car pré-férablement à tout, le Royaume doit être bien peuplé de riches Cultivateurs [b].

[a] On ne doit s'attacher qu'aux manufactures de marchandifes de main-d'œuvre dont on a les matieres premieres, & qu'on peut fabriquer avec moins de dépenfe que dans les autres pays, & il faut acheter de l'étranger les marchandifes de main-d'œuvre qu'il peut vendre à meilleur marché qu'elles ne couteroient à la Nation, fi elle les faifoit fabriquer chez elle. Par ces achats on provoque le commerce réciproque: car fi on vouloit ne rien acheter, & vendre de tout, on éteindroit le commerce extérieur & les avan-tages de l'exportation des denrées du crû, qui eft infiniment plus profitable que eelle des marchandifes de main-d'œuvre. Une Nation agricole doit favorifer le commerce extérieur actif des denrées du crû par le commerce ex-térieur paffif des marchandifes de main-d'œuvre qu'elle peut acheter à profit de l'étranger. Voilà tout le myftere du Commerce: à ce prix ne craignons pas d'être *tributaires des autres Na-tions.*

[b] Le bourg de Goodmans-Chefter en An-g'eterre, eft célébre dans l'Hiftoire pour avoir accompagné fon Roi avec le cortége le plus honorable, ayant conduit 180 charrues à fon paffage: Ce fafte doit paroitre bien ridicule

à nos citadins accoutumés aux décorations frivoles; mais ce font les riches Laboureurs & les riches Commerçans, attachés au com-merce rural, qui animent l'agriculture, qui font exécuter, qui commandent, qui gouvernent, qui font indépendans, qui affurent les revenus de la Nation, qui, après les Propriétaires dif-tingués par la naiffance, par les dignités, par les fciences, forment l'ordre de citoyens le plus honnête, le plus louable & le plus im-portant dans l'Etat. Ce font pourtant ces habi-tans honorables de la campagne, ces maîtres, ces patriarches, ces riches Entrepreneurs d'agricul-ture, que le bourgeois ne connoit que fous le nom dédaigneux de *Payfans*, & auxquels il veut même retrancher les Maitres d'école qui leur apprennent à lire, à écrire, à mettre de la fureté & de l'ordre dans leurs affaires, à étendre leurs connoiffances fur les différentes parties de leur état.

Ces inftructions, dit-on, leur infpirent de la vanité & les rendent proceffifs: la défenfe ju-ridique doit-elle être permife à ces hommes terreftres, qui ofent oppofer de la réfiftance & de la hauteur à ceux qui, par la dignité de leur féjour dans la cité, doivent jouir d'une

19. [114] That the state avoids contracting loans which create rentier incomes, which burden the state with devouring debts, and which bring about a trade or traffic in finance, through the medium of negotiable bills, the discount on which causes a greater and greater increase in sterile monetary fortunes, which separate finance from agriculture, and which deprive the latter of the wealth necessary for the improvement of landed property and the cultivation of the land.

20. [115] That a nation which has a large territory to cultivate, and the means of carrying on a large trade in raw produce, does not extend too far the employment of money and men in manufacturing and trading in luxury goods, to the detriment of the work and expenditure involved in agriculture [a]; for more than anything else the kingdom ought to be well furnished with wealthy cultivators [b].

[a] [116] A nation ought to carry on the production only of those manufactured commodities for which it possesses the raw materials, and which it can make at lower cost than in other countries, and it should purchase from abroad such manufactured commodities as can be sold at a price lower than the cost which would be involved if the nation made them itself. Through these purchases mutual trade is stimulated; for if nations tried to buy nothing and sell everything, this would do away with external trade and the advantages of the export of raw produce, which is infinitely more profitable than that of manufactured commodities. An agricultural nation should facilitate an active external trade in raw produce, by means of a passive external trade in manufactured commodities which it can profitably buy from abroad. This is the whole secret of trade: do not be afraid that by incurring this cost you will become *a tributary of other nations.*[117]

[b] [118] The borough of Goodmans-chester, in England, is renowned in history for escorting its king with the most worthy procession, having accompanied his passage with 180 ploughs. This magnificent display is likely to appear completely absurd to our townsmen, accustomed as they are to frivolous ornamentation. But it is wealthy husbandmen and wealthy merchants engaged in rural trade who stimulate agriculture, who conduct its operations, who control, who direct, who are independent, who safeguard the nation's revenue, and who, after the proprietors who are distinguished by their birth, titles, and learning, constitute the most honourable, praiseworthy, and important order of citizens in the state. It is these worthy inhabitants of the countryside, however, these masters, these patriarchs, these wealthy agricultural entrepreneurs, whom the bourgeois knows only under the contemptuous title of *peasants*, and from whom he even wants to take away the schoolmasters who teach them to read and write, to bring security and order into their businesses, and to extend their knowledge of the different aspects of their calling.

An education of this type, it is claimed, fills them with vanity and makes them fond of going to law: should legal protection be allowed to these earthy men, who presume to set themselves up in haughty opposition to those who, by virtue of the elevated rank which their residence in the city gives them, ought to enjoy a

21.º Que les terres employées à la culture des grains soient réunies, autant qu'il est possible, en grandes fermes exploitées par de riches Laboureurs; car il y a moins de dépense pour l'entretien & réparation des bâtimens, & à proportion beaucoup moins de frais, & beaucoup plus de produit net dans les grandes entreprises de l'agriculture que dans les petites; parce que celles-ci occupent inutilement, & aux dépens des revenus du sol, un plus grand nombre de familles de Fermiers, qui ont peu d'aisance, par l'étendue de leurs emplois & de leurs facultés, pour exercer une riche culture. Cette multiplicité de Fermiers est moins favorable à la population que l'accroissement des revenus : car la population la plus assurée, la plus disponible pour les différentes occupations, & pour les différens travaux qui partagent les hommes en différentes classes, est celle qui est entretenue par le produit net : Toute épargne faite à profit dans les travaux qui peuvent s'exécuter par le moyen des animaux, des machines, des rivières, &c. revient à l'avantage de la population & de l'Etat; parce que plus de produit net procure plus de gain aux hommes pour d'autres services ou d'autres travaux.

distinction & d'une supériorité qui doit en imposer aux villageois. Tels sont les titres ridicules de la vanité du Citadin, qui n'est qu'un mercénaire payé par les richesses de la campagne. *Omnium autem rerum ex quibus aliquid acquiritur, nihil est AGRICULTURA melius, nihil uberius, nihil dulcius, nihil homine, nihil libero dignius.* Cicero de Officiis. . . . . *Meâ quidem sententiâ, haud scio an nulla beatior esse possit, neque solùm officio, quod hominum generi universo cultura agrorum est salutaris; sed & delectatione, & saturitate, copiaque omnium rerum quæ ad victum hominum, ad cultum etiam Deorum pertinent.* Idem, de Senectute.

DE TOUS LES MOYENS DE GAGNER DU BIEN, IL N'Y EN A POINT DE MEILLEUR, DE PLUS ABONDANT, DE PLUS AGRÉABLE, DE PLUS CONVENABLE A L'HOMME, DE PLUS DIGNE DE L'HOMME LIBRE QUE L'AGRICULTURE. . . . POUR MOI, JE NE SAIS S'IL Y A AUCUNE SORTE DE VIE PLUS HEUREUSE QUE CELLE-LA, NON SEULEMENT PAR L'UTILITÉ DE CET EMPLOI, QUI FAIT SUBSISTER TOUT LE GENRE HUMAIN, MAIS ENCORE PAR LE PLAISIR ET PAR L'ABONDANCE QU'IL PROCURE; CAR LA CULTURE DE LA TERRE PRODUIT DE TOUT CE QU'ON PEUT DESIRER POUR LA VIE DES HOMMES ET POUR LE CULTE DES DIEUX.

15

21. [119] That the land employed in the cultivation of corn is brought together, as far as possible, into large farms worked by rich husbandmen; for in large agricultural enterprises there is less expenditure required for the upkeep and repair of buildings, and proportionately much less cost and much more net product than in small ones, because the latter employ uselessly, and at the expense of the revenue of the land, a greater number of the families of farmers, the extent of whose activities and means hardly puts them in a position to carry on wealthy cultivation. This multiplicity of farmers is less favourable to population than is the increase of revenue, because the population whose position is most assured, and which is most readily available for the different occupations and different kinds of work which divide men into different classes, is that maintained by the net product. All economies profitably made use of in work which can be done with the aid of animals, machines, rivers, etc., bring benefit to the population and the state, because a greater net product procures men a greater reward for other services or other kinds of work.

distinction and superiority which are bound to overawe the rustics? Such are the absurd claims made in his vanity by the townsman, who is nothing but a hireling paid by the wealth of the countryside. *Omnium autem rerum ex quibus aliquid acquiritur, nihil est* AGRICULTURA *melius, nihil uberius, nihil dulcius, nihil homine, nihil libero dignius.* Cicero, De Officiis. . . . *Mea quidem sententia, haud scio an nulla beatior esse possit, neque solum officio, quod hominum generi universo cultura agrorum est salutaris, sed et delectatione, et saturitate, copiaque omnium rerum quae ad victum hominum, ad cultum etiam Deorum pertinent.* Cicero, De Senectute.

OF ALL THE OCCUPATIONS BY WHICH GAIN IS SECURED, NONE IS BETTER THAN Agriculture, NONE MORE PROFITABLE, NONE MORE DELIGHTFUL, NONE MORE BECOMING TO A FREEMAN. . . . FOR MY PART, AT LEAST, I AM INCLINED TO THINK THAT NO LIFE CAN BE HAPPIER THAN THAT OF THE FARMER, NOT MERELY FROM THE STANDPOINT OF THE DUTY PERFORMED, WHICH BENEFITS THE ENTIRE HUMAN RACE, BUT ALSO BECAUSE OF ITS CHARM, AND THE PLENTY AND ABUNDANCE IT GIVES OF EVERYTHING THAT TENDS TO THE NURTURE OF MAN AND EVEN TO THE WORSHIP OF THE GODS.[120]

16

22.º Que chacun soit libre de cultiver dans son champ telles productions que son intérêt, ses facultés, la nature du terrein lui suggerent, pour en tirer le plus grand produit qu'il lui soit possible : On ne doit point favoriser le monopole dans la culture des biens-fonds ; car il est préjudiciable au revenu général de la Nation [a]. Le préjugé qui porte à favoriser l'abondance des denrées de premier besoin, préférablement à celle de moindre besoin,

[a] Des vûes particulieres avoient fait croire pendant un temps qu'il falloit restraindre en France la culture des vignes pour augmenter la culture du blé, dans le temps même où le commerce extérieur du blé étoit prohibé, où la communication même du commerce des grains entre les provinces du Royaume étoit empêchée, où la plus grande partie des terres étoit en friches, parce que la culture du blé y étoit limitée à la consommation de l'intérieur de chaque province du Royaume ; & où la dégradation des vignes augmentoit de plus en plus les friches : D'ailleurs des Provinces éloignées de la capitale étoient obligées de faire des représentations pour s'opposer à l'accroissement de la culture des grains, qui faute de débit tomboient dans leur pays en non-valeur ; ce qui causoit la ruine des Propriétaires & des Fermiers, & anéantissoit l'impot, dont les terres étoient chargées. Tout conspiroit donc à la dégradation des deux principales cultures du Royaume, & à faire tomber de plus en plus les biens-fonds en non-valeur ; une partie des Propriétaires des terres, au préjudice des autres, tendoit au privilége exclusif de la culture : Funestes effets des prohibitions & des empêchemens du commerce des productions des biens-fonds, dans un Royaume où les Provinces se communiquent par les rivieres & les mers, où la Capitale, & toutes les autres villes, peuvent être facilement approvisionnées des productions de toutes les parties du territoire, & où la facilité de l'exportation assure le débit du superflu.

La culture des vignes est la plus riche culture du royaume de France, car le produit net d'un arpent de vignes, évalué du fort au foible, est au moins double de celui du meilleur arpent de terre cultivé en grains : Mais on doit encore remarquer que les frais compris dans le produit total de l'une & de l'autre culture, sont plus avantageux dans la culture des vignes que dans la culture des grains ; parce que dans la culture des vignes, les frais fournissent, avec profit, beaucoup plus de salaire pour les hommes, & parce que la dépense pour les échalats & les tonneaux est au profit du débit des bois, & que les hommes occupés à la culture des vignes n'y sont pas employés dans les temps de la moisson, où ils sont alors d'une grande ressource aux Laboureurs pour la récolte des grains. D'ailleurs cette classe d'hommes payés de leurs travaux par la terre, en devenant fort nombreuse, augmente le débit des blés & des vins, & en soutient la valeur vénale à mesure que la culture s'étend ; & que l'accroissement de la culture augmente les richesses : car l'augmentation des richesses augmente la population dans toutes les classes d'hommes d'une Nation, & cette augmentation de population soutient de toutes parts la valeur vénale des produits de la culture.

On doit faire attention que la facilité du commerce extérieur des denrées du crû délivrées d'impositions dispendieuses, est un grand avantage pour une Nation qui a un grand territoire, où elle peut varier la culture pour en obtenir différentes productions de bonne valeur ; sur-tout celles qui ne peuvent pas naître chez les Nations voisines. La vente du vin & des eaux-de-vie à l'étranger étant pour nous un commerce privilégié, que nous devons à notre territoire & à notre climat, il doit spécialement être protégé par le Gouvernement ; ainsi il ne doit pas être assujéti à des impositions

au

22. [121] That each person is free to cultivate in his fields such products as his interests, his means, and the nature of the land suggest to him, in order that he may extract from them the greatest possible product. Monopoly in the cultivation of landed property should never be encouraged, for it is detrimental to the general revenue of the nation [a]. The prejudice which leads to the encouragement of an abundance of produce of primary necessity in preference to that of less necessary

[a] [122] As a result of interested attitudes it was believed for a period that it was necessary in France to restrict the cultivation of vineyards in order to increase the cultivation of corn, at the very time when external trade in corn was prohibited, when trade suffered even from restrictions on the passage of corn between the provinces of the kingdom, when the greater part of the land was lying fallow because the cultivation of corn on it was confined to the internal consumption of each of the provinces of the kingdom, and when the deterioration of the vineyards was increasing to a greater and greater degree the amount of land lying fallow. The provinces which were distant from the capital, moreover, were obliged to make representations in order to resist the extension of the cultivation of corn, which for lack of a market was going to waste in their districts; this was bringing about the ruin of the proprietors and the farmers, and wiping out the taxes with which the land was burdened. Thus everything was conspiring to bring about the deterioration of the two main branches of cultivation in the kingdom, and to cause more and more landed property to become valueless; and one section of the proprietors of the land, to the detriment of the others, was aiming at exclusive privileges in cultivation. These were the disastrous effects of prohibitions and impediments to trade in the produce of landed property, in a kingdom where the provinces are linked with one another by rivers and seas, where the capital and all the other towns can easily be supplied with the produce of all parts of the territory, and where facility of export guarantees that the surplus will be sold.

The cultivation of vineyards is the most wealthy branch of cultivation in the French kingdom, for the net product of an *arpent* of land given over to vineyards, valued on an average basis, is at least double that of an *arpent* of the best land given over to the cultivation of corn. But it should also be noted that the expenses which are included in the total product of each branch of cultivation are more advantageous in the case of the cultivation of vineyards than in that of the cultivation of corn, because in the cultivation of vineyards the expenses provide, with profit, much greater wages for men; because the expenditure for vine-props and casks favours the sale of wood; and because the men engaged in the cultivation of vineyards are not employed in it at harvest-time, when they can very usefully be drawn on by husbandmen in order to gather in the corn. In addition, when this class of men, paid for its work by the land, becomes very numerous, it widens the market for corn and wine, and maintains their market value, in the proportion that cultivation is extended and the expansion of cultivation increases wealth. For the increase in wealth increases the number of people in all the classes of men in a nation, and this increase in population maintains the market value of the produce of cultivation on all sides.

It should be noted that an unobstructed external trade in raw produce, released from costly duties, is very advantageous to a nation with a large territory, where the pattern of cultivation can be varied in order to obtain different assortments of highly-valued products, above all those which cannot be produced in neighbouring countries. Since the sale of wines and spirits abroad is for us a privileged trade, owing to the nature of our soil and our climate, it should receive special protection from the Government. Thus it should not be subjected, for taxation purposes, to a

au préjudice de la valeur vénale des unes ou des autres, eſt inſpiré par des vûes courtes qui ne s'étendent pas juſqu'aux effets du commerce extérieur réciproque, qui pourvoit à tout, & qui décide du prix des denrées que chaque Nation peut cultiver avec le plus de profit. Ce ſont les revenus & l'impôt qui ſont les richeſſes de premier beſoin dans un Etat pour défendre les Sujets contre la diſette & contre l'ennemi, & pour ſoutenir la gloire & la puiſſance du Monarque, & la proſpérité de la Nation [a].

multipliées en pure perte pour l'impôt, & trop préjudiciables au débit des productions qui ſont l'objet d'un grand commerce extérieur, capable de ſoutenir l'opulence du Royaume : L'impôt doit être pur & ſimple, aſſigné ſur le ſol qui produit ces richeſſes ; & dans la compenſation de l'impoſition générale, on doit avoir égard à celles dont il faut aſſurer, par un prix favorable, le débit chez l'étranger ; car alors l'Etat eſt bien dédommagé de la modération de l'impôt, par l'influence avantageuſe de ce commerce ſur toutes les autres ſources de richeſſes du Royaume.

[a] En quoi conſiſte la proſpérité d'une Nation agricole ? *EN DE GRANDES AVANCES POUR PERPÉTUER ET ACCROITRE LES REVENUS, ET L'IMPOT ; EN UN COMMERCE INTÉRIEUR ET EXTÉRIEUR LIBRE ET FACILE ; EN JOUISSANCE DES RICHESSES ANNUELLES DES BIENS-FONDS ; EN PAYEMENS PÉCUNIAIRES ET OPULENS DU REVENU, ET DE L'IMPOT.* L'abondance des productions s'obtient par les grandes avances ; la conſommation & le commerce ſoutiennent le débit & la valeur vénale des productions ; la valeur vénale eſt la meſure des richeſſes de la Nation ; les richeſſes reglent le tribut qui peut être impoſé, & fourniſſent la finance qui le paye, & qui doit circuler dans le commerce ; mais qui ne doit point ſurabonder dans un pays au préjudice de l'uſage & de la conſommation des productions annuelles, qui doivent y perpétuer, par la reproduction & le commerce réciproque, les véritables richeſſes.

L'argent monnoyé eſt une richeſſe qui eſt payée par d'autres richeſſes, qui *eſt*, dans les Nations, *un gage intermédiaire entre les ventes & les achats*, qui ne contribue plus à perpétuer les richeſſes dans un Etat, lorſqu'il eſt retenu hors de la circulation, & qu'il ne rend plus richeſſe pour richeſſe : Alors plus il s'accumuleroit, plus il couteroit de richeſſes, qui ne ſe renouvelleroient pas, & plus il apauvriroit la Nation : L'argent n'eſt donc une richeſſe active & réellement profitable dans un Etat qu'autant qu'il rend continuellement richeſſe pour richeſſe ; parce que la Monnoie n'eſt par elle-même qu'une richeſſe ſtérile, qui n'a d'autre utilité dans une Nation que ſon emploi pour les ventes & les achats, & pour les payemens des revenus & de l'impôt, qui le remettent dans la circulation ; en ſorte que le même argent ſatisfait tour à tour & continuellement à ces payemens, & à ſon emploi dans le commerce.

Ainſi la maſſe du pécule d'une Nation agricole ne ſe trouve qu'à peu près égale au produit net ou revenu annuel des biens-fonds ; car dans cette proportion il eſt plus que ſuffiſant pour l'uſage de la Nation ; une plus grande quantité de finance ne ſeroit point une richeſſe utile pour l'Etat. Car quoique l'impôt ſoit payé en argent, ce n'eſt pas l'argent qui le fournit, ce ſont les richeſſes du ſol qui renaiſſent annuellement ; c'eſt dans ces richeſſes renaiſſantes, & non, comme le penſe le vulgaire, dans le pécule de la Nation, que conſiſte la proſpérité & la force d'un Etat. On ne ſupplée point au renouvellement ſucceſſif de ces richeſſes par le pécule,

E

produce, to the detriment of the market value of one or the other, is inspired by short-sighted views that do not extend as far as the effects of mutual external trade, which makes provision for everything and determines the price of the produce which each nation can cultivate with the most profit. It is revenue and taxes which are the wealth of primary necessity in a state, in order to defend subjects against scarcity and against the enemy, and to maintain the glory and power of the monarch and the prosperity of the nation [a].

useless multiplicity of duties, which are very harmful to the sale of these products, with which a large part of our external trade, capable of maintaining the kingdom's opulence, is concerned. The tax should be pure and simple,[123] and charged on the land which produces this wealth. In considering the question of compensation for the loss of general tax revenue, account should be taken of the fact that the sale of these items of wealth to foreign countries has to be ensured by means of a favourable price; for then the state is fully recompensed for its action in moderating the taxes by the favourable influence of this trade on all the other sources of wealth in the kingdom.[124]

[a] [125] In what does the prosperity of an agricultural nation consist? IN LARGE ADVANCES TO PERPETUATE AND INCREASE REVENUE AND TAXES; IN A FREE AND UNOBSTRUCTED INTERNAL AND EXTERNAL TRADE; IN THE ENJOYMENT OF THE ANNUAL WEALTH FROM LANDED PROPERTY; AND IN AMPLE MONETARY PAYMENTS OF REVENUE AND TAXES. An abundance of products is obtained through large advances; consumption and trade maintain the sales and market value of the products; the market value is the measure of the nation's wealth; the wealth regulates the contributions which can be levied, and provides the money which pays them. This money ought to circulate in trading transactions; it ought never to superabound in a country to the detriment of the use and consumption of the annual

product, which ought through reproduction and mutual trade to perpetuate true wealth there.[126]

Coined money is a form of wealth which is paid for by other forms of wealth, which is in nations a *token intermediating between sales and purchases*, and which no longer contributes to the perpetuation of a state's wealth when it is kept out of circulation and no longer returns wealth for wealth. Thus the more it is accumulated the more it costs in terms of wealth which is not renewed, and the more it impoverishes the nation. Thus money is an active and really profitable form of wealth in a state only so far as it continually returns wealth for wealth, because money in itself is only sterile wealth. It possesses no utility for a nation other than its employment in sales and purchases, and in the payment of revenue and taxes, which puts it back into circulation in such a way that the same money continually and by turns meets these payments and fulfils its function in trade.[127]

Thus the total money stock of an agricultural nation is only about equal to the net product of annual revenue of its landed property, for when it stands in this proportion it is more than sufficient for the nation's use. A greater quantity of money would not be a useful item of wealth for the state at all. Although taxes are paid in money, it is not money which provides them: it is the wealth annually regenerated from the land. It is in this renascent wealth, and not as the vulgar believe in the nation's money stock, that the prosperity and power of a state consist. You can never make up for the successive renewal of this wealth with the money

23.° Que le Gouvernement soit moins occupé des soins d'épargner que des opérations nécessaires pour la prospérité du Royaume ; car de trop grandes dépenses peuvent cesser d'être excessives par l'augmentation des richesses.

mais le pécule est facilement suppléé dans le commerce par des engagemens par écrit, assurés par les richesses que l'on possede dans le pays, & qui se transportent chez l'étranger : L'avidité de l'argent est une passion vive dans les particuliers ; parce qu'ils sont avides de la richesse qui représente les autres richesses ; mais cette sorte d'avidité, distraite de son objet, ne doit pas être la passion de l'Etat. La grande quantité d'argent n'est à desirer dans un Etat qu'autant qu'elle y est proportionnée au revenu, & qu'elle marque par-là une opulence perpétuellement renaissante, dont la jouissance est effective & bien assurée : Telle étoit sous Charles V, dit le Sage, l'abondance de l'argent qui suivoit l'abondance des autres richesses du Royaume. On peut en juger par celles qui sont détaillées dans l'inventaire immense de ce Prince, indépendamment d'une réserve de 27 millions (près de 300 millions, valeur actuelle de notre monnoie) qui se trouva dans ses coffres. Ces grandes richesses sont d'autant plus remarquables que les domaines des Rois de France ne comprenoient pas alors un tiers du Royaume.

L'argent n'est donc pas la véritable richesse d'un Etat, la richesse qui se consomme & qui renaît continuellement ; car l'argent n'engendre pas de l'argent : Un écu bien employé peut à la vérité faire naître une richesse de deux écus, mais c'est la richesse, & non pas l'argent, qui s'est multipliée ; ainsi l'argent ne doit pas séjourner dans des mains stériles : Il n'est donc pas aussi indifférent, qu'on le croit, pour l'Etat, que l'argent passe dans la poche de Pierre ou de Paul ; car il est essentiel qu'il ne soit pas enlevé à celui qui l'emploie au profit de l'Etat. Mais à parler rigoureusement, l'argent qui a cet emploi dans la Nation, n'a point de Propriétaire ; il appartient aux besoins de l'Etat, lesquels le font circuler pour la reproduction des richesses qui font subsister la Nation, & qui fournissent le tribut au Souverain.

Il ne faut pas confondre cet argent avec la finance dévorante qui se trafique en prêts à intérêts, & qui élude la contribution que tout revenu annuel doit à l'Etat. Cet argent de besoin a, dis-je, chez tous les particuliers une destination à laquelle il appartient décisivement : Celui qui est destiné au payement actuel de l'impôt appartient à l'impôt : Celui qui est destiné au besoin de quelqu'achat appartient à ce besoin : Celui qui vivifie l'agriculture, le commerce & l'industrie appartient à cet emploi : Celui qui est destiné à payer une dette échûe, ou prête à écheoir, appartient à cette dette, &c. & non à celui qui le possede : C'est l'argent de la Nation ; personne ne peut le prêter, parce qu'il n'appartient à personne : Cependant c'est cet argent dispersé qui forme la principale masse du pécule d'un Royaume vraiment opulent, où il est toûjours employé à profit pour l'Etat. On n'hésite pas même à le vendre à plus haut prix qu'il n'a couté, c'est-à-dire, à le laisser passer chez l'étranger pour des achats de marchandises, où l'on trouve un gain assuré ; & l'étranger n'ignore pas non plus les avantages de ce commerce, où le profit décide des échanges de l'argent en marchandises, & des marchandises en argent. Car par-tout l'argent & les marchandises ne sont richesses qu'à raison de leur valeur vénale.

L'argent qui est oisif, qui ne peut pas renaître, est un petit objet, qui est bien-tôt épuisé par les emprunts un peu multipliés. Cependant c'est cet argent oisif qui fait illusion au bas peuple ; c'est lui que le vulgaire regarde comme les richesses de la Nation, & comme une grande ressource dans les besoins d'un Etat ; même d'un grand Etat, qui réellement ne peut être opulent que par le produit net des richesses qui naissent annuellement de son territoire, & qui, pour ainsi dire, fait renaître l'argent, en le renouvellant, & en accélérant continuellement sa circulation.

D'ailleurs quand un Royaume est riche & florissant par le commerce de ses productions, il a, par ses correspondances, des richesses dans les autres pays, & le papier lui tient lieu par-

23. [128] That the Government troubles itself less with economising than with the operations necessary for the prosperity of the kingdom; for an expenditure that is too high may cease to be excessive by virtue of the increase of wealth. But abuses must not be confused with simple expendi-

stock; but in trade the money stock is readily made up for with written pledges, guaranteed by the wealth which is possessed in the country and transported abroad. Greed for money is an ardent passion among individuals, because they are greedy for the form of wealth which represents other forms of wealth. But this kind of greed, in abstraction from its object, ought not to be a passion indulged in by the state. A great quantity of money in a state is to be desired only so far as it is proportionate to the revenue, and denotes in this way a state of opulence which is perpetually being renewed, and the enjoyment of which is effective and fully guaranteed. Of such a type was the abundance of money which, in the reign of Charles V, called the Wise, followed upon an abundance of the other forms of wealth in the kingdom. We can see this from the items of wealth which are set out in this prince's huge inventory, independently of a reserve of 27 millions[129] (about 300 millions according to the present value of our money) which was held in his treasury. This great quantity of wealth is still more remarkable when we recall that the properties of the kings of France at this time did not include one-third of the kingdom.[130]

Thus money does not constitute the true wealth of a state, the wealth which is consumed and regenerated continually, for money does not breed money. It is true that an écu which is properly employed can cause wealth worth two écus to be generated, but then it is wealth and not money which has increased. Thus money should not remain in sterile hands. So it is not a matter of such indifference to the state as people believe whether money goes into Peter's pocket or into Paul's, for it is essential that it should not be taken away from the man who employs it to the benefit of the state. Strictly speaking, money which is employed in this way in a nation has no owner at all: it belongs to the needs of the state, which cause it to circulate for the purpose of reproducing the wealth which enables the nation to subsist and provides contributions for the sovereign.[131]

This money must not be confused with the funds which are the subject of the ruinous traffic in loans at interest, and which escape the contributions which all annual revenue ought to pay to the state. This money held to meet needs, I maintain, has in the case of all individuals a destination to which it decisively belongs. That which is destined for the payment of current taxes belongs to the taxes; that which is destined to meet the need for some purchase belongs to this need; that which invigorates agriculture, trade, and industry belongs to this employment; and that which is destined to pay a debt which has fallen due or a loan which is about to expire belongs to this debt, etc., and not to the man who possesses it. It is the nation's money, and no one is entitled to lend it, because it belongs to no one; yet it is money dispersed in this way which constitutes the main part of the money stock of a really opulent kingdom, where it is always employed to the benefit of the state. People do not even hesitate to sell it at a higher price than it has cost, that is, to allow it to go abroad for the purchase of commodities when there is an assured gain; and foreign countries too are not unaware of the advantages of this trade, in which considerations of profit determine the exchange of money for commodities and of commodities for money. For money and commodities everywhere constitute wealth only in proportion to their market value.[132]

The quantity of money which is idle and which cannot be regenerated is small, and it is soon exhausted when borrowing increases a little. It is this idle money, however, which deludes the rabble; it is this which the vulgar regard as the nation's wealth and as an important means for meeting a state's needs – even those of a great state which in actual fact can be opulent only as a result of the net product of the wealth which is annually generated from its territory, and which, so to speak, causes money to be regenerated by renewing it and continually accelerating its circulation.[133]

Moreover, when a kingdom is wealthy and thriving as a result of trade in its products, it has, as a result of its intercourse, wealth in other countries, and paper everywhere takes the place of money for it. The abundance

Mais il ne faut pas confondre les abus avec les simples dépenses : car les abus pourroient engloutir toutes les richesses de la Nation & du Souverain.

24.° Que l'on soit moins attentif à l'augmentation de la population qu'à l'accroissement des revenus : car plus d'aisances que procurent de grands revenus sont préférables à plus de besoins pressans de subsistance qu'exige une population qui excède les revenus ; & il y a plus de ressources pour les besoins de l'Etat quand le peuple est dans l'aisance, & aussi plus de moyens pour faire prospérer l'agriculture [a].

tout d'argent. L'abondance & le débit de ses productions lui assurent donc par-tout l'usage du pécule des autres Nations ; & jamais l'argent ne manque non plus dans un Royaume bien cultivé, pour payer au Souverain, & aux Propriétaires les revenus fournis par le produit net des denrées commerçables, qui renaissent annuellement de la terre : Mais quoique l'argent ne manque point pour payer ces revenus, il ne faut pas prendre le change, & croire que les revenus de l'Etat puissent être imposés sur l'argent.

L'argent est une richesse qui se dérobe à la vûe. L'imposition du tribut ne peut être établie que sur des richesses ostensibles, toujours renaissantes & commerçables. Elles fournissent les revenus du Souverain ; & il peut y trouver de plus des ressources assurées dans des besoins pressans de l'Etat. Le produit net des biens-fonds se distribue à trois propriétaires, à l'Etat, aux possesseurs des terres, & aux décimateurs. Il n'y a que la partie du possesseur du bien qui soit aliénable, & elle ne se vend qu'à raison du revenu qu'elle produit ; car c'est ce produit qui regle le prix de l'acquisition : La propriété du possesseur ne s'étend donc pas au delà. Ce n'est donc pas lui qui paye les autres Propriétaires qui ont part au bien, puisque leurs parts ne lui appartiennent pas, qu'il ne les a pas acquises, & qu'elles ne sont pas aliénables. Le possesseur du bien ne doit donc pas regarder l'impôt ordinaire comme une charge établie sur sa portion ; car ce n'est pas lui qui paye ce revenu, c'est la partie du bien qu'il n'a pas acquise, & qui ne lui appartient pas, qui le paye à qui il est dû. Mais dans les cas de nécessité, tous Propriétaires doivent contribuer sur leurs portions à la subvention passagère que les besoins pressans de l'Etat peuvent exiger. Ainsi dans les Nations agricoles, où l'agriculture est opulente, il y a pour l'Etat des ressources assurées dans les revenus des biens-fonds.

Les vûes du Gouvernement ne doivent donc pas s'arrêter à l'argent, elles doivent s'étendre plus loin, & se fixer à l'abondance & à la valeur vénale des productions de la terre, pour accroître les revenus. C'est dans cette partie de richesses visibles & annuelles que consiste l'opulence & la domination du Monarque, & la prospérité de la Nation : c'est elle qui fixe & qui attache les Sujets au sol. L'argent, l'industrie, le commerce mercantil, & de trafic ne forment qu'un domaine postiche & indépendant, qui sans les richesses du sol, ne constitueroit qu'un Etat républicain : Constantinople même, qui n'en a pas le gouvernement, mais qui est réduit aux richesses mobiliaires du commerce de trafic, en a, au milieu du Despotisme, le génie & l'indépendance dans les correspondances & dans l'état libre de ses richesses de commerce.

[a] L'idée dominante de la guerre dans les Nations, fait penser que la force des Etats consiste dans une grande population ; mais la partie militaire d'une Nation ne peut ni subsister ni agir que par la partie contribuable : Supposeroit-on que les grandes richesses d'un

ture, for abuses could swallow up all the wealth of the nation and the sovereign.

24. [134] That less attention is paid to increasing the population than to increasing the revenue; for the greater well-being which a high revenue brings about is preferable to the greater pressure of subsistence needs which a population in excess of the revenue entails; and when the people are in a state of well-being there are more resources to meet the needs of the state, and also more means to make agriculture prosper [a].

of its products and their sale thus assure to it everywhere the use of the money stock of other nations; and money is never lacking, either, in a kingdom which is properly cultivated, for the purpose of paying to the sovereign and the proprietors the revenue provided by the net product of the exchangeable produce which is annually regenerated from the land. But although money is never lacking for the purpose of paying this revenue, we must not make the mistake of believing that the state's revenue can be imposed on money.[135]

Money is a form of wealth which steals away on sight. The assessment of contributions can be based only on palpable wealth which is always renascent and exchangeable. It provides revenue for the sovereign, who will moreover find in it assured means for meeting the pressing needs of the state. The net product of landed property is distributed to three proprietors — the state, the possessors of land, and the tithe-owners. It is only the portion of the property belonging to the possessor which is transferable, and its selling price is no more than in proportion to the revenue which it produces, for it is the latter which regulates the purchase price. The ownership of the possessor, therefore, does not extend any further than this. Thus it is not he who pays the other proprietors who have shares in the property, since their shares do not belong to him, he has not acquired them, and they are not transferable. Thus the possessor of the property should not regard ordinary taxes as a charge laid on his portion, for it is not he who pays this revenue: it is the portion of the

property which he has not acquired and which does not belong to him which pays it to those to whom it is due. But in cases of necessity all the proprietors should make contributions out of their portions to the temporary subsidy which the pressing needs of the state may require. Thus in agricultural nations, where agriculture is affluent, the state will find assured means in the revenue from landed property.[136]

Thus the Government's gaze should not stop short at money, but should extend further and fix itself upon the abundance and market value of the produce of the land, in order to increase the revenue. It is in this part of visible and annual wealth that the affluence and power of the monarch and the prosperity of the nation consist; it is this which binds and attaches the subjects to the land. Money, industry, and mercantile trade[137] and traffic constitute only an artificial and independent realm, which in the absence of the land's wealth would be only a republican state; Constantinople itself, which has control over no such wealth, but is reduced to the movable wealth associated with the re-export trade, gains from it, in the midst of despotism, considerable ability and independence in its intercourse and in the free state of its commercial wealth.[138]

[a] [139] The predominant idea which nations have about war makes it thought that the strength of states consists in a large population; but the military part of a nation can neither subsist nor operate except through the tax-paying part. One would imagine that the great wealth of a state is obtained through an abundance of

Sans ces conditions, l'agriculture qu'on ſuppoſe dans le Tableau produire comme en Angleterre cent pour cent,

Etat s'obtiennent par l'abondance des hommes ? mais les hommes ne peuvent obtenir & perpétuer les richeſſes que par les richeſſes, & qu'autant qu'il y a une proportion convenable entre les hommes & les richeſſes.

Une Nation croit toûjours qu'elle n'a pas aſſez d'hommes, & on ne s'aperçoit pas qu'il n'y a pas aſſez de ſalaire pour ſoutenir une plus grande population, & que les hommes ſans fortune ne ſont profitables dans un pays, qu'autant qu'ils y trouvent des gains aſſurés pour y ſubſiſter par leur travail. Au défaut de gains ou de ſalaire le bas peuple des campagnes peut à la vérité faire naître, pour ſe nourrir, quelques productions de vil prix, qui n'exigent pas de dépenſes ni de longs travaux, & dont la récolte ne ſe fait pas attendre long-temps : Mais ces hommes, ces productions & la terre où elles naiſſent ſont nuls pour l'Etat. Il faut pour tirer de la terre un revenu, que les travaux de la campagne rendent un produit net au delà du ſalaire payé aux Ouvriers ; car c'eſt ce produit net qui fait ſubſiſter les autres claſſes d'hommes néceſſaires dans un Etat. C'eſt ce qu'on ne doit pas attendre des hommes pauvres qui labourent la terre avec leurs bras, ou avec d'autres moyens inſuffiſans ; car ils ne peuvent que ſe procurer à eux ſeuls leur ſubſiſtance en renonçant à la culture du blé, qui exige trop de temps, trop de travaux, & trop de dépenſes pour être exécutée par des hommes dénués de facultés, & réduits à tirer leur nourriture de la terre par le ſeul travail de leurs bras.

Ce n'eſt donc pas à de pauvres Payſans que vous devez confier la culture de vos terres : Ce ſont les animaux qui doivent labourer & fertiliſer vos champs ; c'eſt la conſommation, le débit, la facilité & la liberté du commerce intérieur & extérieur qui aſſurent la valeur vénale, qui forme vos revenus. Ce ſont donc des hommes riches que vous devez charger des entrepriſes de la culture des terres & du commerce rural pour vous enrichir, pour enrichir l'Etat, pour faire renaître des richeſſes intariſſables, par leſquelles vous puiſſiez jouir largement des produits de la terre & des arts, entretenir une riche défenſe contre vos ennemis, & ſubvenir avec opulence aux dépenſes des travaux publics pour les commodités de la Nation, pour la facilité du commerce de vos denrées, pour les fortifications de vos frontieres, pour l'entretien d'une Marine redoutable, pour la décoration du Royaume, & pour procurer aux hommes de travail des ſalaires & des gains qui les attirent & qui les retiennent dans le Royaume. Ainſi le gouvernement politique de l'agriculture & du commerce de ſes productions eſt la baſe du Miniſtere des finances & de toutes les autres parties de l'adminiſtration d'une Nation agricole.

Les grandes armées ne ſuffiſent pas pour former une riche défenſe ; il faut que le Soldat ſoit bien payé, pour qu'il puiſſe être bien diſcipliné, bien exercé, vigoureux, content & courageux. La guerre ſur terre & ſur mer emploie d'autres moyens que la force des hommes, & exige d'autres dépenſes bien plus conſidérables que celles de la ſubſiſtance des Soldats : Ainſi ce ſont bien moins les hommes que les richeſſes qui ſoutiennent la guerre ; car tant qu'on a des richeſſes pour bien payer les hommes, on n'en manque pas pour réparer les armées. Plus une Nation a de richeſſes pour faire renaître annuellement les richeſſes, moins cette reproduction annuelle occupe d'hommes, plus elle rend de produit net, plus le Gouvernement a d'hommes à ſa diſpoſition pour le ſervice & les travaux publics ; & plus il y a de ſalaire pour les faire ſubſiſter, plus ces hommes ſont utiles à l'Etat par leur emploi, & par leurs dépenſes qui font rentrer leur paye dans la circulation.

Les batailles gagnées où l'on ne tue que des hommes, ſans cauſer d'autres dommages, affoibliſſent peu l'ennemi, ſi le ſalaire des hommes qu'il a perdus lui reſte, & s'il eſt ſuffiſant pour attirer d'autres hommes. Une armée de cent mille hommes bien payés, eſt une armée d'un million d'hommes ; car toute armée où la ſolde attire des hommes ne peut être détruite ; c'eſt alors aux Soldats à ſe défendre courageuſement ; ce ſont eux qui ont le plus à perdre ; car ils ne manqueront pas de ſucceſſeurs bien déterminés à affronter les dangers de la guerre. C'eſt donc la richeſſe qui ſoutient l'honneur des armes : Le Héros qui gagne des batailles, qui prend des villes, qui acquiert de la gloire, &

ſeroit

Without[140] these conditions, an agriculture producing 100 per cent, as we have assumed it to do in the *tableau* and as it does in England, would

men; but men can obtain and perpetuate wealth only by means of wealth, and to the extent that there is a proper proportion between men and wealth.[141]

Nations always believe that they do not have enough men: it is not perceived that there are not enough wages to maintain a larger population, and that men without means are of benefit to a country only to the extent that they receive assured gains there which enable them to live by their work. In the absence of gains or wages, it is true, the common people in the countryside may generate for their subsistence certain very low-priced products which do not demand expenses or protracted labour, and which one does not have to wait a long time before gathering in. But these men, these products, and the land on which they are grown, are worth nothing to the state. In order that the land should yield a revenue, work in the countryside must render a net product over and above the wages paid to the workmen, for it is this net product which enables the other classes of men who are necessary in a state to subsist. This should not be expected from poor men who work the land with their hands, or with other insufficient resources; for they can procure subsistence for themselves alone only by giving up the cultivation of corn, which demands too much time, too much labour, and too much expense to be carried on by men who are destitute of means and reduced to obtaining their food from the land simply by the work of their hands.[142]

Thus it is not to these poor peasants that you should entrust the cultivation of your land. It is animals which should plough and fertilise your fields; it is consumption, sales, and free and unobstructed internal and external trade which ensure the market value which constitutes your revenue. Thus it is wealthy men whom you should put in charge of the enterprises of agriculture and rural trade, in order to enrich yourselves, to enrich the state, and to enable inexhaustible wealth to be generated. With the aid of this wealth you may enjoy in abundance the products of the land and the arts, maintain powerful defences against your enemies, and provide amply for the expenses of public works devoted to the conveniences of the nation, to the facilitation of trade in your produce, to the fortification of your frontiers, to the maintenance of a formidable navy, to the beautification of the kingdom, and to the procuring for working men of wages and gains which attract them into the kingdom and keep them there. Thus the political administration of agriculture and of trade in its produce is the foundation of the department of finance, and of all the other branches of administration in an agricultural nation.[143]

Large armies are not sufficient to provide a powerful defence. The soldier must be well paid if he is to be well disciplined, well trained, energetic, happy, and fearless. War on land and sea employs other resources besides men's strength, and demands other expenditure much greater than that necessary for the soldiers' subsistence. Thus it is much less men than wealth which sustains a war, for so long as wealth is available to pay the men well, men will not be lacking as reinforcements for the army. The more wealth a nation possesses for the purpose of enabling wealth to be annually regenerated, the fewer men does this annual reproduction employ, the more net product it yields, and the more men the Government has at its disposal for services and public works; and the more wages there are to enable them to subsist, the more useful are these men to the state by virtue of their occupations, and by virtue of their expenditure, which causes their pay to be brought back into circulation.[144]

Battles which are won simply by killing men, without causing any other damage, do little to weaken the enemy if he still has the wages of the men he has lost, and if they are sufficient to attract other men. An army of 100,000 well-paid men is an army of a million men, for no army to which men are attracted by the pay can be destroyed. It is then up to the soldiers to defend themselves bravely; they are the ones who have most to lose, for they will not lack bold successors fully prepared to face the dangers of war. Thus it is wealth which sustains the honour of the troops. The hero who wins battles, who takes cities, who acquires glory, and who is the soonest

feroit une fiction ; mais les principes n'en font pas moins certains, ni moins les vrais principes de la fcience du Gouvernement économique, que l'on ne confond pas ici avec la fcience triviale des opérations fpécieufes de finance, qui n'ont pour objet que le pécule de la Nation & le mouvement de l'argent, par un trafic d'argent ; où le crédit, l'appas des intérêts, &c. ne produifent, comme

qui eft le plus tôt épuifé, n'eft pas le Conquérant : l'Hiftorien qui fe borne au merveilleux dans le récit des exploits militaires, inftruit peu la Poftérité fur les fuccès des événemens décififs des guerres, s'il lui laiffe ignorer l'état des forces fondamentales & de la politique des Nations dont il écrit l'hiftoire ; car c'eft dans l'aifance permanente de la partie contribuable des Nations, & dans les vertus patriotiques que confifte la puiffance permanente des Etats.

Il faut penfer de même à l'égard des travaux publics qui facilitent l'accroiffement des richeffes, tels font la conftruction des canaux, la réparation des chemins, des rivières, &c. qui ne peuvent s'exécuter que par l'aifance des contribuables, en état de fubvenir à ces dépenfes, fans préjudicier à la reproduction annuelle des richeffes de la Nation : autrement de tels travaux fi étendus, quoique fort defirables, feroient par les impofitions déréglées, ou par les corvées continuées, des entreprifes ruineufes dont les fuites ne feroient pas réparées par l'utilité de ces travaux forcés & accablans. Car le dépériffement d'un Etat fe répare difficilement ; les caufes deftructives, qui augmentent de plus en plus, rendent inutiles toute la vigilance & tous les efforts du Miniftère, lorfqu'on s'attache qu'à en réprimer les effets, & qu'on ne remonte pas jufqu'au principe : ce qui eft bien prouvé par l'Auteur du Livre intitulé *Le Détail de la France fous Louis XIV,* imprimé en 1699, où cet Auteur rapporte les commencemens de la décadence du Royaume à l'année 1660, & où il en examine les progrès jufqu'au temps où il a publié fon Livre : Et il démontre

que les revenus des biens-fonds, qui étoient de 700 millions (1400 millions de notre monnoie d'aujourd'hui) avoient diminué de moitié depuis 1660 jufqu'à 1699 : Il obferve que ce n'eft pas à la quantité d'impôts, mais à la mauvaife forme d'impofition, & à fes defordres qu'il faut imputer cette énorme dégradation. On doit juger de-là des progrès de cette diminution, par la continuation du même genre d'adminiftration. L'impofition devint fi défordonnée qu'elle monta fous Louis XIV à plus de 750 millions ¶, qui ne rendoient au Tréfor royal que 250 millions ; ce qui enlevoit annuellement aux contribuables la jouiffance de 500 millions, dont la reproduction de plus de 200 millions étoit anéantie fans retour chaque année : ce qui diminuoit d'autant tous les ans la maffe des richeffes du royaume, fans y comprendre la deftruction annuelle que caufoit la taille arbitraire établie fur les Fermiers : ce qui montoit enfemble annuellement à plus de 300 millions de déprédation. Ainfi tous les trois ans la dégradation étoit d'environ un milliard, (à peu près deux milliards, monnoie d'aujourd'hui). Cette impofition ruineufe qui s'étendoit fur la dépenfe de l'impot même, le réduifoit en valeur réelle environ à 170 millions : Auffi remarque-t-on que par une meilleure adminiftration on auroit pû, en un mois, augmenter beaucoup l'impot, & enrichir les Sujets, en aboliffant une impofition fi deftructive, & en ranimant le commerce extérieur des grains, des vins, des laines, des toiles, &c. Qui auroit ofé entreprendre une telle réforme dans des temps où l'on n'avoit plus d'idée du gouvernement économique d'une Nation agricole ? On auroit cru alors renverfer les colonnes de l'édifice.

¶ *Mémoires pour fervir à l'Hiftoire générale des Finances,* par M. DEON DE BEAUMONT.

F

be fictitious; but the principles would be no less certain, nor any less the true principles of the science of economic administration. This science is not confused here with the trivial and specious science of financial operations whose subject-matter is only the money stock of the nation and the monetary movements resulting from traffic in money, in which credit, the lure of interest, etc., as in the case of gambling, bring about

exhausted, is not the conqueror. The historian who confines himself to a description of marvellous happenings in his account of military exploits does little to instruct posterity about the results of decisive events in war, if he allows himself to ignore the state of the basic resources and policy of the nations whose history he is writing. For it is in the permanent well-being of the tax-paying section of a nation, and in the patriotic virtues, that the permanent power of a state consists.[145]

One should consider in the same light the public works which facilitate the increase of wealth, such as the construction of canals, the putting into order of roads, rivers, etc., which can be carried out only as a result of the comfortable situation of tax-payers who are in a position to meet these expenses without detrimentally affecting the annual reproduction of the nation's wealth. Otherwise works of such an extensive character, although very desirable, would as a result of ill-regulated taxes or continual *corvées* become ruinous enterprises, whose consequences would not be made up for by the utility of these resource-straining and burdensome works; for it is not easy to make up for the decline of a state. Destructive causes, which increase more and more, render all the vigilance and exertions of the administration useless, when attention is devoted only to keeping the effects in check instead of going back to the causes. This is fully proved by the author[146] of the book entitled *A Detailed Account of France under Louis XIV*, published in 1699. This author dates the beginning of the kingdom's decline back to the year 1660, and he examines its course down to the time when his book was published. He shows that the revenue from landed property, which was formerly 700 millions (1400

millions in terms of our money today) diminished by one-half between 1660 and 1699. He notes that it is not to the level of taxes but to the injurious form of assessment and the disorder which it brought about that this huge decline must be attributed. One is bound to impute the continuation of this contraction to the continuation of the same form of administration. The assessment became so irregular that under Louis XIV it rose to more than 750 millions¶ but yielded to the royal treasury only 250 millions, which meant that the tax-payers were deprived every year of the enjoyment of 500 millions, the reproduction of more than 200 millions of which was irretrievably destroyed each year. This correspondingly reduced every year the mass of the kingdom's wealth, without taking into account the annual destruction caused by the arbitrary *taille* which was imposed on the farmers. Taken together, the annual depredations amounted to more than 300 millions. Thus in each three-year period the deterioration amounted to about a milliard (nearly two milliards in terms of our money today). This ruinous assessment, which spread out over the expenditure of the taxes themselves, reduced their real value to about 170 millions. Thus we see that by a better form of administration tax revenue could have been greatly increased in a month, and the subjects could have been enriched, by abolishing such a destructive imposition, and by reviving external trade in corn, wine, wool, cloth, etc. Who would have dared to attempt such a reform at a time when no one any longer had a proper conception of the economic administration of an agricultural kingdom? At that time it would have been considered as overthrowing the pillars of the building.[147]

¶ *Memoranda on the General History of Finance*, by M. D'ÉON DE BEAUMONT.

au jeu, qu'une circulation stérile : ce qui ne peut être de quelqu'avantage que dans des cas extraordinaires. C'est dans la connoissance des véritables sources des richesses, & des moyens de les multiplier & de les perpétuer, que consiste la science du gouvernement économique d'un Royaume.

Le Gouvernement économique ouvre les sources des richesses ; les richesses attirent les hommes ; les hommes & les richesses font prospérer l'agriculture, étendent le commerce, animent l'industrie, accroissent & perpétuent les richesses : Le Gouvernement économique prévient le dépérissement de l'opulence & des forces de la Nation. De ses ressources abondantes dépendent les succès des autres parties de l'administration du Royaume : le Gouvernement économique affermit la puissance de l'Etat, attire la considération des autres Nations, assure la gloire du Monarque & le bonheur du Peuple. Ses vûes embrassent tous les principes essentiels d'un Gouvernement parfait, où l'autorité est toûjours protectrice, bienfaisante, tutélaire, adorable ; elle n'est point susceptible d'écarts, elle ne sauroit trop s'étendre, elle ne peut inquiéter, elle soutient par-tout les intérêts de la Nation, le bon ordre, le droit public, la puissance & la domination du Souverain.

F I N.

nothing but a sterile circulation which only in exceptional circumstances can be of any benefit. It is in a knowledge of the true sources of wealth, and of the means of increasing and perpetuating them, that the science of the economic administration of a kingdom consists.

Economic administration opens up the sources of wealth; wealth attracts men; men and wealth make agriculture prosper, expand trade, give new life to industry, and increase and perpetuate wealth. Economic administration forestalls a decline in the affluence and strength of the nation. Upon the means which it abundantly provides, the success of the other branches of the kingdom's government depends. Economic administration strengthens the power of the state, attracts the respect of other nations, and safeguards the glory of the monarch and the happiness of the people. It includes in its scope all the essential principles of a perfect system of government, in which authority is always a benevolent protectress and a beloved guardian, which can never be diverted from its course, which will not spread its influence too far, and which cannot cause anxiety. It maintains everywhere the interests of the nation, good order, the rights of the public, and the power and dominion of the sovereign.[148]

THE END

4

Notes to the 'Third Edition'

4

Notes to the 'Third Edition'

Diagram   1   This *tableau* is identical with the first of the four documents reproduced in B.E.A. It is clearly a revised and developed version of the *tableaux* included in the 'first edition' (see below, App. A) and the 'second edition' (see below, App. B). The 'zigzag' form employed in these three 'editions' was also extensively used in *A.D.H*. In *P.R.*, however, the 'zigzag' gave way in the main to a simplified '*précis*'. In the *Analyse*, a new '*formule*' was introduced, and this was also employed in the *Premier Problème Économique* and the *Second Problème Économique*. For details, see Meek, passim. Cf. Higgs, *The Physiocrats* (London, 1897) pp. 42–3.

  The *tableau* of the 'third edition' does not fully reflect the set of figures incorporated in the *Explication*, p. v (para. 4) and pp. vi (para. 3)–vii (para. 1), since the figure given for interest at the foot of the *tableau* is only 300 (million) livres, this being the total (apparently rounded to the nearest 100) of the interest on the original advances alone. Cf. the developed and partially corrected formulation in the *tableau* opposite p. 23 of *A.D.H.*, in which a total sum of 345 livres is quoted for the interest on the original advances and the annual advances taken together.

i   2   This *Explication*, of which the second of the four documents reproduced in B.E.A. is probably best regarded as a proof copy, clearly grew out of the abbreviated explanatory comments which accompanied the *tableaux* of the 'first edition' and the 'second edition' (q.v.).

  The proof copy reproduced in B.E.A. contains a number of corrections in Quesnay's hand. The corrections actually made in the final version reproduced here include some (although by no means all) of these, but they also include quite a large number which are not noted on the proof copy. It is clear, therefore, that this proof copy was a relatively early one, and that it must eventually have been superseded by another. One possible explanation of what happened is that Quesnay, having taken this proof copy, began to correct it in the normal way, noting a number of alterations on pp. i–iv. After p. iv, however, he began to read it simply for sense, indicating only two corrections of any consequence in the whole of the rest of the document – the insertions on pp. vi and vii (see notes 10 and 21 below). He then sent the proof copy to Mirabeau. In his final revision Quesnay made the indicated insertions on pp. vi and vii, corrected some of the arithmetical errors on p. viii, and while he was about it made a number of additional corrections, of a relatively minor character, on each of these three pages. He also made a few corrections – only one of them of any real significance – on pp. ix–xi; but he evidently forgot about pp. i–iv, making none of the corrections he himself had indicated in the original proof copy which he had sent to Mirabeau. Realising his mistake before the copies were bound, he inserted a note of errata at the end of the *Explication* in which he made the only one of these corrections which was of any real importance – an alteration of two figures on p. ii. This reconstruction of

the course of events, it goes without saying, is wholly speculative, and all that can really be claimed for it is that it seems to be consistent with the facts.

The corrections in Quesnay's hand on p. i of the proof copy were the insertion of a comma after '*productives*' in l. 1; the insertion of a comma after '*stériles*' in l. 5; the insertion of a comma at the end of l. 12; and the alteration of '*de matière première d'ouvrage*' in l. 14 to '*des matières premières des ouvrages*'. None of these corrections was made in the final version.

ii   3, 4   In the printed text, of both the proof copy and the final version, the figures are 400 and 800 respectively. In the proof copy they are corrected in Quesnay's hand to 500 and 700. In the final version, they are similarly corrected in the errata at the end of the *Explication,* and the correction has also been made by hand on p. ii itself.

iii   5   The amount taken for external trade is assumed to be 150 in accordance with the supposition, made a few lines below, that one-eighth of the total product of the productive class enters into external trade.

The proof copy contains a number of corrections to this sentence in Quesnay's hand. In l. 22 '*il*' is changed to '*Il*'; and commas are inserted after '*moitié*' in l. 23, after '*liv.*' in l. 24, and after '*moitié*' and '*liv.*' in l. 25. None of these corrections was made in the final version.

iv   6   The proof copy contains three corrections to this passage, two of which were struck out again. The one which was allowed to remain affects l. 5, where '*en exportation, ou en matières premières*' has been changed to '*soit en exportation, soit en matières premières*'. This correction was not made in the final version.

   7   Cf. note 33 below.

v   8   The figure should of course be 105 millions. The correct figure was substituted in *A.D.H.* (p. 77).

   9   In the light of the correction mentioned in the last note, this figure is changed to 2,205,000,000 in *A.D.H.* (p. 77).

vi   10   In the proof copy, the text of this paragraph reads as follows: '*Cette culture peut s'étendre en France à plus de 60 millions d'arpens.*' The words '*avec 5 ou 6 milliards d'avances*' have been written in the margin in Quesnay's hand, with an indication that they should be inserted after '*peut*'. In the final version the text of the paragraph reads: '*Cette culture pourroit, avec 5 ou 6 milliards d'avances, s'étendre en France à plus de 60 millions d'arpens.*'

The first four lines of p. vi contain a number of differences in punctuation, as compared with the proof copy. In l. 1 the comma after '*mille*' does not appear in the proof copy. In l. 2 the semi-colon after '*charrue*' has replaced a comma in the proof copy. In l. 3 the comma after '*mille*' does not appear in the proof copy. In l. 4 the semi-colon after '*conduire*' has replaced a comma in the proof copy.

vi   11   The text seems to be imperfect here, and Quesnay's meaning is not immediately obvious. (Cf. the more complete formulation at the foot of the *tableau* opposite p. 23 of *A.D.H.*, where the relevant phrase reads '*la moitié du produit de l'emploi d'une charrue*'.) Here and in the next paragraph, it would seem, Quesnay is using '*charrue*' to mean a plough *of land* (a carucate or ploughland), this being a measure of the amount of land which can be tilled with one plough in a year. In the present context, what Quesnay is saying in effect is that the amount of the total agricultural

product has been worked out by estimating the value of the harvest which each plough of land could yield under conditions of large-scale cultivation, and then dividing the total by two – the latter operation being necessary because each unit of land is assumed to be fallow in alternate years.

This paragraph contains two differences in punctuation, as compared with the proof copy. The comma after '*mêmes*' in l. 14, and that after '*ingrate*' in l. 18, do not appear in the proof copy.

vi   12   The ampersand at the beginning of l. 27, before the word '*nourriture*', does not appear in the proof copy. Quesnay may have used it to improve the spacing of the words in the line, or perhaps to link '*semence*' and '*nourriture*' as coming mainly from the same source – in which case, of course, the comma after '*semence*' should have been deleted. In the corresponding passage in *A.D.H.* (pp. 27–8), the relevant part of the sentence reads '*dépenses en bestiaux, instrumens, fourage, semence & nourriture, entretien, salaire, &c.*'

     13   The comma after '*mille*' in l. 30 does not appear in the proof copy.

vii   14   Vol. v (Paris, 1756) p. 511.

     15   Ibid., p. 528.

     16   The problem of the advances is given special treatment on pp. 816–19 of vol. VII (Paris, 1757), although it is here a question of the annual and not the original advances.

     17   If the interest is to be at least 10 per cent, this figure of 333,322,000 is obviously too low. In *A.D.H.* (p. 78) a figure of 333,340,000 is substituted, but it is clear from what follows that this is a misprint for the correct figure, 333,334,000. The latter is in fact used in *A.D.H.* in arriving at the figure for the total annual reproduction including interest (see note 20 below).

     18   '*Ouvrages*' in the final version has replaced '*travaux*' in the proof copy.

     19   In the proof copy this figure appeared as 1,000,0000,000. The superfluous zero was crossed out by hand, and the correction was duly made in the final version.

     20   This represents the sum of 2,210,000,000 livres estimated (p. v above) for the total annual reproduction, plus the sum of 333,322,000 livres estimated (incorrectly) for the annual interest on the original advances. In *A.D.H.* (p. 79), in the light of the corrections referred to in notes 8, 9 and 17 above, the total becomes 2,538,334,000.

     21   In the proof copy, the text of this paragraph reads as follows: '*Le territoire de la France pourroit produire autant & même beaucoup plus.*' The words '*avec des avances et du débit*' have been written in the margin in Quesnay's hand, with an indication that they should be inserted after '*France*'. In the final version, the text of the paragraph reads: '*Le territoire de la France pourroit, avec des avances & du débit, produire autant & même beaucoup plus.*'

     22   See note 20 above.

     23   In *A.D.H.* (p. 80), in the light of the corrections referred to above, this figure becomes 2,013,334,000.

This paragraph contains three differences, as compared with the proof copy. In l. 27, the comma after '*lions*' does not appear in the proof copy. In l. 28, the comma after '*annuelles*' does not appear in the proof copy. In l. 28, the word '*bestiaux*' has replaced '*animaux*' in the proof copy.

H

viii   24   It is not clear how Quesnay arrived at the figures 562 and 530.

The difficulty arises, of course, because Quesnay starts with a figure of 2,018,322,000 for total expenditure, divides this by four to obtain a figure of 504,580,500 'for each million heads of families', and then tells us that 'for each individual head of family' this is equivalent, not to 505 as we would expect, but to 562, which 'accidents' (presumably those for which interest at the postulated rate of 10 per cent is a kind of compensation) are said to reduce to 'about 530'.

Each of the editors of the present volume has already made an attempt to solve this problem – Mrs Kuczynski in her German edition of the *Tableau Économique* (pp. 80–1, note 23), and Professor Meek in his *Economics of Physiocracy* (p. 133, fn. 1). Mrs Kuczynski's argument was based on the assumption that the figures applied to those heads of families who were not proprietors. Professor Meek started with the assumption that the figure 530 was a misprint for 505, the latter being roughly one-millionth of 504,580,500. They both now recognise, however, that their respective arguments contained serious mistakes, and they have therefore been seeking for better alternatives.

Mrs Kuczynski, in a new edition of Quesnay's *Works* which she is at present preparing, now suggests that Quesnay's calculation was probably based on his assumption, made explicitly in the 'third edition' (*Extrait*, p. 2 fn.), that 'the expenses of 16 million persons of all ages would be equal to those of only about 11 million adults'. Thus she arrives at a figure of 552, which is fairly near Quesnay's (miscalculated?) 562. By dividing the 333,322,000 livres interest also among 11 million adults, she gets a per capita share of 30. Deducting this from 562 gives her 532, which is very close to Quesnay's 'about 530'. But this procedure rests on the supposition that Quesnay mistakenly deducted only the per capita share of interest and not the pertinent family share. Her reconstructions are thus made at the cost of charging Quesnay (*a*) with an arithmetical error, and (*b*) with an error of thought.

Professor Meek now suggests that Quesnay, when he first tried to divide 2,018,322,000 among four million families, may have wrongly obtained 562,000,000 (approximately) instead of 505,000,000. (This would be an easy error for a bad arithmetician to make if he did the operation in two stages, since 504 + 58 = 562.) Dividing 562,000,000 by one million he immediately obtained the figure of 562 'for each individual head of family'. He then also divided the interest of 333,322,000 by one million, obtaining (wrongly, as usual) a figure of 33 which he thereupon deducted from 562 to obtain the net figure of 'about 530'. Later, having discovered his initial error, he altered the figure of 562,000,000 to the correct figure of 504,580,500, but forgot (as he frequently did) to make consequential alterations in the two figures 'for each individual head of family'. Professor Meek's reconstructions are thus made at the cost of assuming (*a*) an initial calculating mistake and its later correction, and (*b*) the overlooking of consequential corrections.

25   The words '*puissant en tribut & en ressources*' in the final version have been substituted for the word '*riche*' in the proof copy; and '530�.' has been substituted for '*530 liv.*'.

viii   26   This figure of 2,018,322,000 has been substituted for the figure 2,543,322,000 in the proof copy. Cf. *A.D.H.*, p. 81.

27   i.e. at a rate of $3\frac{1}{3}$ per cent. Quesnay has tried to work out the capital sum which would yield 1,050,000,000 livres per annum at this rate of interest, but the figure of 33,455,000,000 at which he arrives is obviously incorrect. In *A.D.H.* (p. 81) the figure is given correctly as 31,500,000,000.

28   The total of 36,788,340,000, on the basis of the figures being used by Quesnay, ought obviously to be 37,788,340,000. The most plausible explanation of the error is that Quesnay began by including in the figure for the original advances only the 3,333,340,000 livres estimated on p. vi for corn production, and worked out his total of 36,788,340,000 on this basis. He then realised that he ought also to include in the figure for the original advances the 1,000,000,000 livres estimated on p. vii for meadows, vineyards, etc., but having done this forgot to amend the total. In *A.D.H.* (pp. 80–1) the addition is correct, and the sum total includes the 1,000,000,000 for meadows, vineyards, etc.

29   There are several differences in the last two lines of this paragraph, as compared with the proof copy. The full stop after '36,788,340,000*l*' has been substituted for a comma; '*En*' has been substituted for '*en*'; and the comma after '*produit annuel*' has been substituted for a full stop. In addition to these grammatical corrections, the figure 2,543,322,000 has been substituted for 2,210,500,000. The latter figure in the proof copy was no doubt intended to be 2,210,000,000, the first figure given (on p. v) for the annual reproduction (excluding interest on the original advances). In the final version, Quesnay substitutes the figure of 2,543,322,000 given on p. vii, which includes interest on the original advances. Cf. *A.D.H.*, pp. 81–2.

30   Instead of '*sera* . . . 40,331,662,000*l*' in the final version, the proof copy has '*sera* 40,331,660,000*l*'.

31   A duplicate '*des*' in front of '*bestiaux*' in the proof copy has been removed in the final version, and the paragraph reset.

32   In the proof copy, '*la culture; car*'; in the final version, '*la culture. Car*'.

33   This is apparently made up of the sterile class's assumed annual advances of 300 million, plus a proportionate share of the taxes and tithes.

ix   34   '*Usances*', which appears here in both the final version and the proof copy, is probably a misprint for *usines*, which is the word appearing in the corresponding passage in *A.D.H.* (p. 82). It is interesting to note that the word *usine* was not contained in the fourth edition of the *Dictionnaire de l'Académie Française* which appeared in 1762.

35   In the proof copy, '*du commerce* . . . 1,000,000,000'; in the final version, '*du commerce. Ainsi* . . . 1,000,000,000'.

36   The portion of this footnote on p. ix contains the following differences, as compared with the proof copy. In l. 12, left side, the semi-colon after '*dettes*' has replaced a comma in the proof copy. In l. 13, left side, the comma after '*ruinée*' has replaced a semi-colon in the proof copy. In l. 26, left side, the semi-colon after '*Nations*' has replaced a comma in the proof copy. In l. 31, left side, the full stop after '*l'argent*' has replaced a semi-colon in the proof copy. In l. 29, right side, the comma after '*44 ans*' does not appear in the proof copy.

Page	Note	
x	37	In *A.D.H.* (p. 83) this figure is changed to 2,000,000,000. No explanation is given for this alteration, or for those described in notes 38 and 39 below.
	38	In *A.D.H.* (p. 84) this figure is changed to 2,000,000,000.
	39	In *A.D.H.* (p. 84) this figure is changed to 3,000,000,000.
	40	In the proof copy the full stop after '*prix*' appeared as a colon, and the following words (omitted in the final version) were added immediately thereafter: '*Tel est l'intérêt en France depuis long-temps.*'
xi	41	In the proof copy there is no '*Le*' before '*Total*'; the words '*peut être environ*' do not appear; and the description of the figure is set in only two lines of type instead of three.
	42	The total of the figures used by Quesnay is actually 17,525,000,000. In *A.D.H.* (p. 85) the net effect of the alterations mentioned in notes 37, 38 and 39 above is to reduce it to 16,525,000,000.
	43	This is intended to be the sum of the wealth of the productive expenditure class (p. viii) and the wealth of the sterile expenditure class. The actual sum of the figures used by Quesnay is 57,856,662,000.
	44	In *A.D.H.*, on the basis of the amended figures used in that work, the total comes out at 54,896,674,000, and is described (p. 85) simply as '*environ* 55,000,000,000', without any attempt to make a specific allowance for possible error.
xii	45	This note of errata does not appear in the proof copy. The emblem has been lowered to make room for it, and a rule has been inserted at the end of the text. The word '*corrigé*' appears in handwriting beside the errata. Cf. note 2 above.
1	46	Quesnay's first attempt to present certain basic Physiocratic premises and policies in the form of a set of numbered maxims was made in his *Encyclopedia* article 'Grains' (see I.N.E.D., II 496–504, translated in Meek, pp. 72–81). Towards the end of 'Grains' we find, under the title '*Maximes de Gouvernement Économique*', a set of fourteen numbered maxims (together with explanatory comments), which were designed by Quesnay to help his readers obtain 'a better understanding of the advantages of foreign trade in *corn*'. Some of the material in this early set of maxims eventually found its way in one form or another into later sets; but the range of the early set was relatively narrow, and naturally it had no connection with the *Tableau Économique,* which had not yet been formulated.

In the 'first edition' of the *Tableau Économique* Quesnay again used the device of a set of numbered maxims, this time under the title 'Remarques sur les Variations de la Distribution des Revenus Annuels d'une Nation' (see App. A of the present volume). There are twenty-two of these *remarques*; their range is much wider than that of the maxims in 'Grains'; and they are presented as the basic conditions or assumptions underlying the particular 'order of circulation' postulated in the *tableau.* The idea here is, of course, that France will not be able to achieve the height of prosperity which this 'order of circulation' implies unless she adopts the policies embodied in the maxims. These twenty-two *remarques* of the 'first edition' formed the basis of all the subsequent sets of maxims, and many of them survived more or less unchanged right through to the 'Maximes Générales' in *Physiocratie.*

In the 'second edition' of the *Tableau Économique,* the maxims are based

1   46   directly on those of the 'first edition' and are presented in the same kind
(cont.)   of setting (see I.N.E.D., II 669–73, translated in Meek, pp. 120–5). The
alterations in the content of the maxims themselves were relatively small:
fourteen of them were reproduced without any amendment at all, and the
changes made in the remaining eight were on the whole relatively slight. A
number of new footnotes were added, however; a new maxim concerning
freedom of cultivation was inserted, bringing the total number of maxims
to twenty-three; and the title was changed to 'Extrait des Œconomies
Royales de M. de Sully'. This latter alteration, as Oncken points out (p.
329 fn.), may possibly have been due to the influence of Mirabeau, who
in the first edition of his *L'Ami des Hommes* had drawn the public's
attention to the thirty-six maxims which Sully had addressed to Henry IV
in 1604 (see *A.D.H.*, second part, II 502–12). On the other hand the author
of 'Grains', in which there are several commendatory references to Sully
(to say nothing of a set of 'Maximes de Gouvernement Économique'),
could well have decided quite independently to change the title.

In the 'third edition' of the *Tableau Économique*, the maxims are based
on those of the 'second edition', and are once again presented as the
assumptions underlying the 'order of circulation' of the *tableau*. Fifteen
of the maxims of the 'second edition' were reproduced without any
alterations of substance, but there were certain changes of importance made
in some of the remaining eight. A new maxim concerning the economic
advantages of large farms was inserted, bringing the total number of maxims
to twenty-four. The notes were very considerably extended, and a great
deal of new material was incorporated in them. There was no further
change in the title, however, except that 'Œconomies' became 'Économies'.

The maxims were destined to appear three more times in basic Physiocratic texts, although never again under the title 'Extrait des Économies
Royales de M. de Sully'. In the sixth part of *L'Ami des Hommes* the
twenty-four maxims of the 'third edition' were republished in a chapter
headed 'Tableau Œconomique Considéré dans les Conditions Nécessaires
au Libre Jeu de la Machine de Prospérité' (*A.D.H.*, pp. 86 ff.). The maxims
appeared here without the extensive notes which had accompanied them
in the 'third edition', although much of the actual content of these notes
was scattered through other parts of the extensive exposition. A number of
amendments were made to some of the maxims, not always of an exclu-
sively stylistic character.

In *Philosophie Rurale*, where the titles of the twelve chapters were made
to correspond with the twelve 'objects to be considered' at the head of the
tableau of the 'third edition', the maxims were again republished, this time
under the heading 'MAXIMES GÉNÉRALES du Gouvernement économique' (*P.R.*, II 341–55). Mirabeau, in introducing the maxims in this
context, said that in order to conclude the chapter (chap. 9, on the relation
between expenditure and agriculture) he could not do better than tran-
scribe the 'twenty-four conditions' as they had appeared in the sixth part
of *L'Ami des Hommes*. 'These twenty-four conditions,' he wrote,
'immutable as the principles from which they spring and which they
embody, tell us everything we need to know to ensure the prosperity of
states; and to attempt even to touch this treasure of economic science

1 46
(cont.)

would be to falsify it with a sacrilegious hand' (*P.R.*, II 340). In spite of this, the maxims in *Philosophie Rurale* are by no means identical with those in *L'Ami des Hommes*: there are a large number of stylistic changes; in the case of nine maxims there are quite important alterations in individual words; and one maxim (v) is appreciably shortened.

In their final appearance in *Physiocratie*, however, the maxims underwent a much more substantial change. It is true that all the twenty-four maxims of the 'third edition' have their counterparts in *Physiocratie*, where they appear under the title 'Maximes Générales du Gouvernement Économique d'un Royaume Agricole'. But only in half a dozen or so cases are the maxims of *Physiocratie* identical with those of the 'third edition'; and in several cases quite substantial changes have been made. In addition the order of the maxims has been completely altered; six new maxims have been added, bringing the total number to thirty; and their former connection with the *Tableau Économique* has been completely severed. So far as the notes of the 'third edition' are concerned, most of these have found their way into *Physiocratie*, but here too there are some quite substantial changes in order, form and content.

The six new maxims added in *Physiocratie* are as follows:

I. QUE l'autorité souveraine soit unique, & supérieure à tous les individus de la société & à toutes les entreprises injustes des intérêts particuliers; *car l'objet de la domination & de l'obéissance est la sûreté de tous, & l'intérêt licite de tous. Le systême des contreforces dans un Gouvernement est une opinion funeste, qui ne laisse appercevoir que la discorde entre les Grands & l'accablement des Petits. La division des sociétés en différens ordres de Citoyens dont les uns exercent l'autorité souveraine sur les autres, détruit l'intérêt général de la Nation, & introduit la dissension des intérêts particuliers entre les différentes classes de Citoyens: cette division intervertiroit l'ordre du Gouvernement d'un Royaume agricole qui doit réunir tous les intérêts à un objet capital, à la prospérité de l'agriculture, qui est la source de toutes les richesses de l'État & de celles de tous les Citoyens.*

II. QUE la Nation soit instruite des loix générales de l'ordre naturel qui constituent le Gouvernement évidemment le plus parfait. *L'étude le la Jurisprudence humaine ne suffit pas pour former les hommes d'Etat; il est nécessaire que ceux qui se destinent aux emplois de l'administration soient assujettis à l'étude de l'ordre naturel le plus avantageux aux hommes réunis en société. Il est encore nécessaire que les connoissances pratiques & lumineuses que la Nation acquiert par l'expérience & la réflexion, se réunissent à la science générale du Gouvernement; afin que l'autorité souveraine, toujours éclairée par l'évidence, institue les meilleures loix & les fasse observer exactement pour la sûreté de tous, & pour parvenir à la plus grande prospérité possible de la société.*

III. QUE le Souverain & la Nation ne perdent jamais de vue, que la terre est l'unique source des richesses, & que c'est l'agriculture qui les multiplie. *Car l'augmentation des richesses assure celle de la population; les hommes & les richesses font prospérer l'agriculture, étendent le commerce, animent l'industrie, accroissent & perpétuent les*

1   46
(cont.)   *richesses. De cette source abondante dépend le succès de toutes les parties de l'administration du Royaume.*

IV.   QUE la propriété des biens fonds & des richesses mobiliaires soit assurée à ceux qui en sont les possesseurs légitimes; car LA SURETÉ DE LA PROPRIÉTÉ EST LE FONDEMENT ESSENTIEL DE L'ORDRE ÉCONOMIQUE DE LA SOCIÉTÉ. *Sans la certitude de la propriété le territoire resteroit inculte. Il n'y auroit ni propriétaires ni fermiers pour y faire les dépenses nécessaires pour le mettre en valeur & pour le cultiver, si la conservation du fonds & des produits n'étoit pas assurée à ceux qui font les avances de ces dépenses. C'est la sûreté de la possession permanente qui provoque le travail & l'emploi des richesses à l'amélioration & à la culture des terres, & aux entreprises du commerce & de l'industrie. Il n'y a que la Puissance Souveraine qui assure la propriété des Sujets, qui ait un droit primitif au partage des fruits de la terre, source unique des richesses.*

XVII.   QUE l'on facilite les débouchés & les transports des productions & des marchandises de main d'œuvre, par la réparation des chemins, & par la navigation des canaux, des rivieres & de la mer; *car plus on épargne sur les frais du commerce, plus on accroît le revenu du territoire.*

XXV.   QU'ON maintienne l'entiere liberté du commerce; *CAR LA POLICE DU COMMERCE INTÉRIEUR ET EXTÉRIEUR LA PLUS SURE, LA PLUS EXACTE, LA PLUS PROFITABLE A LA NATION ET A L'ÉTAT, CONSISTE DANS LA PLEINE LIBERTÉ DE LA CONCURRENCE.*

Since the main focus of the present volume is on the 'third edition', the notes which follow will concentrate on comparing the 'Extrait des Économies Royales' of the 'third edition' with (*a*) the 'Extrait des Œconomies Royales' of the 'second edition', and (*b*) the 'Maximes Générales' of *Physiocratie*. Incidental references will also be made from time to time to the versions of the maxims which appeared in the sixth part of *L'Ami des Hommes* and in vol. II of *Philosophie Rurale*. A more comprehensive comparison between the 'third edition' and *L'Ami des Hommes* is made in a special appendix to the notes.

In these comparisons no attention will normally be paid to purely stylistic changes, differences in punctuation and spelling, minor differences in emphasis, small printers' errors, etc.

1   47   The corresponding footnote at this place in the 'second edition' reads as follows down to this point: '*Si on ajoûtoit l'impôt aux 600 millions de revenue & que l'impôt fût de 200 millions, il faudroit que les avances annuelles fussent au moins de 1200 millions, sans compter les avances primitives, nécessaires pour former d'abord l'établissement des Laboureurs.*' The footnote then proceeds as it does in the 'third edition' down to '*à leur indigence*' at the end of the paragraph, and finishes at that point.

48   The words from '*il faut remarquer*' to '*à leur indigence*' form the opening sentence of the Note to maxim VI of *Physiocratie* (p. 131).

49   This paragraph, with the words '*aucune régle de proportion avec les richesses de la Nation*' substituted for '*aucune règle proportionnelle avec lui-même*',

constitutes the opening paragraph of the Note to maxim v of *Physiocratie* (p. 124).

1   50   This paragraph, with the words '*& sur ceux du Souverain*' substituted for '*& sur les revenus de l'Etat*', and with a number of stylistic alterations, constitutes all but the first few words of the third paragraph of the Note to maxim v of *Physiocratie* (p. 125).

     51   This paragraph, with a few stylistic alterations, constitutes the fourth paragraph of the Note to maxim v of *Physiocratie* (pp. 125–6).

2   52   The text of this opening paragraph is substantially the same as that of the 'second edition'. It does not appear at all in *Physiocratie*.

     53   This paragraph, with a few stylistic alterations and two alterations of substance, constitutes the fifth paragraph of the Note to maxim v of *Physiocratie* (p. 126). The alterations of substance are:

       (*a*) The words '*assujetti à l'impôt dans ces Etats qui n'ont point de territoire. Et il est encore presque toujours regardé comme une ressource momentanée dans les grands Etats*' are substituted for '*assujéti à l'impôt; ou des grands Etats*'.

       (*b*) The words '*Mais alors cette ressource insidieuse*' are substituted for '*Mais dans le dernier cas, cette ressource*'.

     54   This paragraph, with the words '*plus il seroit onéreux, injuste et désastreux*' substituted for '*plus il est onéreux & injuste*', constitutes the sixth paragraph of the Note to maxim v of *Physiocratie* (p. 127).

     55   The last sentence of this paragraph does not appear in *Physiocratie*. The earlier part of the paragraph, with the words '*au produit net*' inserted after '*proportionellement*', is almost exactly the same as the seventh paragraph of the Note to maxim v of *Physiocratie* (p. 127).

     56   In the corresponding footnote at this point in the 'second edition', the words '*ce que leur fourniroit la dépense de leur revenu*' appear in place of '*ce que leur revenu fourniroit pour leurs dépenses*'. Otherwise, apart from some stylistic differences, the footnote in the 'second edition' is the same down to '*des hommes des autres classes*', where it finishes. No part of the present footnote appears in *Physiocratie*.

     57   Taking into account the correction mentioned in note 8 above, the rounded total should properly be 438,300,000.

     58   The rounded total should properly be 2,013,300,000. Cf. note 23 above.

3   59   This maxim corresponds to (*a*) maxim I of the 'second edition', with the words after '*au préjudice*' appearing as '*de la réproduction du revenu & de l'aisance du Peuple*'; and (*b*) maxim VII of *Physiocratie* (pp. 110–11), which reads as follows: 'QUE la totalité des sommes du revenu rentre dans la circulation annuelle & la parcourre dans toute son étendue; *qu'il ne se forme point de fortunes pécuniaires, ou du moins, qu'il y ait compensation entre celles qui se forment & celles qui reviennent dans la circulation; car autrement ces fortunes pécuniaires arrêteroient la distribution d'une partie du revenu annuel de la Nation, & retiendroient le pécule du Royaume au préjudice de la rentrée des avances de la culture, de la rétribution du salaire des artisans, & de la consommation que doivent faire les différentes classes d'hommes qui exercent des professions lucratives: cette interception du pécule diminueroit la réproduction des revenus & de l'impôt.*' The reference made here to the consumption of '*les différentes classes d'hommes qui exercent des*

professions lucratives' was first made in the version of this maxim in *A.D.H.* (p. 87).

  3   60   This maxim corresponds to (*a*) maxim 2 of the 'second edition', with the word '*ou*' appearing in place of '&', and with one stylistic difference; and (*b*) maxim X of *Physiocratie* (p. 112), with the word '*ou*' substituted for '&'.

         61   This maxim corresponds to (*a*) maxim 3 of the 'second edition', with which it is virtually identical; and (*b*) maxim XXIII of *Physiocratie* (p. 118), with the word '*fort*' in the third line deleted, and with several stylistic alterations.

         62   This footnote does not appear in the 'second edition'. The words after '*trois quarts moins*' constitute the main part of the second half of the first paragraph of the Note to maxim VI of *Physiocratie* (pp. 131-2).

         63   This footnote does not appear in the 'second edition'. With '*améliorer*' substituted for '*acquérir*' in the eighth line, with '*leur circulation stérile ne les empêche point d'être des fortunes*' substituted for '*& qui sont des fortunes*', and with a few stylistic alterations, it constitutes the Note to maxim VII of *Physiocratie* (pp. 135-6).

  4   64   The first sentence of this maxim corresponds to maxim 4 of the 'second edition', with one or two stylistic differences. The first sentence also corresponds to maxim XXIV of *Physiocratie* (pp. 118-19), with '*se trouve*' substituted for '*se tourne*'. The versions in *A.D.H.* (pp. 88-9) and *P.R.* (pp. 343-4) also have '*se trouve*' substituted for '*se tourne*', and in addition include the second sentence of the maxim, with some slight modifications, as well as the first. The second sentence does not appear either in the 'second edition' or in *Physiocratie*.

         65   This maxim corresponds to (*a*) maxim 5 of the 'second edition', with a few stylistic differences; and (*b*) maxim XXI of *Physiocratie* (p. 117), with '*ne se livrent pas*' substituted for '*ne soient pas portés, par quelqu'inquiétude qui ne seroit pas prévûe par le Gouvernement, à se livrer*', and with one stylistic amendment. This shortening of the maxim had already been effected in *P.R.* (p. 344), but not in *A.D.H.* (p. 89).

         66   This maxim corresponds to (*a*) maxim 6 of the 'second edition', with one stylistic difference; and (*b*) maxim XXVIII of *Physiocratie* (pp. 120-1), with which it is substantially identical.

         67   This maxim corresponds to (*a*) maxim 7 of the 'second edition', which reads as follows: '*Que l'impôt ne soit pas destructif ou disproportionné à la masse du revenu de la Nation, que son augmentation suive l'augmentation du revenu de la Nation, qu'il soit établi immédiatement sur le revenu des propriétaires, & non sur des denrées où il multiplieroit les frais de perception, & préjudicieroit au commerce; qu'il ne se prenne pas non plus sur les avances des fermiers des biens fonds, dont les richesses doivent être conservées précieusément pour les dépenses de la culture, & éviter les pertes des revenus.*'; and (*b*) maxim V of *Physiocratie* (p. 109), which reads as follows: '*QUE l'impôt ne soit pas destructif, ou disproportionné à la masse du revenu de la Nation; que son augmentation suive l'augmentation du revenu; qu'il soit établi immédiatement sur le produit net des biens fonds & non sur le salaire des hommes, ni sur les denrées, ou il multiplieroit les frais de perception, préjudicieroit au commerce, & détruiroit annuellement une partie des richesses de la Nation. Qu'il ne se prenne pas non plus sur les richesses des fermiers des*

biens fonds; car LES AVANCES DE L'AGRICULTURE D'UN ROYAUME DOIVENT ÊTRE ENVISAGÉES COMME UN IMMEUBLE, QU'IL FAUT CONSERVER PRÉCIEUSEMENT POUR LA PRODUCTION DE L'IMPÔT, DU REVENU, ET DE LA SUBSISTANCE DE TOUTES LES CLASSES DE CITOYENS: autrement l'impôt dégénére en spoliation, & cause un dépérissement qui ruine promptement un Etat.' Many (but not all) of the alterations incorporated in the version in *Physiocratie* had already been made in *A.D.H.* (pp. 89–90) and *P.R.* (pp. 345–6).

5 68 This footnote does not appear in the 'second edition'.

  69 This paragraph, with the words '*qui forme le revenu de la Nation*' substituted for '*qui fournit le revenu des Propriétaires*', and with '*devenu très foible, n'est qu'en raison de l'état misérable*' substituted for '*est borné à l'état*', constitutes the eighth paragraph of the Note to maxim v of *Physiocratie* (pp. 127–8). Cf. the final paragraph of *Premier Problème Économique* (I.N.E.D., II 875–7), translated in Meek, pp. 184–5.

  70 In place of this paragraph, only the last few words of which have been included, we find in *Physiocratie* (p. 128) the following:

'*Une imposition établie également sur les terres, sur leurs produits, sur les hommes, sur leur travail, sur les marchandises & sur les animaux de service, présenteroit une gradation de six impositions égales, posées les unes sur les autres, portant toutes sur une même base, & néanmoins payées chacune à part, mais qui toutes ensemble fourniroient beaucoup moins de revenu au Souverain qu'un simple impôt réel, établi uniquement & sans frais sur le produit net, & égal dans sa proportion à celle des six impositions qu'on pourroit regarder comme réelle. Cet impôt indiqué par l'ordre naturel & qui augmenteroit beaucoup le revenu du Souverain coûteroit cependant cinq fois moins à la Nation & à l'Etat que les six impositions ainsi répétées, lesquelles anéantiroient tous les produits du territoire & sembleroient exclure tout moyen de rentrer dans l'ordre. Car les impositions illusoires pour le Souverain & ruineuses pour la Nation paroissent aux esprits vulgaires, de plus en plus inévitables a mesure que le dépérissement de l'agriculture augmente.*'

In this passage, the words '*un simple impôt réel, établi uniquement & sans frais sur le produit net*' should be especially noted. The commentary in *Physiocratie* seems to come a good deal nearer to the '*impôt unique*' than does that of the 'third edition' in this particular place. (Cf., however, the formulation on p. 17 of the 'third edition', where Quesnay says, towards the end of first footnote to maxim 22, that '*L'impôt doit être pur & simple, assigné sur le sol qui produit ces richesses*'.)

It is strange that in the reformulation in *Physiocratie* quoted above, use was not made of the expression '*impôt unique et direct*' – the most succinct form of words which Quesnay himself managed to find for the idea. He seems to have employed it for the first time in the *Second Problème Économique* (I.N.E.D., II 983), which was the only new work included in *Physiocratie*. In the preceding year Quesnay had employed the slightly less succinct formulation '*impôt unique, régulier & direct*' in the original version of his *Analyse* in the *Journal de l'Agriculture, du Commerce et des Finances* (June 1766, p. 41), but the relevant passage was omitted from the version of this article published in *Physiocratie*.

Du Pont also avoided the expression later on, even in a place where the most succinct formulation would have been very apt – i.e. in the *Table Raisonnée des Principes de l'Économie Politique* which he prepared for the Margrave of Baden in 1773 – where he used the clumsy phrase '*contribution aux avances sociales*' or the even vaguer abbreviation '*contribution sociale*'.

5   71   This paragraph, with a number of extensive modifications and additions, and with several stylistic amendments, constitutes the tenth paragraph of the Note to maxim v of *Physiocratie* (pp. 128–30). The modifications and additions are as follows:

(a) In the first sentence, the words '*des terres*' are inserted after '*Fermiers*', and '*d'anéantir*' is substituted for '*de détruire*'.

(b) For the words between '*non par le Fermier*' and '*seroient attentifs*' the following passage is substituted: '*si ce n'est en déduction du fermage, comme cela arrive naturellement lorsque le Fermier est instruit avant de passer son bail de la quotité de l'impôt. Si les besoins de l'État y nécessitent des augmentations, elles doivent être uniquement à la charge des Propriétaires; car le Gouvernement seroit en contradiction avec lui-même s'il exigeoit que les Fermiers remplissent les engagemens de leurs baux, tandis que par l'impôt imprévu dont il les chargeroit il les mettroit dans l'impossibilité de satisfaire à ces engagemens. Dans tous les cas le payement de l'impôt doit être garanti par la valeur même des biens fonds, & non par celle des richesses d'exploitation de la culture, qui ne peuvent sans déprédation être assujetties à aucun service public, autre que celui de faire renaître les richesses de la Nation & du Souverain, & qui ne doivent jamais être détournées de cet emploi naturel & nécessaire. Les Propriétaires, fixés a cette régle par le Gouvernement*'.

6   72   This maxim corresponds to (a) maxim 8 of the 'second edition', with which it is substantially identical; and (b) maxim vi of *Physiocratie* (p. 110), with the following words substituted for the first half of the maxim before the semi-colon: '*QUE les avances des cultivateurs soient suffisantes pour faire renaître annuellement par les dépenses de la culture des terres le plus grand produit possible*'.

73   This paragraph, with a number of substantial modifications and one or two stylistic amendments, constitutes the last paragraph of the Note to maxim v of *Physiocratie* (pp. 130–1). The substantial modifications are as follows:

(a) The first three lines are shortened to '*Il y a une Nation qui a su*'.

(b) The words '*qui pendant ces temps orageux peuvent restraindre leurs dépenses*' are omitted.

(c) On p. 6, the word '*extérieur*' in l. 3 is omitted.

(d) The last sentence of the paragraph is omitted.

The country which Quesnay has in mind is presumably England.

74   The corresponding footnote at this point in the 'second edition' reads as follows:

'*Dans tel Royaume les avances ne produisoient du fort au foible, l'impôt à part, qu'environ 20 pour cent, qui se distribuoient à la dixme, au propriétaire, au fermier, pour son gain, les intérêts de ses avances, & ses risques : Ainsi* deficit *de trois quarts sur le produit net.*

'L'impôt étoit presque tout établi sur les fermiers & sur les marchandises, ainsi il portoit sur les avances des dépenses, ce qui les chargeoit d'environ 500 millions pour l'impôt, les gains, les frais de regie, &c. Et elles ne rendoient à la Nation, à en juger par la taxe d'un dixiéme, qu'environ 400 millions de revenu. Les dépenses productives étoient enlevées successivement par l'impôt, au préjudice de la réproduction. Le sur-faix de l'impôt sur le prix naturel des denrées ajoûtoit un tiers en sus au prix des marchandises dans la dépense du revenu de 400 millions; ce qui le réduisoit, en valeur réelle, à 300 millions, & portoit le même préjudice au commerce extérieur, & à l'emploi de l'impôt qui rentroit dans la circulation.

'Le commerce réciproque avec l'étranger raporte des marchandises qui sont payées par les revenus de la Nation en argent ou en échange; ainsi il n'en faut pas faire un objet à part qui formeroit un double emploi. Il faut penser de même des loyers de maisons & des rentes d'intérêt d'argent: car ce sont des dépenses pour ceux qui les payent, excepté les rentes placées sur les terres, qui sont assignées sur un fonds productif; mais ces rentes sont comprises dans le produit du revenu des terres.'

6   75   This paragraph, with some substantial modifications at the beginning, and with a number of stylistic amendments, constitutes the second paragraph of the Note to maxim VI of *Physiocratie* (pp. 132–3). The substantial modifications are embodied in the substitution, for the first seven lines of the footnote, of the following: *'Autrefois dans tel Royaume les avances annuelles ne faisoient renaître de produit net, du fort au foible, l'impôt sur le Laboureur compris, qu'environ* vingt-cinq *pour cent, qui se distribuoient à la dixme, à l'impôt, & au Propriétaire: distraction faite des reprises annuelles du Laboureur. Si les avances primitives avoient été suffisantes, la culture auroit pu y rendre aisément* cent *de produit net & même davantage pour* cent *d'avances annuelles. Ainsi la Nation souffroit un* deficit *des quatre cinquiemes au moins sur le produit net de ses avances annuelles, sans compter la perte sur'*. The country to which Quesnay is referring here is of course France.

In the 'third edition' it is stated in this paragraph that the advances produce only 'about 20 per cent', whereas in the fourth paragraph of the same footnote it is said that the *'dépenses de la culture'* produce no more than '25 per cent'. In *Physiocratie*, in the corresponding passage, the figure appears as 25 per cent in both places, so that the apparent ambiguity in the 'third edition' is removed. At first sight, therefore, it might appear that the figure of 20 per cent in the 'third edition' was simply a misprint, which was corrected in *Physiocratie*. This would seem unlikely, however, in view of the fact that the figure used in the corresponding place in the 'second edition' was also 20 per cent. It is interesting to note, too, that in the 'first edition' a figure of 30 per cent was used (see below, App. A).

These discrepancies are a little puzzling, since Quesnay, when making calculations of this kind, normally relied on one and the same set of figures – those in 'Grains'. At least part of the explanation would seem to be that the figure you get for the ratio of surplus to costs will obviously depend upon the way in which you define these two categories and assign various constituents of the total product to them; and Physiocratic practice varied appreciably from time to time in this respect. Take, for example, the table in 'Grains' in which Quesnay gives figures purporting to show the

way in which the value of the total product of French agriculture was divided up between *'les propriétaires'*, *'la taille'*, *'les fermiers'*, *'la dîme'* and *'les frais'* (I.N.E.D., II 478). On the basis of these figures one can obtain widely varying figures for the 'percentage yield' of the 'costs'. The ratio of the proprietors' revenue to *'les frais'*, for example, is 18 per cent; the ratio of the proprietors' revenue plus the farmers' income to *'les frais'* is 25 per cent; the ratio of the proprietors' revenue plus the *taille* and the *dîme* to *'les frais'* plus the farmers' income is 37 per cent, and so on. Once again, however, it would be unwise to seek for too sophisticated an explanation of the divergences, which after all are not *very* great. Much can clearly be put down to human frailty, and to the variations in the categories which have been mentioned above.

6   76   This paragraph, with the figure of 200 in l. 6 changed to 300, with *'net'* inserted after *'revenu'* in l. 13, and with a number of stylistic amendments, constitutes the third paragraph of the Note to maxim VI of *Physiocratie* (p. 133).

The amended figure of 300 million in the version of the paragraph in *Physiocratie* presumably includes the 100 million mentioned a little later in the 'third edition' (p. 7, first line of footnote) as originating in taxes on commodities. This supposition would seem to be confirmed by a comparison with the first two sentences of the second paragraph of footnote (*a*) to maxim 8 of the 'second edition', cited in note 74 above. It should be noted, however, that in *Physiocratie* it is assumed that the costs of administration and collection are of the same size as the tax itself, making a total of 600 million as opposed to the 500 million of the two earlier 'editions'.

77   Cf. the more arithmetically correct version in *A.D.H.*, pp. 194–6.

7   78   This maxim corresponds to (*a*) maxim 9 of the 'second edition', with one or two stylistic differences; and (*b*) maxim XII of *Physiocratie* (pp. 112–13), with several substantial alterations and a few stylistic changes. The substantial alterations are as follows:

(i) In the first line, *'riches'* is inserted in front of *'Fermiers'*. (This alteration had already been made in *P.R.* (p. 346), but not in *A.D.H.*)

(ii) In the eighth line, *'des grains'* is deleted.

(iii) In the ninth line, *'revenu'* is substituted for *'profit net'* and the words *'par exemple, pour les grains'* are inserted after *'Telle est'*.

79   The substance of much of this paragraph and of the following paragraph of the present footnote is included in the fourth paragraph of the Note to maxim VI in *Physiocratie* (p. 134). The version in *Physiocratie*, however, is very much shorter: a great deal of stylistic tightening-up has been carried out, and most of Quesnay's figures have been omitted. The text of the relevant paragraph in *Physiocratie* reads as follows:

'*Les avances des dépenses productives étoient enlevées successivement par l'impôt arbitraire & par les charges indirectes, à l'anéantissement de la réproduction & de l'impôt même; les enfans des Laboureurs abandonnoient les campagnes; le sur-faix de l'impôt sur les denrées en haussoit le prix naturel, & ajoutoit un surcroit de prix onéreux aux marchandises & aux frais de salaire dans les dépenses de la Nation; ce qui retomboit encore en déchet sur les reprises des Fermiers, sur le produit net des biens fonds, & sur l'impôt sur la*

culture, &c. La spoliation, causée par la partie de l'impôt arbitraire établie sur les Fermiers, causoit d'ailleurs un dépérissement progressif, qui, joint au défaut de liberté de commerce, faisoit tomber les terres en petite culture & en friche. C'étoit à ce dégré de décadence où les dépenses de la culture ne produisoient plus, l'impôt territorial compris, que 25 pour cent, ce qui n'étoit même dû qu'au bénéfice de la grande culture qui existoit encore pour un quart dans le Royaume. On ne suivra pas ici la marche rapide des progrès de cette décadence, il suffit de calculer les effets de tant de causes destructives, procédant les unes des autres, pour en prévoir les conséquences funestes.'

7   80   See note 79 above.

    81   This paragraph, with the words '*pour l'avantage commun du Souverain & de la Nation*' substituted for '*pour la sûreté d'un Etat*', and with a few stylistic amendments, constitutes the final paragraph of the Note to maxim VI of *Physiocratie* (p. 135).

        Quesnay wrote this appeal for reform in the middle of the Seven Years War, which was imposing very heavy burdens on the French people, particularly in the sphere of finance. This made the appeal for a reform of the taxation system as urgent as it was hopeless. Just how hopeless it was is shown by the fact that we find the appeal virtually unaltered in *Physiocratie*, four years after the end of the war.

    82   This paragraph, with the words '*des Entrepreneurs de la culture*' substituted for '*des Fermiers pour la culture*' in the last line but two, with '*unique*' inserted after '*source*' in the last line but one, and with one or two stylistic amendments, constitutes the Note to maxim III of *Physiocratie* (p. 123).

    83   This note does not appear either in the 'second edition' or in *Physiocratie*. Cf. the *tableau* in *A.D.H.*, opposite p. 185, which is based on the premises described in the note, and the commentary ibid., pp. 194–5.

8   84   This maxim corresponds to (*a*) maxim 10 of the 'second edition', with which it is identical; and (*b*) maxim XI of *Physiocratie* (p. 112), with two stylistic amendments. In the version of the maxim in *A.D.H.* (p. 91), the word '*emploiroient*' is substituted for '*emportent*'.

    85   This maxim corresponds to (*a*) maxim 11 of the 'second edition', with which it is substantially identical; and (*b*) maxim XVI of *Physiocratie* (p. 115), with which too it is substantially identical.

    86   The corresponding footnote at this point in the 'second edition' reads as follows: '*Dans la grande culture, un homme seul conduit une charrue tirée par des chevaux, qui fait autant de travail que trois charrues tirées par des bœufs, & conduites par six hommes: Dans ce dernier cas, faute d'avances pour l'établissement d'une grande culture, la dépense annuelle est excessive, & ne rend presque point de produit net. On dit qu'il y a une nation qui est réduite à cette petite culture dans les trois quarts de son territoire, & qu'il y a d'ailleurs un tiers des terres cultivables qui sont en non valeur. Mais le Gouvernement est occupé à arrêter les progrès de cette dégradation, & à pourvoir aux moyens de la réparer.* Voyez dans *l'Encyclopédie* les articles *FERMIERS, FERME, GRAINS.*'

    87   This footnote, with the word '*infructueusement*' inserted after '*emploie*' in the eighth line, with the words '*presque entierement en pure perte*' substi-

tuted for '*& tout en pure perte*', and with a number of stylistic amendments, constitutes the Note to maxim XII of *Physiocratie* (pp. 143–4).

The fact that the last sentence of this footnote, which had first appeared in the 'second edition', was retained unaltered in *Physiocratie* in 1767 shows how little the Government had in fact been doing along the lines suggested.

8   88   This footnote does not appear in the 'second edition'.

9   89   This maxim corresponds to (*a*) maxim 12 of the 'second edition', with the words after '*tel est le revenu*' omitted, and with one or two stylistic differences; and (*b*) maxim XVIII of *Physiocratie* (p. 116), with which it is substantially identical.

The set of economic 'equations' with which this maxim concludes recurs frequently, in one form or another, in Quesnay's work. It appears for the first time in 'Grains' (I.N.E.D., II 507, translated in Meek, p. 84), in the section of that article entitled 'Observations sur le Prix des Grains'. Quesnay's ambiguous use of the word *cherté* should be noted here: sometimes he uses it to mean an excessively high price, whereas in other place- he uses it to describe a state of affairs in which the *bon prix* has been established.

90   See note 91 below.

91   This footnote, with a large number of stylistic modifications, but with very few substantial changes, constitutes the Note to maxim XVI of *Physiocratie* (pp. 158–61). The substantial changes are:

(*a*) In para. 3, line 4, '*dixieme*' is substituted for '*sixième*'.

(*b*) In the final paragraph, the words '*par permissions particulières ou furtives*' and (three lines further on) '*dans un Royaume*' are omitted.

The reason for the substitution of '*dixieme*' for '*sixième*' is not clear. So far as the figure in the 'third edition' is concerned, one would naturally suppose that Quesnay derived it, as he quite frequently did in such cases, from the calculations in 'Grains'. In that article Quesnay tried to show that free export in itself would raise the average price of corn in sales at first hand from 15*l*. 9*s*. to 17*l*. 13*s*. 4*d*. per *setier* (cf. I.N.E.D., II 462 and 475). This increase, elsewhere rounded off to 2*l*. 4*s*. (p. 475, fn. 11), actually amounts to almost one-seventh. This is 'more than one-tenth' and *not* 'more than one-sixth', but it is nevertheless much closer to one-sixth than to one-tenth. If we take the increase in the average price *to the purchaser* we get a similar result: the calculated increase was from 15*l*. 9*s*. to 18*l*. (ibid., pp. 474 and 475, fn. 11), which is just under one-sixth.

92   This footnote does not appear in the 'second edition'.

93   This footnote corresponds to the Note to maxim XVIII of *Physiocratie* (p. 161), with which it is substantially identical.

94   This footnote does not appear in the 'second edition'.

95   This footnote, with the words '*toutes les autres choses dont elle peut avoir besoin*' substituted for '*toutes autres sortes de richesses, & de l'or & de l'argent*', constitutes the second Note to maxim XVIII of *Physiocratie* (pp. 161–2).

The stronger anti-mercantilist emphasis, it will be noted, disappears in *Physiocratie*.

10   96   This maxim corresponds to (*a*) maxim 13 of the 'second edition', with which it is substantially identical; and (*b*) maxim XIX of *Physiocratie* (pp.

116–17), with the words '*le salaire des gens du Peuple*' substituted for '*leur salaire*', with '*anéantit*' substituted for '*diminue*' in the last line, and with several stylistic alterations. The footnote reference in *Physiocratie* comes after '*menu peuple*', instead of at the end of the maxim.

10　97　This maxim corresponds to (*a*) maxim 14 of the 'second edition', with which it is substantially identical; and (*b*) maxim XX of *Physiocratie* (p. 117), which reads as follows: 'QU'ON ne diminue pas l'aisance des dernieres classes de Citoyens; *car elles ne pourroient pas assez contribuer à la consommation des denrées qui ne peuvent être consommées que dans le pays, ce qui feroit diminuer la réproduction & le revenu de la Nation.*'

98　This maxim corresponds to (*a*) maxim 15 of the 'second edition', with which it is identical; and (*b*) maxim XIV of *Physiocratie* (p. 114), with which it is also identical. The footnote reference in *Physiocratie*, however, comes after '*bestiaux*', instead of at the end of the maxim.

99　This footnote does not appear in the 'second edition'.

100　This footnote, with the words '*assez naturellement*' inserted after '*s'établit*' and the word '*ordinairement*' inserted before '*le vingtième*' (ll. 5–6), and with some stylistic alterations, constitutes the Note to maxim XIX of *Physiocratie* (pp. 162–3).

101　This footnote does not appear in the 'second edition'.

102　This footnote, with the words '*La véritable cause*' substituted for '*Une autre cause*', and with several stylistic alterations, constitutes the Note to maxim XX of *Physiocratie* (pp. 163–4).

　　　The famous formula with which this maxim ends, although appearing for the first time in Mirabeau's *Réponse sur la Voierie* – the essay immediately preceding the explanation of the *Tableau Économique* in the sixth part of *A.D.H.* – was nevertheless written by Quesnay himself. Along with other amendments and additions, he had inserted it in Mirabeau's manuscript draft of the *Réponse*, and from there it passed into the printed text.

11　103　Obviously a misprint for '(*a*)'.

104　This footnote does not appear in the 'second edition'.

105　As mentioned in note 108 below, the version of this passage in *Physiocratie* has '*d'après le revenu*' instead of '*par le revenu*'. Strictly speaking, since Quesnay usually derives the revenue from the product rather than the other way about, it ought properly to be '*pour le revenu*' instead of '*par le revenu*'. Cf. Quesnay's statement, in the previous paragraph, that '*le prix du loyer d'une ferme s'établit à raison du produit qu'elle peut donner*'. Cf. also the statement in the footnote on p. 19 of the 'third edition' (ll. 24–5, left side): '*car c'est ce produit qui regle le prix de l'acquisition*'.

12　106　This maxim corresponds to (*a*) maxim 16 of the 'second edition', with which it is substantially identical; and (*b*) maxim XXII of *Physiocratie* (pp. 117–18), which reads as follows: 'QU'ON ne provoque point le luxe de décoration *au préjudice des dépenses d'exploitation & d'amélioration d'agriculture, & des dépenses en consommation de subsistance, qui entretiennent le bon prix & le débit des denrées du crû, & la réproduction des revenus de la Nation.*'

107　This maxim corresponds to (*a*) maxim 17 of the 'second edition', with which it is substantially identical; and (*b*) maxim VIII of *Physiocratie* (p. 111), with the word '*extérieur*' deleted.

108　This footnote, with a large number of stylistic amendments, and some

substantial alterations, constitutes the Note to maxim XIV of *Physiocratie* (pp. 154–8). The substantial alterations are as follows:

(*a*) *1st paragraph:* In l. 5, the words '*celle que doit faire*' are inserted before '*le menu peuple*'; in l. 8, the words '*c'est l'engrais que les bestiaux fournissent à la terre*' are substituted for '*c'est encore cette consommation*'; and in l. 12, '*fécond*' is substituted for '*fertile*'.

(*b*) *2nd paragraph:* In l. 12, the words '*la crainte que ces bestiaux, qui sont des objets visibles*' are substituted for '*la crainte qu'ils*'.

(*c*) *3rd paragraph:* In l. 2, '*s'obtient*' is substituted for '*se mesure*'; and in l. 5, '*d'après*' is substituted for '*par*' (see note 105 above).

(*d*) *4th paragraph:* In l. 2, the words '*l'emploi visible des richesses à la culture de la terre*' are substituted for '*l'emploi des richesses à la culture*'.

(*e*) *5th paragraph:* In the last line but one, '*dégradé*' is substituted for '*d[éparé*'.

12   109 This footnote does not appear in the 'second edition', and the first paragraph does not appear in *Physiocratie*.

110 The second paragraph of this footnote, with several substantial alterations and a number of stylistic modifications, constitutes the Note to maxim XXII of *Physiocratie* (pp. 165–6). The substantial alterations are as follows:

(*a*) In the first line, '*Ce que l'on remarque ici*' is substituted for '*Ce qui nous venons de remarquer*'.

(*b*) In the sixth line, '*leur intérêt les oblige d'épargner*' is substituted for '*elles doivent épargner*'.

(*c*) The last words of the note, after '*Commerçans étrangers*', are expanded into the following: '*car ce n'est que par la plus grande concurrence possible, permise à tous les Négocians de l'univers, qu'une Nation peut s'assurer le meilleur prix & le débit le plus avantageux possible des productions de son territoire & se préserver du monopole des Commerçans du pays.*'

111 The corresponding footnote at this point in the 'second edition' consists essentially of the first three paragraphs of the present note, running on without any break. There are a number of stylistic differences, and one substantial one: the words in the first three lines of the second paragraph appear as: '*Il y a des Royaumes où la plûpart des manufactures ne peuvent se soutenir que par des privilèges exclusifs, & en*'.

13   112 This maxim corresponds to (*a*) maxim 18 of the 'second edition', with which it is substantially identical; and (*b*) maxim XXIX of *Physiocratie* (p. 121), with one stylistic amendment.

113 This footnote, with a number of substantial amendments and stylistic modifications, constitutes the Note to maxim VIII of *Physiocratie* (pp. 136–140). The substantial amendments are as follows:

(*a*) *1st paragraph:* In ll. 5 and 6, '*net*' is deleted and '*qu'aux seuls pays*' is substituted for '*que dans les pays*'; and in ll. 13–14, '*profit*' is substituted for '*produit net*'.

(*b*) *2nd paragraph:* The second sentence is deleted and the following substituted: '*Ces prohibitions toujours préjudiciables à la Nation sont encore plus funestes quand l'esprit de monople & d'erreur qui les a fait naître les étend jusques sur la culture & le commerce des productions des*

I

biens fonds, où la la [sic] *concurrence la plus active est indispensablement nécessaire pour multiplier les richesses des Nations.'*

    (*c*) *5th paragraph:* In l. 11, '*ce qui fit tomber*' is substituted for '*on laissa tomber*'; in ll. 16–17, '*touchoit à l'impossibilité d'y subvenir*' is substituted for '*ne pouvoit plus y subvenir*'; the sentence between semi-colons in ll. 19–21 is amended to '*il se multiplia en dépenses dans la perception et en déprédations destructives de la reproduction*'; and in ll. 27 '*minoit*' is substituted for '*rongeoit*'.

14	114	This maxim corresponds to (*a*) maxim 19 of the 'second edition', with the words '*qui chargent l'Etat de dettes dévorantes*' not appearing, and with one or two stylistic differences; and (*b*) maxim XXX of *Physiocratie* (pp. 121–2), with the words '*privent les campagnes*' substituted for '*qui la privent*', with '*l'exploitation de*' inserted before '*la culture des terres*', and with several stylistic modifications. The two changes of substance had already been made in *P.R.* (p. 351), but not in *A.D.H.*
	115	This maxim corresponds to (*a*) maxim 20 of the 'second edition', with the last word appearing as '*laboureurs*' instead of '*Cultivateurs*', and with one or two stylistic differences; and (*b*) maxim IX of *Physiocratie* (p. 111), with which it is substantially identical.
	116	The corresponding footnote in the 'second edition' (the reference to which in the latter is at the end of the maxim instead of after '*l'agriculture*') follows the present one, with one or two stylistic differences, down to '*l'exportation des denrées du crû*', and finishes at that point.
	117	This footnote substantially constitutes the first Note to maxim IX of *Physiocratie* (pp. 140–1).
	118	This footnote does not appear in the 'second edition'.
15	119	This maxim does not appear either in the 'first edition' or the 'second edition'. It corresponds to maxim XV of *Physiocratie* (pp. 114–15), with several stylistic modifications and one substantial alteration. The latter consists of the condensation of all the material between '*que dans les petites:*' and '*la population la plus assurée*' into the following short sentence: '*La multiplicité de petits fermiers est préjudiciable à la population*'.

    In *A.D.H.*, as compared with the 'third edition', the words '*ces dernieres occupent*' were substituted for '*parce que celles-ci occupent*'; and the words '*& dont le terrein & les facultés sont trop bornées*' were substituted for '*par l'étendue de leurs emplois & de leurs facultés*' (p. 95). In *P.R.*, as compared with *A.D.H.*, the words '*est préjudiciable à la population, & à l'accroissement des revenus*' were substituted for '*est moins favorable à la population que l'accroissement des revenus*' (p. 352).

	120	This footnote, with three changes of substance and a number of stylistic modifications, constitutes the second Note to maxim IX of *Physiocratie* (pp. 141–3). The changes of substance are as follows:

    (*a*) In the first paragraph, after '*aux décorations frivoles*', the following words are substituted for '*mais*': '*On voit encore des hommes stupidement vains, ignorer que*'.

    (*b*) In the first line of the footnote which appears on p. 15, '*particuliere*' is inserted after '*distinction*'.

    (*c*) The Latin quotation from Cicero ends with '*nihil homini libero dignius*' instead of with '*nihil homine, nihil libero dignius*'.

The Latin sources are as follows: Cicero, *De Officiis* (Loeb Classical Library ed., 1938, p. 155; English translation by Walter Miller); and Cicero, *De Senectute* (Loeb Classical Library ed., 1938, p. 69; English translation by W. A. Falconer).

16   121   This maxim corresponds to maxim 21 of the 'second edition', with several stylistic differences, and with the final sentence appearing as follows: '*Ce sont donc les revenus & l'impôt qui sont de premier besoin pour défendre les sujets contre la disette, & contre l'ennemi, & pour soutenir la gloire & la puissance du Monarque.*'

The maxim also corresponds to maxim XIII of *Physiocratie* (pp. 113–14), with three changes of substance and a few stylistic modifications. The changes of substance are as follows:

(*a*) In l. 4 of the maxim, the words '*qu'il lui soit*' are deleted.

(*b*) The words '*aux autres productions*' are substituted for '*à celle de moindre besoin*'.

(*c*) The words '*Après les richesses d'exploitation de la culture*' are inserted before '*ce sont les revenus & l'impôt*'.

    122   This footnote does not appear in the 'second edition'.

17   123   Cf. note 70 above.

    124   This footnote, with several substantial amendments, and quite a large number of stylistic modifications, constitutes the first Note to maxim XIII of *Physiocratie* (pp. 144–7). The substantial amendments are as follows:

(*a*) *1st paragraph:* In ll. 11–12, the word '*destruction*' is substituted for '*dégradation*'; in ll. 22–3, the words '*& à détruire de plus en plus la valeur des biens fonds*' are substituted for '*& à faire tomber de plus en plus les biens-fonds en non-valeur*'; and in the last two lines of the paragraph the words '*débouché de l'excedent*' are substituted for '*débit du superflu*'.

(*b*) *2nd paragraph:* In l. 4, the words '*environ le triple*' are substituted for '*au moins double*'; and in l. 13 '*à l'avantage*' is substituted for '*au profit*'.

(*c*) *3rd paragraph:* In l. 3, '*onéreuses*' is substituted for '*dispendieuses*'; and in the third line from the end the words '*sur ces parties*' are inserted after '*l'impôt*'.

    125   This footnote does not appear in the 'second edition'.

    126   This paragraph, with '*s'accumuler*' substituted for '*surabonder*' in the fifth line from the end, and with a few stylistic modifications, constitutes the first paragraph of the second Note to maxim XIII of *Physiocratie* (p. 148).

    127   This paragraph, with one or two stylistic modifications, constitutes the second paragraph of the second Note to maxim XIII of *Physiocratie* (pp. 148–9).

18   128   The first sentence of this maxim corresponds to maxim 22 of the 'second edition', with which it is substantially identical. The whole maxim corresponds to maxim XXVII of *Physiocratie* (p. 120), with '*très grandes*' substituted for '*trop grandes*', and with one or two stylistic modifications.

    129   This figure reappears in the text of *Physiocratie* as '27 millions', but in the list of errata it is replaced by '17 millions' (see note 130 below). We do not know what Quesnay's source was for the '27 millions'. A few years later he uses this figure again in a marginal note to Mirabeau's manuscript of

Philosophie Rurale (Weulersse, *Manuscrits Économiques,* p. 83); but in the printed version of *Philosophie Rurale* the figure of 17 millions is used in the corresponding place (*P.R.,* III 297). Claude Villaret, in vol. XI of his *Histoire de France,* which appeared (as did *Philosophie Rurale*) in 1763, also speaks, although very cautiously, of 17 millions (p. 102), and this may well be the source of Du Pont's later correction.

18   130   This paragraph, with several alterations of substance, and with a number of stylistic modifications, constitutes the third paragraph of the second Note to maxim XIII of *Physiocratie* (pp. 149–50). The alterations of substance are as follows:

       (*a*) In l. 6, '*monnoye*' is substituted for '*finance*'.

       (*b*) In the eighth line of the portion of the paragraph which appears on p. 18, the words '*qui le soustrait de son emploi*' are substituted for '*distraite de son object*'.

       (*c*) As stated in note 129 above, a figure of 17 millions is substituted (in the errata) for the figure of 27 millions in the sixth line from the end.

       (*d*) In the third line from the end, '*Etats*' is substituted for '*domaines*'.

    131   This paragraph, with '*d'une Nation*' substituted for '*d'un Etat*' in l. 2, with '*production*' substituted for '*richesse*' in l. 6, and with one or two stylistic modifications, constitutes the fourth paragraph of the second Note to maxim XIII of *Physiocratie* (pp. 150–1).

    132   This paragraph, with a number of substantial changes, and with a few stylistic modifications, constitutes the fifth paragraph of the second Note to maxim XIII of *Physiocratie* (pp. 151–2). The substantial changes are as follows:

       (*a*) In l. 15, the words '*doit le retenir*' are substituted for '*peut le prêter*'.

       (*b*) In l. 20, '*au même*' is substituted for '*à plus haut*'.

       (*c*) In l. 23, the words '*dont a besoin*' are substituted for '*où l'on trouve un gain assuré*'.

       (*d*) In l. 25, the words '*où le besoin des échanges décide de l'emploi*' are substituted for '*où le profit décide des échanges*'.

       (*e*) In l. 27, '*par-tout*' is deleted.

    133   This paragraph, with the first line altered to '*L'argent détourné & retenu hors de la circulation*', and with a few stylistic modifications, constitutes the sixth paragraph of the second Note to maxim XIII of *Physiocratie* (p. 152).

19   134   This maxim corresponds to (*a*) maxim 23 of the 'second edition', with a number of stylistic differences; and (*b*) maxim XXVI of *Physiocratie* (pp. 119–20), with a number of stylistic modifications.

    135   This paragraph, with the more comprehensible words '*l'impôt puisse être établi sur la circulation de l'argent*' substituted for '*les revenus de l'Etat puissent être imposés sur l'argent*' at the end, and with a number of stylistic modifications, constitutes the seventh paragraph of the second Note to maxim XIII of *Physiocratie* (pp. 152–3).

In *Physiocratie,* a footnote at the end of the paragraph refers the reader to what has been said above on taxation, the particular reference being to the Note to maxim V.

19 136   The first three sentences of this paragraph form the material from which the first three sentences of the eighth (and final) paragraph of the second Note to maxim XIII of *Physiocratie* (pp. 153–4) are constituted. The version in *Physiocratie* reads as follows: '*L'argent est une richesse qui se dérobe à la vûe. Le tribut ne peut être imposé qu'à la source des richesses disponibles, toujours renaissantes, ostensibles & commerçables. C'est là que naissent les revenus du Souverain; & qu'il peut trouver de plus des ressources assurées dans des besoins pressans de l'Etat.*' This version was presumably less open to the interpretation that it sanctioned taxes on commodities.

  The remainder of the paragraph, with the exception of the last sentence which does not appear in *Physiocratie*, constitutes the second paragraph of the Note to maxim v of *Physiocratie* (pp. 124–5). There are a few stylistic modifications, and the following substantial amendments:

(*a*) In l. 10 of the paragraph, '*portion*' is substituted for '*partie*'.

(*b*) In ll. 12–13 of the paragraph, the words '*car c'est ce produit qui regle le prix de l'acquisition*' are omitted.

(*c*) In the last sentence but one of the paragraph, the words before '*contribuer sur leurs portions*' are replaced by '*Et ce n'est que dans les cas de nécessité, dans les cas où la sûreté de la propriété seroit exposée, que tous les Propriétaires doivent pour leur propre intérêt*'.

137   For a succinct statement of Quesnay's distinction between '*pur commerce*' and '*trafic*', see his *Lettre de M. Alpha* (I.N.E.D., II 936).

138   This paragraph, with the words in l. 7 replaced by '*la puissance de l'Etat &*', with '*productions*' substituted for '*richesses*' in l. 12, and with a few stylistic modifications, constitutes the remaining part of the eighth (and final) paragraph of the second Note to maxim XIII of *Physiocratie* (pp.153–4), running straight on from the three sentences referred to in note 136 above.

  The last sentence of this paragraph, which is very obscure as it stands, will be more comprehensible if it is read in conjunction with the passage from the eighth chapter of *Philosophie Rurale* which is translated in Meek, pp. 63–4.

139   The corresponding footnote at this point in the 'second edition' consists essentially of the first paragraph of the present note and the first sentence of the second paragraph, running on without a break. There are a number of stylistic differences, and the following substantial ones:

(*a*) In ll. 4–5, the words '*ni subsister ni agir*' appear simply as '*subsister*'.

(*b*) The second half of the first sentence of the second paragraph, after the words '*une plus grande population*', appears in the 'second edition' as '*& que les hommes n'abondent dans un pays, qu'autant qu'ils y trouvent des gains assurés pour y subsister*'.

20 140   The corresponding concluding remarks at this point in the 'second edition' read as follows: '*Sans ces conditions, l'agriculture, qu'on suppose, dans le Tableau, produire comme en Angleterre cent pour cent, seroit une fiction: Mais les principes n'en sont pas certains*'. The 'third edition' restores the missing '*moins*' in the final phrase.

  These concluding remarks were not included in *Physiocratie*.

141   This paragraph constitutes the material upon which the first two paragraphs of the Note to maxim XXVI of *Physiocratie* (pp. 166–7) are based. These two paragraphs are as follows:

> '*Le désir qu'ont toutes les Nations d'être puissantes à la guerre, &*
> *l'ignorance des moyens de faire la guerre, parmi lesquels le vulgaire n'envisage*
> *que les hommes, ont fait penser que la force des Etats consiste dans une grande*
> *population. On n'a point assez vu que pour soutenir la guerre il ne falloit pas à*
> *beaucoup près une si grande quantité d'hommes qu'on le croit au premier coup-*
> *d'œil; que les armées très nombreuses doivent être & sont ordinairement bien*
> *plus funestes à la Nation, qui s'épuise pour les employer, qu'à l'ennemi qu'elles*
> *combattent; & que la partie militaire d'une Nation, ne peut ni subsiter, ni*
> *agir que par la partie contribuable.*
>
> '*Quelques esprits superficiels supposent que les grandes richesses d'un Etat*
> *s'obtiennent par l'abondance des hommes; mais leur opinion vient de ce qu'ils*
> *oublient que les hommes ne peuvent obtenir & perpétuer les richesses que par les*
> *richesses, & qu'autant qu'il y a une proportion convenable entre les hommes &*
> *les richesses.*'

20   142   This paragraph, with '*une partie du peuple*' substituted for '*le bas peuple*' in l. 8, with '*grandes*' inserted before '*dépenses*' in l. 11, and with a number of stylistic modifications, constitutes the third paragraph of the Note to maxim XXVI of *Physiocratie* (pp. 167–8).

    143   This paragraph, with a few stylistic modifications, constitutes the fourth paragraph of the Note to maxim XXVI of *Physiocratie* (p. 168).

    144   This paragraph, with a few stylistic modifications, constitutes the fifth paragraph of the Note to maxim XXVI of *Physiocratie* (p. 169).

21   145   This paragraph, with a few stylistic modifications, constitutes the sixth paragraph of the Note to maxim XXVI of *Physiocratie* (pp. 169–70). Cf. the miscellaneous extracts from Quesnay's unpublished writings which are translated in Meek, pp. 65–8.

    146   Boisguillebert. Several editions of this work had appeared before the one to which Quesnay refers here, the first being in 1695.

    147   This paragraph, with several substantial changes, and a large number of stylistic modifications, constitutes the seventh (and last) paragraph of the Note to maxim XXVI of *Physiocratie* (pp. 170–2). The substantial changes are as follows:

       (*a*) In l. 20, the words '*pour le tems*' are inserted after '*prouvé*'.

       (*b*) In l. 25, '*expose*' is substituted for '*démontre*'.

       (*c*) The words between '*la jouissance de 500 millions*' and '*Aussi remarque-t'on*' are replaced by the following: '*sans compter la dégradation annuelle que causoit la taille arbitraire établie sur les Fermiers. Les impositions multipliées & ruineuses sur toute espece de dépenses s'étendoient par repompement sur la dépense de l'impôt même, au détriment du Souverain pour lequel une grande partie de ses revenus devenoit illusoire.*'

       (*d*) In the ninth line from the end, '*en très peu de tems*' is substituted for '*en un mois*'.

       (*e*) In the third line from the end, '*où l'on n'avoit nulle idée*' is substituted for '*où l'on n'avoit plus d'idée*' – i.e. than in Sully's time.

22   148   Some of the material in this final paragraph forms the basis of maxim III of *Physiocratie* (pp. 107–8), which reads: '*QUE le Souverain & la Nation ne perdent jamais de vue, que la terre est l'unique source des richesses, & que c'est l'agriculture qui les multiplie. Car l'augmentation des richesses*

assure celle de la population; les hommes & les richesses font prospérer l'agriculture, étendent le commerce, animent l'industrie, accroissent & perpétuent les richesses. De cette source abondante dépend le succès de toutes les parties de l'administration du Royaume.'

5

Appendix to the Notes

5

Appendix to the Notes

A summary comparison between the 'third edition' of Quesnay's *Tableau Économique* and the revised and enlarged version published by Mirabeau in *L'Ami des Hommes*.[1]

GENERAL COMPARISON.

Abstracting from the diagram, the 'third edition', pp. (i)-xij and (1)–22, contains *157 paragraphs* of varying lengths. Of these, we could trace in *A.D.H.* *131 paragraphs*, or roughly five paragraphs out of every six. Of the number not so traced, i.e. *26 paragraphs*, approximately *12 paragraphs* which consist mainly of quotations, references and repetitions may be disregarded, leaving *14 paragraphs* which seem not to have been used for other reasons.

FOR DETAILED COMPARISON
see pp. 32–5 below

[1] The sections of *A.D.H.* which are largely or entirely additional to the 'third edition' (apart from five new diagrams) are as follows: pp. 1–30, introductory remarks and chapter on the construction of the *Tableau*; pp. 41–50, chapter on population; pp. 119–30, chapter on *spoliation*; pp. 209–28, *résultat* and *résumé*.

Quesnay's Tableau Économique

DETAILED COMPARISON[1]

(1) 'Third Edition' page and paragraph numbers	(2) L'Ami des Hommes page and paragraph numbers of passages taken over or worked in	(3) Comments[2] on (2)
A. Diagram	Unnumbered page preceding p. (i)	Opposite p. 23	Printed, not engraved. Further development of analysis of expenditure needed for the production of rent, the total net product, and the total product.
B. 'Explication du Tableau Économique'	(i)/1–5	29/1–2; 30/2; 31/2; 32/2	
	(i)/6–ij/1	103/1–2; 104/1; 105/1 and 3	Text and figures substantially enlarged and amended.
	ij/2–iij/2	32/3–34/2	
	iij/3–iv/1	34/3–35/1; 38/3–39/1; 35/2–36/1	Some divergences, particularly in the additional footnote on p. 36.
	iv/2	39/2	
	iv/3–v/3	41/1–43/1	
	v/4–vi/2	76 76/2–77/3	Heading added. Figures corrected.
	vi/3	25/2–26/1	
	vi/4–vij/7	77/4–80/1	Figures corrected, and reference deleted.
	viii/1	48/3	Text and calculations amended.
	viii/2–ix/1	80/2–82/2; 82/4–6	Order changed; figures and printing errors amended.
	ix/2	64/2	First sentence enlarged.
	ix–x (footnote*)	68/1; 69/1–74/1	On p. 71, 'variétés générales' is replaced by 'vérités générales'.
	x/1–xj/5	83/2–85/2	Figures corrected or changed; xj/4 deleted.
	xj/6–xij(1.°–8.°)	86/1–86/2	Only fragments taken over.
	xij, Errata		Deleted; not relevant.

[1] Parts of paragraphs at the beginning or end of a normal page have each been counted as one paragraph. Where the text is printed in two columns the same method has been used, but the two columns are covered by one set of figures only.

[2] No comments are made on changes which seem (*a*) to result from an endeavour to present problems in a less summary fashion, or (*b*) to be purely stylistic.

(1) 'Third Edition' page and paragraph numbers	(2) L'Ami des Hommes page and paragraph numbers of passages taken over or worked in	(3) Comments on (2)
C. 'Extrait des Économies Royales' (a) *Text* (*excluding notes*)		
1. Introductory Remarks (1)/1; 3/1 2/1	86/3 48/3	Basic figure changed. Text amended. Para. 1 of footnote* on p. (1) of 'Extrait' partially included.
2. Maxims 3/2–19/2	86/4–98/1	Basic figure changed. Text amended, e.g. in maxims 1 and 7 additions are made; in maxim 16 the order of a few words is changed; and in maxim 18 'richesses clandestines' is replaced by 'fortunes clandestines'.
3. Concluding Remarks 20/1–22/1	98/2–100/1	In 98/2 'ce qui . . . extraordinaires' is not included.
(b) *Notes to Text* (1)/1 (first part)		See above, Introductory Remarks, p. (1).
(1)/1 (second part)		Not traced.
(1)/2–2/2	187/2–190/3	
2/3	203/3–204/1	
2/4	49/2–50/1	
2/5		Probably deleted; in part a repetition of pp. iv, v and vi of 'Explication'.
3 (footnote*); 5/1–5/3		Not traced.
5/4–6/1	204/2–205/2	
6/2	135/3–136/1	
6/3–7/1	191/2–196/1	Figures corrected; other small changes.
7/2	196/3–198/2; 199/2	Figures changed.

(1) 'Third Edition' page and paragraph numbers	(2) *L'Ami des Hommes* page and paragraph numbers of passages taken over or worked in	(3) *Comments* on (2)
7/3		Not traced.
7/4	174, almost entirely	
7 (note at foot of page)		{ Deleted; replaced by *Tableau* opposite p.185.
8/1	{ 110/2–111/1; 111/2 (second sentence)	
8/2–9/3	167/3–171/2	
9/4		Not traced.
9/5	172/4–173/2	
10/1–2	171/3–172/1	{ Only briefly men- tioned; reference made to Mirabeau's *Mémoire sur l'Agriculture*.
10/3–4		Not traced.
11/1–3	115/1–117/1	
11/4–12/1		Not traced.
12/2 (up to '*successivement*')	103/2	{ Condensed; in part a repetition of paras. (i)/ 6 –ij/1 of 'Explication'.
12/2 (remainder) –12/3	106/3–107/1; 177/2	
12/4–13/2	181/3–183/1	
13/3 (from '*ébloui*' – 13/5 ('*Hé*')	178/1–181/1	
14/1	183/2–184/1	
14/2	109/2; 110/1	{ Considerably shortened.
14/3–15/1 (first part)		Not traced.
15/1 (remainder); 15/2		Quotations not used.
16/1–17/1	162/3–167/1	
17/2	108/2–109/1	
17/3–19/1	146/1–153/1	{ In para. 148/3, '250' is substituted for '300' (para. 18/1 of the 'third edition').
19/2 (up to '*pressans de l'Etat*')		Not traced.
19/2 (remainder)	55/3–56/1	
19/3	153/2–154/1	
19/4–20/5 (up to '*Le Héros*')	138/2–143/1	

(1) *'Third Edition'* page and paragraph numbers	(2) *L'Ami des Hommes* page and paragraph numbers of passages taken over or worked in	(3) *Comments* on (2)
20/5 (remainder) − 21/1 }		{ Not taken over. Cf. the passages translated in Meek, pp. 66 and 68.
21/2 (first part)		Not traced.
21/2 (from '*l'Auteur*') }	200/2–203/1	

6

Appendix A: The 'First Edition'

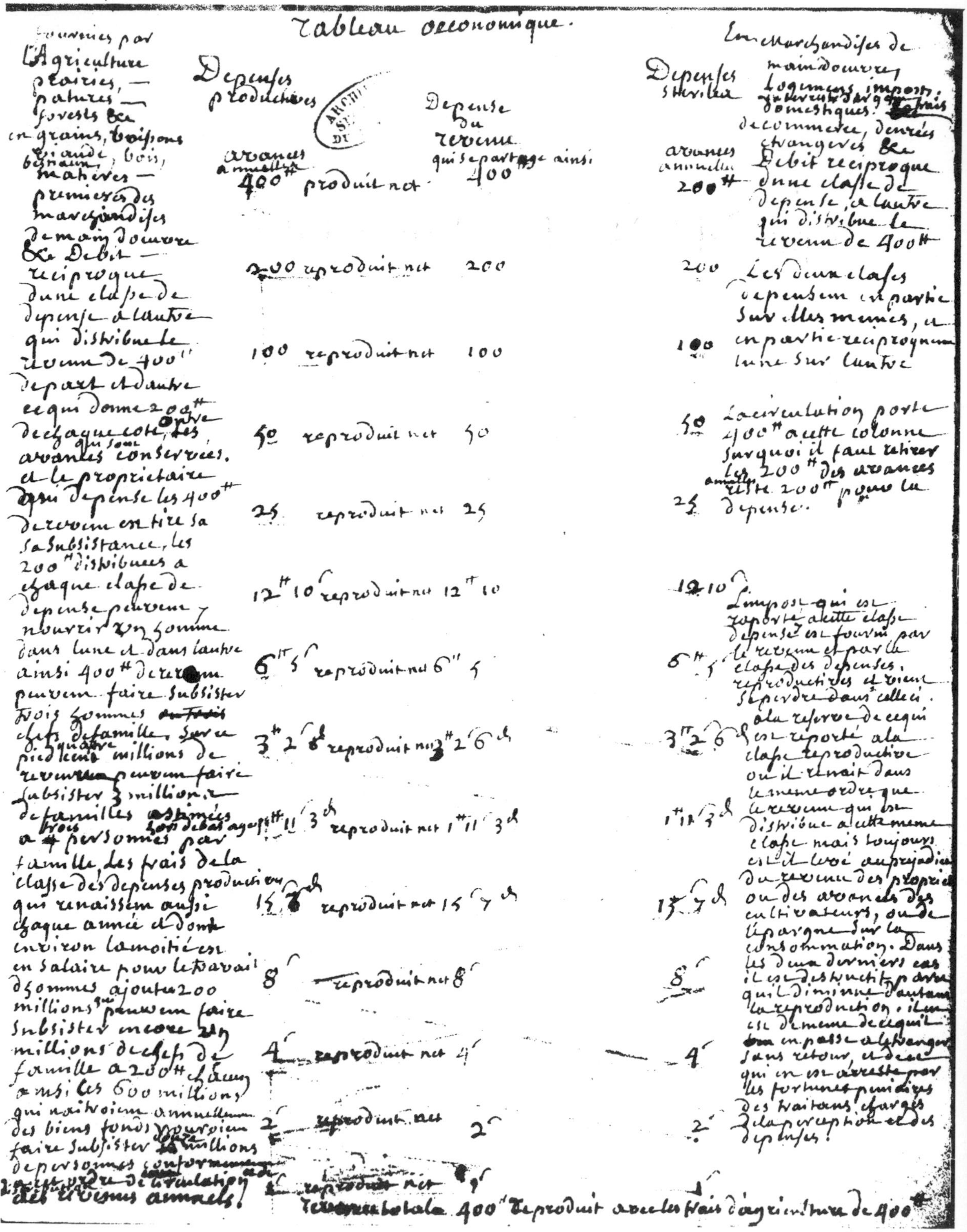

Tableau oeconomique.

Fournies par l'Agriculture prairies, patures, forests &c en grains, boissons viande, bois, bestiaux, matieres premieres des marchandises de main d'oeuvre &c Debit reciproque d'une classe de depense a l'autre qui distribue le revenu de 400ll de part et d'autre ce qui donne 200ll de chaque coté outre les avances qui sont conservées. et le proprietaire qui depense les 400ll de revenu en tire sa subsistance, les 200ll distribuées a chaque classe de depense peuvent y nourrir un homme dans l'une et dans l'autre ainsi 400ll de revenu peuvent faire subsister trois hommes chefs de famille. sur ce pied quatre millions de revenu peuvent faire subsister 3 millions de familles estimées a 4 personnes par famille les frais de la classe des depenses productives qui renaissent aussi chaque année et dont environ la moitié est en salaire pour le travail d'hommes ajoutent 200 millions qui peuvent faire subsister encore un million de chefs de famille a 200ll chacun ainsi les 600 millions qui naitroient annuellement des biens fonds pourroient faire subsister 12 millions de personnes conformement a cet ordre de circulation des revenus annuels.

Depenses productives		Depense du revenu qui se partage ainsi	Depenses steriles
avances annuelles 400ll	produit net	400ll	avances annuelles 200ll
200	reproduit net	200	200
100	reproduit net	100	100
50	reproduit net	50	50
25	reproduit net	25	25
12ll 10s	reproduit net	12ll 10	12 10s
6ll 5s	reproduit net	6ll 5	6ll 5s
3ll 2s 6d	reproduit net	3ll 2 6d	3ll 2 6
1ll 11 3d	reproduit net	1ll 11 3d	1ll 11 3d
15s 7d	reproduit net	15s 7d	15 7d
8s	reproduit net	8s	8s
4s	reproduit net	4s	4s
2s	reproduit net	2s	2s
1s	reproduit net	1s	1

Revenu total 400ll reproduit avec les frais d'agriculture de 400ll.

En marchandises de main d'oeuvre, logements, impots, interets d'argent, domestiques, frais de commerce, denrées etrangeres &c Debit reciproque d'une classe de depense a l'autre qui distribue le revenu de 400ll

Les deux classes depensent en partie sur elles memes, et en partie reciproquement l'une sur l'autre

La circulation porte 400ll a cette colonne sur quoi il faut retirer les 200ll des avances annuelles reste 200ll pour la depense.

L'impost qui est raporté a cette classe depense est fourni par le revenu et par la classe des depenses reproductives et vient se perdre dans celle ci. a la reserve de ce qui est raporté a la classe reproductive ou il renait dans le meme ordre que le revenu qui se distribue a cette meme classe mais toujours est il levé au prejudice du revenu des proprietaires ou des avances des cultivateurs, ou de l'epargne sur la consommation. Dans les deux derniers cas il est destructif parce qu'il diminue d'autant la reproduction. il en est de meme de ce qui en passe a l'etranger sans retour, et de ce qui en est arresté par les fortunes pecuniaires des traitans chargés de la perception et des depenses.

The 'First Edition' of the *Tableau Économique* (in the Archives Nationales)

TABLEAU OECONOMIQUE

Provided by agriculture, grasslands, pastures, forests, etc. On corn, drink, meat, wood, live-stock, raw materials for manufactured commodities, etc. Mutual sales from one expenditure class to the other, which distribute the revenue of 400 livres to both sides, giving 200 livres to each, in addition to the advances which are maintained intact. The proprietor, who spends the revenue of 400 livres, draws his subsistence from it. The 200 livres distributed to each expenditure class can support one man in each; thus 400 livres of revenue can enable three heads of families to subsist. On this basis 400 millions of revenue can enable three million families to subsist, estimated at three persons above the age of infancy per family. The costs of the productive expenditure class which are also regenerated each year, and about half of which consists of wages for men's labour, add 200 millions, which can enable another one million heads of families to subsist at 200 livres each. Thus these 600 millions which are annually generated from landed property could enable 12 million persons to subsist, in conformity with this order of circulation and distribution of the annual revenue.

PRODUCTIVE EXPENDITURE

STERILE EXPENDITURE

EXPENDITURE
OF THE
REVENUE
which is divided
thus:

Annual
Advances

Annual
Advances

On manufactured commodities, house-room, taxes, interest on money, servants, commercial costs, foreign produce, etc. Mutual sales from one expenditure class to the other, which distribute the revenue of 400 livres.

The two classes spend in part on their own products and in part mutually on the products of one another.

The process of circulation sends 400 livres to this column, from which 200 livres have to be kept back for the annual advances. 200 livres remain for expenditure.

The taxes which are included in this expenditure class are provided by the revenue and by the reproductive expenditure class. They get lost in the latter class, except for those which are brought back to the reproductive class, where they are regenerated in the same way as the revenue which is distributed to this same class. But they are always levied to the detriment of the proprietors' revenue, or of the cultivators' advances, or of economy in consumption. In the two latter cases they are destructive, because they reduce reproduction in the same proportion. It is just the same with those which are transferred abroad without any return, or which are held back in the monetary fortunes of the tax-farmers who are responsible for their collection and expenditure.

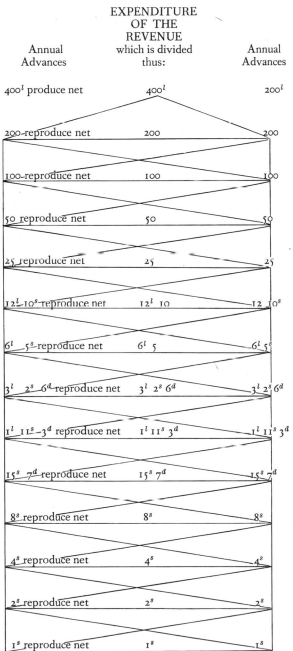

Annual Advances	EXPENDITURE OF THE REVENUE	Annual Advances
400^l produce net	400^l	200^l
200–reproduce net	200	200
100–reproduce net	100	100
50 reproduce net	50	50
25 reproduce net	25	25
$12^l 10^s$ reproduce net	$12^l 10$	$12^l 10^s$
$6^l 5^s$ reproduce net	$6^l 5$	$6^l 5^s$
$3^l 2^s 6^d$ reproduce net	$3^l 2^s 6^d$	$3^l 2^s 6^d$
$1^l 11^s 3^d$ reproduce net	$1^l 11^s 3^d$	$1^l 11^s 3^d$
$15^s 7^d$ reproduce net	$15^s 7^d$	$15^s 7^d$
8^s reproduce net	8^s	8^s
4^s reproduce net	4^s	4^s
2^s reproduce net	2^s	2^s
1^s reproduce net	1^s	1^s

Total revenue of 400 livres reproduced together with agricultural costs of 400 livres.

French Text of the 'Remarks' following the Tableau in the 'First Edition'[1]

Remarques sur les variations de la distribution des revenus annuels dune nation

On voit dans le tableau precedent que dans lordre de la circulation reguliere de 400 millions de revenu annuel ces quatre cens millions sobtiennent au moyen de 600 millions davances, et se distribuent annuellement a quatre millions de chefs de famille, il y a un million de proprietaires dont la depense est estimee du fort au foible 400^{ll} pour chacun, et trois millions de chefs de famille occupés aux travaux ou emplois lucratifs qui chacun du fort au foible retire 200^{ll} pour sa depense. Mais dans cette distribution on supose 1º que la totalité des quatre cens millions de revenu entre dans la circulation annuelle et la parcourt dans toute son etendue quils ne se forment point de fortunes pecuniaires qui arrêtent le cours dune partie de ce revenu annuel de la nation et qui retiennent le pecul ou la finance du royaume au prejudice de la reproduction du revenu, et de l'aisance du peuple 2º quune partie de la somme du revenu ne passe pas chez letranger sans retour en argent ou en marchandises 3º que la nation ne souffre pas de perte dans son commerce reciproque avec letranger, quand meme ce commerce seroit fort profitable aux commerçans en gagnant sur leurs concitoyens dans la vente des marchandises quils rapportent; car alors laccroissement de la fortune de ces commerçans est un retranchement dans la circulation des revenus, qui est prejudiciable a la distribution et a la reproduction. 4º Quon ne soit pas trompé par un avantage aparent du commerce reciproque avec letranger, en en jugeant simplement par la balance des sommes en argent, sans examiner le plus ou le moins de profit qui resulte des marchandises memes que lon a vendues et de celles que lon achettées; car souvent la perte est pour la nation qui reçoit un surplus en argent, et cette perte tourne au prejudice de la distribution et de la reproduction des revenus 5º que les proprietaires et ceux qui exercent les proffessions lucratives ne retranchent de la circulation et de la distribution, par une epargne sterile, une partie de leur revenu et de leur gain. 6º que l'administration des finances, soit dans la perception des imposts, soit dans les depenses du gouvernement, n'occasionnent point de fortunes pecuniaires qui derobent une partie des revenus a la circulation a la distribution et a la reproduction. 7º que limpost ne soit pas destructif, ou disproportionné a la masse du revenu de la nation; que son

---

[1] Taken from the original manuscript in the Archives Nationales. No attempt has been made to rationalise the punctuation, to insert the many missing accents, or to correct or modernise the spelling, so that the text as printed is a very close approximation to that of the original.

Remarks on the Variations in the Distribution of the Annual Revenue of a Nation

From the preceding *Tableau*, it can be seen that in the order of the regular circulation of 400 millions of annual revenue, these 400 millions are obtained by means of 600 millions of advances, and are distributed annually to four million heads of families. There are one million proprietors, whose average expenditure is estimated at 400 livres each; and three million heads of families engaged in remunerative work or employment, each of whom draws on the average 200 livres for his expenditure. But in this distribution it is assumed: (1) That the whole of the 400 millions of revenue enters into the annual circulation, and runs through it to the full extent of its course; and that it is never formed into monetary fortunes, which check the flow of a part of this annual revenue of the nation and hold back the money stock or finance of the kingdom, to the detriment of the reproduction of the revenue and the well-being of the people; (2) That no part of the sum of revenue passes into the hands of foreign countries without return in money or commodities; (3) That the nation does not suffer any loss in its mutual trade with foreign countries, even if this trade is very profitable to the merchants through the gains they make out of their fellow-citizens on the sale of the commodities they import; for then the increase in the fortunes of these merchants represents a deduction from the circulation of the revenue, which is detrimental to distribution and reproduction; (4) That people are not taken in by a seeming advantage in mutual trade with foreign countries, through judging it simply with reference to the balance of the sums of money involved and not examining the greater or lesser profit which results from the particular commodities which are sold and purchased; for the loss often falls on the nation which receives a surplus in money, and this loss operates to the detriment of the distribution and reproduction of the revenue; (5) That the proprietors and those engaged in remunerative occupations do not, by means of sterile saving, deduct from circulation and distribution a part of their revenue and gains; (6) That the administration of finance, whether in the collection of taxes or in the expenditure of the Government, never brings about the formation of monetary fortunes, which steal a portion of the revenue away from circulation, distribution, and reproduction; (7) That taxes are not destructive or disproportionate to the total of the nation's revenue; that their increase is in accordance with the increase in the nation's revenue; that they are laid directly on the revenue of the proprietors, and not on the produce, where they increase the

augmentation suive laugmentation du revenu de la nation qu'il soit etabli immediatement sur le revenu des proprietaires et non sur les denrees où il multiplieroit les frais de perception et prejudicieroit au commerce; quil ne se prenne pas non plus sur les avances des fermiers des biens fond dont les richesses doivent etre conservees pretieusement pour les depenses de la culture. 8º Que les avances des fermiers soit suffisantes pour que les depenses de la culture reproduissent au moins cent pour cent; car si les avances ne sont pas suffisantes les depenses de la culture sont plus grandes et produissent peu de revenu net. en france elles ne produissent en proffit net quenviron — trente pour cent 9º que les enfans des fermiers setablissent dans les campagnes pour y perpetuer les laboureurs car si quelques vexations leur font abandonner les campagnes et les determinent a se retirer dans les villes ils y emportent les richesses de leurs peres qui etoient employés a la culture 10º Que lon evite la desertion des habitans qui emportent leurs richesses hors du Royaume 11º Que lon empeche point le commerce exterieur des denrées du cru car tel est le debit telle est la reproduction 12º Qu'on ne fasse point baisser le prix des denrees et des marchandises dans le Royaume car le commerce reciproque avec letranger deviendroit desavantageux a la nation 13º Que lon ne croye pas que le bon marché des denrees soit profitable au menu peuple car le bas prix des denrées fait baisser leur salaire diminue leur aisance, leur procure moins de travail ou doccupation lucrative et diminue le revenu de la nation. 14º Quon ne diminue pas laisance du bas peuple, car il ne pouroit pas assez contribuer a la consommation des denrées qui ne peuvent etre consommees que dans le pays, et la reproduction et le revenu de la nation diminueroit. 15 Quon favorise la multiplication des Bestiaux, car cest eux qui fournissent aux terres les engrais qui procurent les riches moissons. 16º Que lon ne provoque point le luxe de decoration, parce quil ne se soutient quau prejudice du luxe de subsistance qui entretient le debit et le bon prix des denrees du cru, et la reproduction des revenus de la nation. 17 Que le gouvernement oeconomique ne soccupe qua favoriser les depenses productives et du commerce exterieur des denrées du cru, et quil laisse aller delles memes les depenses steriles. 18 Quon n'espere des ressources pour les besoins extraordinaires de létat que de la prosperité de la nation et non du credit des financiers, car les fortunes pecuniaires sont des richesses clandestines qui ne connoissent ni Roi ni patrie 19º Que létat evite les emprunts qui forment des rentes financieres et qui occasionnent un commerce de finance ou dagiot par lentremise de papiers commerçables où l'escomte augmente de plus en plus les fortunes pecuniaires steriles; car on prefere ces rentes et ces gains usuriers aux revenus de l'agriculture que lon abandonne et que lon prive des richesses necessaires pour l'amelioration des biens fond et pour la culture des terres. 20º Quune nation qui a un grand territoire a cultiver et la facilité dexercer un grand commerce de denrees du cru, netende pas trop lemploy de largent et des hommes aux manufactures et au commerce de luxe, au prejudice des travaux et des depenses

costs of collection and operate to the detriment of trade; and, in addition, that they are not taken from the advances of the farmers of landed property, whose wealth ought to be very carefully safeguarded in order to meet the expenses of cultivation; (8) That the advances of the farmers are sufficient to enable the expenses of cultivation to reproduce at least 100 per cent; for if the advances are not sufficient, the expenses of cultivation are higher and produce little net revenue; in France they reproduce in the form of net profit only about 30 per cent; (9) That the children of farmers are settled in the countryside, so that there are always husbandmen there; for if they are harassed into abandoning the countryside and withdrawing to the towns, they take there their fathers' wealth which used to be employed in cultivation; (10) That the desertion of inhabitants who take their wealth out of the kingdom is avoided; (11) That no barriers at all are raised to external trade in raw produce; for as the market is, so is the reproduction; (12) That the prices of produce and commodities in the kingdom are never made to fall; for then mutual foreign trade would become disadvantageous to the nation; (13) That people do not believe that cheapness of produce is profitable to the lower classes; for a low price of produce causes a fall in their wages, reduces their well-being, makes less work or remunerative occupations available for them, and reduces the nation's revenue; (14) That the well-being of the lower orders is not reduced; for then they would not be able to contribute sufficiently to the consumption of the produce which can be consumed only within the country, and the reproduction and revenue of the nation would be reduced; (15) That the increase of livestock is encouraged; for it is livestock which provides the land with the manure which procures abundant crops; (16) That no encouragement at all is given to luxury in the way of ornamentation; for this is maintained only to the detriment of luxury in the way of subsistence, which sustains the market for raw produce, its proper price, and the reproduction of the nation's revenue; (17) That the Government's economic policy is concerned only with encouraging productive expenditure and external trade in raw produce, and that it refrains from interfering with sterile expenditure; (18) That means to meet the extraordinary needs of the state are expected to be found only in the prosperity of the nation and not in the credit of financiers; for monetary fortunes are a clandestine form of wealth which knows neither king nor country; (19) That the state avoids contracting loans which result in the formation of rentier incomes and which bring about an agio trade in finance through the medium of negotiable bills, the discount on which causes a greater and greater increase in sterile monetary fortunes; for these incomes and usurious gains are preferred to the revenue of agriculture, which is abandoned and deprived of the wealth necessary for the improvement of landed property and the cultivation of the land; (20) That a nation which has a large territory to cultivate, and the means of carrying on a large trade in raw produce, does not extend too far the employment of money and men in manufacturing and trading in luxury goods,

de lagriculture car preferablement a tout le royaume doit etre bien peuplé de riches laboureurs. 21. Que le gouvernement soit moins occupe des soins depargner que des operations necessaires pour la prosperité du Royaume; car de trop grandes depenses peuvent cesser detre excessives par laugmentation des richesses 22. Qu'on soit moins attentifs a laugmentation de la population qu'a laccroissement des revenus; car laisance que procure de grands revenus est preferable aux besoins pressans de subsistance quexige une trop grande population, et il y a plus de ressources pour les besoins de letat quand le peuple est dans laisance.

Il y a sans doute des royaumes où aucune de ces conditions n'existe; et on dit que tout est bien; cela est vray, car independamment de ces conditions un grand etat peut etre egal a un petit, et avec ces conditions un petit etat peut etre egal a un grand: De la nait cet equilibre de puissances entre les nations, recherché dans lordre politique.

to the detriment of the work and expenditure involved in agriculture; for more than anything else the kingdom ought to be well furnished with wealthy husbandmen; (21) That the Government troubles itself less with economising than with the operations necessary for the prosperity of the kingdom; for expenditure which is too high may cease to be excessive by virtue of the increase of wealth; (22) That less attention is paid to increasing the population than to increasing the revenue; for the well-being which a high revenue brings about is preferable to the pressure of subsistence needs which too great a population entails; and when the people are in a state of well-being there are more resources to meet the needs of the state.

There are no doubt kingdoms where none of these conditions is present, and it is said that all is well; this is true, for independently of these conditions a great state may be equal to a small one; and with these conditions a small state may be equal to a great one; whence springs that balance of power between nations which is sought after in the order of political policy.

7

Appendix B: The 'Second Edition'

A Note on the Two Extant Versions of the Tableau of the 'Second Edition'

The *tableau* reproduced in facsimile on the opposite page is that contained in the Bibliothèque Nationale copy of the 'third edition', to which a number of corrections have been made in Quesnay's hand. As will be seen, the column of text on the right-hand side has been mutilated, apparently by a careless binder.

The *tableau* reproduced on the following page is that contained in the Archives Nationales copy of the 'third edition'. The text is complete, but there are no corrections, and no zigzag lines joining the figures.

The English translation of the *tableau* which follows is in effect a conflated version – i.e. it follows the complete text of the Archives Nationales copy, but embodies the corrections and zigzag lines of the Bibliothèque Nationale copy.

The French text of the *Extrait* which is reproduced after the *tableaux* is that of the Archives Nationales copy. It is exactly the same as the text of the Bibliothèque Nationale copy, except that in the latter, at the very end, '*n'en sont pas certains*' has been corrected in Quesnay's hand to '*n'en sont pas moins certains*'. This correction has been embodied in the English translation.

TABLEAU ŒCONOMIQUE.

FOurnies par l'agriculture, prairies, pâtures, forêts, mines, pêche, &c. En grains, boissons, viandes, bois, bestiaux, matieres premieres des marchandises de main d'œuvre, &c.

Débit réciproque d'une classe de dépense à l'autre qui distribue le revenu de 600 liv. de part & d'autre, ce qui donne 300 liv. de chaque côté : outre les avances qui sont conservées. Le Propriétaire subsiste par les 600 liv. qu'il dépense. Les 300 livres distribuées à chaque classe de dépense peuvent y nourrir un homme dans l'une & dans l'autre : ainsi 600 livres de revenu peuvent faire subsister trois hommes chefs de famille. Sur ce pied 600 millions de revenu peuvent faire subsister 3 millions de familles estimées à 3 personnes, ~~tous de~~ par famille. Les frais de la classe des dépenses productives qui renaissent aussi chaque année, & dont environ la moitié est en salaire pour le travail d'homme, ajoutent 300 millions qui peuvent faire subsister encore un million de chefs de famille à 300 liv. chacun. Ainsi ces 900 millions qui naîtroient annuellement des biens fonds, pourroient faire subsister 12 millions de personnes ~~tous de~~ ~~tous~~ âge, conformément à cet ordre de circulation & de distribution des revenus annuels. Par circulation on entend ici les achats payés par le revenu, & la distribution qui partage le revenu entre les hommes par le payement des achats de la premiere main, abstraction faite du commerce qui multiplie les ventes & les achats, sans multiplier les choses, & qui n'est qu'un surcroit de dépenses stériles.

DEPENSES PRODUCTIVES.

DEPENSES DU REVENU, l'Impôt prélevé, se partagent aux Dépenses productives & aux Dépenses stériles.

DEPENSES STERILES.

Avances annuelles.	Revenu.	Avances annuelles.
††	††	††
600 produisent · · · · · · · · · · 600		300
Productions.		*Ouvrages, &c.*
††	††	††
300 reproduisent net · · · · 300		300
150 reproduisent net · · · · 150		150
75 reproduisent net · · · · 75		75
ſ	ſ	ſ
37·10 reproduisent net · · · · 37·10		37·10
18·15 reproduisent net · · · · 18·15		18·15
℈	℈	℈
9···7···6 reproduisent net · · · · 9···7···6		9···7···6
4···13···9 reproduisent net · · · · 4···13···9		4···13···9
2···6···10 reproduisent net · · · · 2···6·10		2···6·10
1···3···5 reproduisent net · · · · 1···3···5		1···3···5
0···11···8 reproduisent net · · · · 0···11···8		0···11···8
0···5···10 reproduisent net · · · · 0···5·10		0···5·10
0···2···11 reproduisent net · · · · 0···2·11		0···2·11
0···1···5 reproduisent net · · · · 0···1·5		0···1·5

††
REPRODUIT total · · · · · · · 600 de revenu & les frais annuels d'agriculture de 600 livres que la Terre restitue. Ainsi la reproduction est de 1200 livres.

EN marchandises de main d'œuvre, logemens, vêtemens, intérêts d'argent, domestiques, frais de commerce, denrées étrangères, &c.

Les achats réciproques d'une classe de dépense à l'autre distribue le revenu de 600 liv.

Les deux classes dépensent en partie sur elles-mêmes en partie réciproquement l'une sur l'autre.

La circulation porte 600 liv. à cette colonne, sur lequel il faut retirer les 300 liv. des avances annuelles, reste 300 liv. pour le salaire.

L'impôt qui doit être reporté à cette classe, est pris sur le revenu qui s'obtient par les dépenses productives & vient se perdre dans cette classe-ci, à la réserve de ce qui rentre dans la circulation où il renaît dans le même ordre que le revenu, & se distribue de même aux deux classes. Mais il est toujours au préjudice du revenu des propriétaires, ou des avances des cultivateurs, ou de l'épargne sur la consommation. Dans les deux derniers cas il est destructif, parce qu'il diminue d'autant la réproduction ; il en est de même de ce qu'il en passe à l'étranger sans retour, & de ce qui est arrêté par les fortunes pécuniaires des traitans ou autres de la perception & des dépenses ; car ces parties de l'impôt détournées ou dérobées par l'épargne aux dépenses productives, ou prises sur les avances des cultivateurs éteignent la réproduction & retombent doublement en perte sur les propriétaires, & détruisent enfin la masse du revenu qui fournit l'impôt lequel ne doit porter que sur le propriétaire, & non ici sur dépenses réproductives où il ruine le Cultivateur, le Propriétaire, & l'État.

TABLEAU ŒCONOMIQUE.

FOurnies par l'agriculture, prairies, pâtures, forêts, mines, pêche, &c. En grains, boissons, viandes, bois, bestiaux, matieres premieres des marchandises de main d'œuvre, &c.

Débit réciproque d'une classe de dépense à l'autre qui distribue le revenu de 600 liv. de part & d'autre, ce qui donne 300 liv. de chaque côté : outre les avances qui sont conservées. Le Proprietaire subsiste par les 600 liv. qu'il dépense. Les 300 livres, distribuées à chaque classe de dépense peuvent y nourrir un homme dans l'une & dans l'autre : ainsi 600 livres de revenu peuvent faire subsister trois hommes chefs de famille. Sur ce pied 600 millions de revenu peuvent faire subsister 3 millions de familles estimées à 3 personnes, hors de bas âge, par famille. Les frais de la classe des dépenses productives qui renaissent aussi chaque année, & dont environ la moitié est en salaire pour le travail d'homme, ajoûtent 300 millions qui peuvent faire subsister encore un million de chefs de famille à 300 liv. chacun. Ainsi ces 900 millions qui naitroient annuellement des biens fonds, pourroient faire subsister 12 millions de personnes hors de bas âge, conformément à cet ordre de circulation & de distribution des revenus annuels. Par circulation on entend ici les achats payés par le revenu, & la distribution qui partage le revenu entre les hommes par le payement des achats de la premiere main, abstraction faite du commerce qui multiplie les ventes & les achats, sans multiplier les choses, & qui n'est qu'un surcroit de dépenses steriles.

DEPENSES PRODUCTIVES.	DEPENSES DU REVENU, l'Impôt prélevé, se partagent aux Dépenses productives & aux Dépenses steriles.	*DEPENSES STERILES.*
Avances annuelles.	*Revenu.*	*Avances annuelles.*
ᵼᵼ 600 produisent	ᵼᵼ 600	ᵼᵼ 300
Productions.		*Ouvrages,&c.*
ᵼᵼ 300 reproduisent net	ᵼᵼ 300	ᵼᵼ 300
150 reproduisent net	150	150
75 reproduisent net	75	75
37..10 reproduisent net	37..10	37..10
18..15 reproduisent net	18..15	18..15
9....7....6 reproduisent net	9...7...6	9...7...6
4..13....9 reproduisent net	4..13....9	4..13....9
2..6..10 reproduisent net	2....6..10	2....6..10
1...3....5 reproduisent net	1....3....5	1....3....5
0..11....8 reproduisent net	0..11....8	0..11....8
0....5..10 reproduisent net	0....5..10	0....5..10
0..2..11 reproduisent net	0....2..11	0....2..11
0....1....5 reproduisent net	0....1....5	0....1....5

ᵼᵼ
REPRODUIT total.........600 de revenu & les frais annuels d'agriculture de 600 livres que la Terre restitue. Ainsi la réproduction est de 1200 livres.

EN marchandises de main d'œuvre, logemens, vêtemens, intérêts d'argent, domestiques, frais de commerce, denrées étrangeres, &c. Les achats réciproques d'une classe de dépense à l'autre distribue le revenu de 600 liv.

Les deux classes dépensent en partie sur elles-mêmes, & en partie réciproquement l'une sur l'autre.

La circulation porte 600 liv. à cette colomne, sur quoi il faut retirer les 300 liv. des avances annuelles, reste ici 300 liv. pour le salaire.

L'impôt qui doit être rapporté à cette classe, est pris sur le revenu qui s'obtient par les dépenses réproductives, & vient se perdre dans cette classe-ci, à la réserve de ce qui rentre dans la circulation, où il renait dans le même ordre que le revenu, & se distribue de même aux deux classes. Mais il est toujours au préjudice du revenu des propriétaires, ou des avances des cultivateurs, ou de l'épargne sur la consommation. Dans les deux derniers cas il est destructif, parce qu'il diminue d'autant la réproduction ; il en est de même de ce qu'il en passe à l'étranger sans retour, & de ce qui en est arrêté par les fortunes pécuniaires des traitans chargés de la perception & des dépenses ; car ces parties de l'impôt détournées ou dérobées par l'épargne aux dépenses productives, ou prises sur les avances des cultivateurs, éteignent la réproduction, retombent doublement en perte sur les propriétaires, & détruisent enfin la masse du revenu qui fournit l'impôt, lequel ne doit porter que sur le propriétaire, & non sur les dépenses réproductives, où il ruine le Cultivateur, le Propriétaire, & l'Etat.

The 'Second Edition' of the *Tableau Économique* (Archives Nationales copy)

TABLEAU ŒCONOMIQUE

	EXPENDITURE	
PRODUCTIVE EXPENDITURE	OF THE REVENUE after deduction of taxes, is divided between productive expenditure and sterile expenditure	STERILE EXPENDITURE

Provided by agriculture, grasslands, pastures, forests, mines, fishing, etc. On corn, drink, meat, wood, livestock, raw materials for manufactured commodites, etc.

Mutual sales from one expenditure class to the other, which distribute the revenue of 600 livres to both sides, giving 300 livres to each, in addition to the advances which are maintained intact. The proprietor subsists on the 600 livres which he spends. The 300 livres distributed to each expenditure class can support one man in each; thus 600 livres of revenue can enable three heads of families to subsist. On this basis 600 millions of revenue can enable three million families to subsist, estimated at three persons per family. The costs of the productive expenditure class which are also regenerated each year, and about half of which consists of wages for men's labour, add 300 millions, which can enable another one million heads of families to subsist at 300 livres each. Thus these 900 millions which are annually generated from landed property could enable 12 million persons of all ages to subsist, in conformity with this order of circulation and distribution of the annual revenue. By circulation is here meant the purchases paid for by the revenue, and the distribution which shares out the revenue among men by means of the payment for purchases at first hand, abstracting from trade, which increases sales and purchases without increasing things, and which represents nothing but an addition to sterile expenditure.

On manufactured commodities, house-room, clothing, interest on money, servants, commercial costs, foreign produce, etc.

Mutual purchases by one expenditure class from another distribute the revenue of 600 livres.

The two classes spend in part on their own products and in part mutually on the products of one another.

The process of circulation sends 600 livres to this column, from which 300 livres have to be kept back for the annual advances. 300 livres remain here for wages.

The taxes which ought to be included in this class are taken out of the revenue which is obtained through reproductive expenditure, and get lost in the latter class, except for those which come back into circulation, where they are regenerated in the same way as the revenue, and are distributed in the same way to the two classes. But they are always detrimental to the proprietor's revenue, or to the cultivator's advances, or to economy in consumption. In the two latter cases they are destructive, because they reduce reproduction in the same proportion. It is just the same with those which are transferred abroad without any return, or which are held back in the monetary fortunes of the tax-farmers who are responsible for their collection and expenditure; for these parts of the taxes, diverted or stolen from productive expenditure through saving, or taken out of the cultivator's advances, extinguish reproduction, fall back on and cause a double loss to the proprietors, and in the end destroy the mass of revenue which provides the taxes, which ought to fall only on the proprietor, and not on reproductive expenditure, where they ruin the cultivator, the proprietor, and the state.

Annual Advances	Revenue	Annual Advances
600^l produce	600^l	300^l
Products	one-half goes here	Works, etc.
300^l reproduce net	300^l	300^l
	one-half goes here	
150 reproduce net	150	150
	one-half, etc.	
75 reproduce net	75	75
37..10^s reproduce net	37..10^s	37..10^s
18..15 reproduce net	18..15	18..15
9...7..6^d reproduce net	9..7..6^d	9...7..6^d
4.13..9 reproduce net	4.13..9	4.13..9
2..6.10 reproduce net	2..6.10	2..6.10
1..3..5 reproduce net	1..3..5	1..3..5
0..11..8 reproduce net	0..11..8	0..11..8
0..5..10 reproduce net	0..5..10	0..5..10
0..2..11 reproduce net	0..2..11	0..2..11
0..1..5 reproduce net	0..1..5	0..1..5

Total reproduced .... 600^l of revenue and the annual costs of agriculture of 600 livres which the land restores. Thus the reproduction is 1200 livres.

EXTRAIT
DES ŒCONOMIES ROYALES
DE M. DE SULLY.

ON voit dans le tableau précédent que dans l'ordre de la circulation réguliere de 600 millions de revenu annuel, ces 600 millions s'obtiennent au moyen de 900 millions d'avances annuelles (*a*) & qui se distribuent annuellement à quatre millions de chefs de famille. Il y a un million de propriétaires, dont la dépense est estimée du fort au foible à 600 pour chacun (*b*) & trois millions de chefs de famille, occupés aux travaux ou emplois lucratifs qui, chacun du fort au foible, retirent 300 liv. pour leur dépense ; mais dans cette distribution on suppose,

1°. Que la totalité des 600 millions de revenu entre dans la circulation annuelle & la parcourt dans toute son étendue ; qu'il ne se forme point de fortunes pécuniaires, ou du moins qu'il y ait compassation entre celles qui se forment, & celles qui reviennent dans la circulation ; car autrement ces fortunes pécuniaires arrêteroient le cours d'une partie de ce revenu annuel de la Nation, & retiendroient le pécul ou la finance du Royaume, au préjudice de la réproduction du revenu & de l'aisance du Peuple.

2°. Qu'une partie de la somme du revenu ne passe pas chez l'étranger, sans retour en argent ou en marchandises.

3°. Que la Nation ne souffre pas de perte dans son commerce réciproque avec l'étranger, quand même ce commerce seroit fort profitable aux Commerçans en gagnant sur leurs concitoyens dans la vente des marchandises qu'ils rapportent ; car alors l'accroissement de fortune de ces Commerçans est un retranchement dans la circulation des revenus, qui est préjudiciable à la distribution & à la réproduction.

4°. Qu'on ne soit pas trompé par un avantage aparent du commerce réciproque avec l'étranger, en en jugeant simplement par la balance des sommes en argent, sans examiner le plus ou le moins de profit qui résulte des marchandises mêmes que l'on a vendues, & de celles que l'on a achetées : car souvent la perte est pour la Nation qui reçoit un surplus en argent, & cette perte se tourne au préjudice de la distribution & de la réproduction des revenus.

(*a*) Si on ajoûtoit l'impot aux 600 millions de revenu & que l'impôt fût de 200 millions, il faudroit que les avances annuelles fussent au moins de 1200 millions, sans compter les avances primitives, nécessaires pour former d'abord l'établissemement des Laboureurs : ainsi il faut remarquer que les terres les plus fertiles seroient nulles sans les richesses nécessaires pour subvenir aux dépenses de la culture, & que la dégradation de l'agriculture dans un Royaume ne doit pas être imputée à la paresse des hommes, mais à leur indigence.

(*b*) Les 600 millions de revenu peuvent être partagés à un plus petit nombre de propriétaires : Dans ce cas, moins il y auroit de propriétaires, plus la dépense de leur revenu surpasseroit la consommation que chacun d'eux pourroit faire personnellement. Mais ils feroient des libéralités, ou rassembleroient d'autres hommes pour consommer avec eux ce que leur fourniroit la dépense de leur revenu : ainsi cette dépense se trouveroit distribuée à-peu-près, comme s'il y avoit un plus grand nombre de propriétaires bornés chacun à une moindre dépense. On doit penser de même de l'inégalité des gains ou des profits des hommes des autres classes.

A ij

EXTRACT

FROM THE ROYAL ECONOMIC MAXIMS
OF M. DE SULLY

From the preceding *Tableau*, it can be seen that in the order of the regular circulation of 600 millions of annual revenue, these 600 millions are obtained by means of 900 millions of annual advances,[1] and are distributed annually to four million heads of families. There are one million proprietors, whose average expenditure is estimated at 600 livres each,[2] and three million heads of families engaged in remunerative work or employment, each of whom draws on the average 300 livres for his expenditure. But in this distribution it is assumed:

1. That the whole of the 600 millions of revenue enters into the annual circulation, and runs through it to the full extent of its course; and that it is never formed into monetary fortunes, or at least that those which are formed are counterbalanced by those which come back into circulation; for otherwise these monetary fortunes would check the flow of a part of this annual revenue of the nation, and hold back the money stock or finance of the kingdom, to the detriment of the reproduction of the revenue and the well-being of the people.

2. That no part of the sum of revenue passes into the hands of foreign countries without return in money or commodities.

3. That the nation does not suffer any loss in its mutual trade with foreign countries, even if this trade is very profitable to the merchants through the gains they make out of their fellow-citizens on the sale of the commodities they import; for then the increase in the fortunes of these merchants represents a deduction from the circulation of the revenue, which is detrimental to distribution and reproduction.

4. That people are not taken in by a seeming advantage in mutual trade with foreign countries, through judging it simply with reference to the balance of the sums of money involved and not examining the greater or lesser profit which results from the particular commodities which are sold and purchased; for the loss often falls on the nation which receives a surplus in money, and this loss operates to the detriment of the distribution and reproduction of the revenue.

---

[1] If we added taxes to the 600 millions of revenue, and these taxes amounted to 200 millions, the annual advances would require to be at least 1200 millions, without taking account of the original advances necessary in the beginning to set the husbandmen up in their enterprises; thus it should be noted that the most fertile land would be worthless without the wealth necessary to meet the expenses of cultivation, and that the deterioration of a kingdom's agriculture ought to be attributed not to men's idleness but to their poverty.

[2] The 600 millions of revenue may be divided among a smaller number of proprietors: in that case, the fewer proprietors there were the more would the expenditure of their revenue exceed the amount which each of them would personally be able to consume. But then they would indulge in liberality, or gather together other men to consume with them the things with which the expenditure of their revenue would supply them, so that this expenditure would turn out to be distributed in almost the same way as if there had been a greater number of proprietors limited to a smaller individual expenditure. Inequalities in the gains or profits of men in the other classes should be regarded in the same way.

5°. Que les propriétaires & ceux qui exercent les professions lucratives, ne soient pas portés par quelqu'inquiétude, qui ne seroit pas prévue par le Gouvernement, à se livrer à des épargnes stériles qui retrancheroient de la circulation & de la distribution une portion de leur revenu, ou de leurs gains.

6°. Que l'administration des finances, soit dans la perception des impôts, soit dans les dépenses du Gouvernement, n'occasionnent point de fortunes pécuniaires, qui dérobent une partie des revenus à la circulation, à la distribution & à la réproduction.

7°. Que l'impôt ne soit pas destructif ou disproportionné à la masse du revenu de la Nation, que son augmentation suive l'augmentation du revenu de la Nation, qu'il soit établi immédiatement sur le revenu des propriétaires, & non sur les denrées où il multiplieroit les frais de perception, & préjudicieroit au commerce; qu'il ne se prenne pas non plus sur les avances des fermiers des biens fonds, dont les richesses doivent être conservées précieusément pour les dépenses de la culture, & éviter les pertes des revenus.

8°. Que les avances des fermiers soient suffisantes pour que les dépenses de la culture reproduisent au moins cent pour cent : car si les avances ne sont pas suffisantes, les dépenses de la culture sont plus grandes à proportion, & donnent moins de produit net (a).

9°. Que les enfans des fermiers s'établissent dans les campagnes pour y perpétuer les laboureurs. Car si quelques vexations leur font abandonner les campagnes, & les déterminent à se retirer dans les villes, ils y portent les richesses de leurs peres qui étoient employées à la culture. Ce sont moins les hommes que les richesses qu'il faut attirer dans les campagnes ; & plus on emploie de richesses à la culture des grains, moins elle occupe d'hommes, plus elle prospere, & plus elle donne de profit net. Telle est la grande culture des riches fermiers, en comparaison de la petite culture des pauvres métayers qui labourent avec des bœufs ou avec des vaches (b).

(a) Dans tel Royaume les avances ne produisoient du fort au foible, l'impôt à part, qu'environ 20 pour cent, qui se distribuoient à la dixme, au propriétaire, au fermier, pour son gain, les intérêts de ses avances, & ses risques : Ainsi *déficit* de trois quarts sur le produit net.

L'impôt étoit presque tout établi sur les fermiers & sur les marchandises, ainsi il portoit sur les avances des dépenses, ce qui les chargeoit d'environ 500 millions pour l'impôt, les gains, les frais de regie, &c. Et elles ne rendoient à la Nation, à en juger par la taxe d'un dixième, qu'environ 400 millions de revenu. Les dépenses productives étoient enlevées successivement par l'impôt, au préjudice de la réproduction. Le sur-faix de l'impôt sur le prix naturel des denrées ajoûtoit un tiers en sus au prix des marchandises dans la dépense du revenu de 400 millions; ce qui le réduisoit, en valeur réelle, à 300 millions, & portoit le même préjudice au commerce extérieur, & à l'emploi de l'impôt qui rentroit dans la circulation.

Le commerce réciproque avec l'étranger raporte des marchandises qui sont payées par les revenus de la Nation en argent ou en échange; ainsi il n'en faut pas faire un objet à part qui formeroit un double emploi. Il faut penser de même des loyers de maisons & des rentes d'intérêt d'argent : car ce sont des dépenses pour ceux qui les payent, excepté les rentes placées sur les terres, qui sont assignées sur un fonds productif; mais ces rentes sont comprises dans le produit du revenu des terres.

(b) Dans la grande culture, un homme seul conduit une charrue tirée par des chevaux, qui fait autant de travail que trois charrues tirées par des bœufs, & conduites par six hommes : Dans ce dernier cas, faute d'avances pour l'établissement d'une grande culture, la dépense annuelle est excessive, & ne rend presque point de produit net. On dit qu'il y a une nation qui est réduite à cette petite culture dans les trois quarts de son territoire, & qu'il y a d'ailleurs un tiers des terres cultivables qui sont en non valeur. Mais le Gouvernement est occupé à arrêter les progrès de cette dégradation, & à pourvoir aux moyens de la réparer. *Voyez dans l'Encyclopédie les articles* FERMIERS, FERME, GRAINS.

4

5. That the proprietors and those engaged in remunerative occupations are not led by any anxiety, unforeseen by the Government, to give themselves over to sterile saving, which would deduct from circulation and distribution a portion of their revenue or gains.

6. That the administration of finance, whether in the collection of taxes or in the expenditure of the Government, never brings about the formation of monetary fortunes, which steal a portion of the revenue away from circulation, distribution, and reproduction.

7. That taxes are not destructive or disproportionate to the total of the nation's revenue; that their increase is in accordance with the increase in the nation's revenue; that they are laid directly on the revenue of the proprietors, and not on the produce, where they increase the costs of collection and operate to the detriment of trade; and, in addition, that they are not taken from the advances of the farmers of landed property, whose wealth ought to be very carefully safeguarded in order to meet the expenses of cultivation and to avoid the loss of revenue.

8. That the advances of the farmers are sufficient to enable the expenses of cultivation to reproduce at least 100 per cent; for if the advances are not sufficient, the expenses of cultivation are proportionally higher and yield less net product.[1]

9. That the children of farmers are settled in the countryside, so that there are always husbandmen there. For if they are harassed into abandoning the countryside and withdrawing to the towns, they take there their fathers' wealth which used to be employed in cultivation. It is not so much men as wealth which must be attracted to the countryside; and the more wealth is employed in the cultivation of corn, the fewer men it requires, the more it prospers, and the more net profit it yields. Such is the large-scale cultivation carried on by rich farmers, in comparison with the small-scale cultivation carried on by poor *métayers* who plough with the aid of oxen or cows.[2]

[1] In a kingdom of this kind the advances produced, on the average, apart from taxes, only about 20 per cent, which was distributed to the tithes, the proprietor, and to the farmer for his gain, the interest on his advances, and his risks. Thus there was a *deficit* of three-quarters in the net product.

The taxes were almost all laid on the farmers and on commodities, with the result that they fell upon the advances of expenses, which were burdened with about 500 millions for taxes, gains, administration costs, etc. And they yielded to the nation, judging from the tax of one-tenth, only about 400 millions of revenue. Productive expenditure was successively eaten away by taxation, to the detriment of reproduction. The additional burden of taxes on the natural price of produce added one-third to the price of the commodities upon which the revenue of 400 millions was spent, which meant that in real terms its value was reduced to 300 millions; and it did the same damage to foreign trade and to the employment of the taxes which came back into circulation.

Mutual trade with foreign countries brings in commodities which are paid for by the nation's revenue in money or in bartered goods. Thus we do not have to put this down as a separate item, since that would constitute double-counting. House-rent and income derived from interest on money must be regarded in the same way; for these constitute expenditure from the point of view of those who pay them, with the exception of income charged on land, where the liability is placed on a productive fund; but this income is included in the product of the revenue of the land.

[2] In large-scale cultivation, one man alone drives a plough drawn by horses, which does as much work as three ploughs drawn by oxen and driven by six men. In the case of small-scale cultivation, because of a lack of the advances necessary for the introduction of large-scale cultivation, the annual expenses are excessive and yield hardly any net product at all. It is said that there is a nation which is reduced to this small-scale cultivation over three-quarters of its territory, and in which, in addition, a third of the cultivable land is going to waste. But the Government is engaged in stopping the course of this decline, and in providing the means for setting things right again. See the articles 'Farmer', 'Farm', and 'Corn' in the *Encyclopedia*.

10°. Que l'on évite la défertion des habitans qui emportent leurs richeffes hors du Royaume.

11°. Que l'on n'empêche point le commerce extérieur des denrées du crû ; car tel eft le débit , telle eft la réproduction.

12°. Qu'on ne faffe point baiffer le prix des denrées & des marchandifes dans le Royaume ; car le commerce réciproque avec l'étranger deviendroit défavantageux à la Nation. *Telle eft la valeur vénale , tel eft le revenu.*

13°. Que l'on ne croye pas que le bon marché des denrées foit profitable au menu peuple ; car le bas prix des denrées fait baiffer leur falaire , diminue leur aifance , leur procure moins de travail ou d'occupations lucratives , & diminue le revenu de la Nation.

14°. Qu'on ne diminue pas l'aifance du bas peuple , car il ne pourroit pas affez contribuer à la confommation des denrées qui ne peuvent être confom-mées que dans le pays , & la réproduction & le revenu de la Nation dimi-nueroient.

15°. Qu'on favorife la multiplication des beftiaux ; car ce font eux qui fourniffent aux terres les engrais qui procurent les riches moiffons.

16°. Que l'on ne provoque point le luxe de décoration , parce qu'il ne fe foutient qu'au préjudice du luxe de fubfiftance , qui entretient le débit & le bon prix des denrées du crû , & la réproduction des revenus de la Nation.

17°. Que le gouvernement œconomique ne s'occupe qu'à favorifer les dépenfes productives & le commerce extérieur des denrées du crû , & qu'il laiffe aller d'elles-mêmes les dépenfes ftériles (a).

18°. Qu'on n'efpere de reffources pour les befoins extraordinaires de l'Etat, que de la profpérité de laNation,& nondu crédit desFinanciers;car les fortunes pécuniaires font des richeffes clandeftines qui ne connoiffent ni Roi ni patrie.

19°. Que l'Etat évite les emprunts qui forment des rentes financieres, & qui occafionnent un commerce, ou trafic de finance, par l'entremife des papiers commerçables, où l'efcompte augmente de plus en plus les fortunes pécuniaires ftériles, qui féparent la finance de l'agriculture, & qui la pri-

(a) Les travaux des marchandifes de main d'œuvre & d'induftrie pour l'ufage de la Nation, ne font qu'un objet difpendieux & non une fource de revenu. Ils ne peuvent procurer de profit net dans la vente à l'étranger, que dans les pays où la main d'œuvre eft à bon marché par le bas prix des denrées qui fervent à la fubfiftance des ouvriers; condition fort défavantageufe au produit des biens-fonds; auffi ne doit-elle pas exifter dans les Etats qui ont la liberté & la facilité d'un com-merce extérieur qui foutient le débit & le prix des denrées du crû, & qui heureufement détruit le petit produit net qu'on pourroit retirer d'un commerce extérieur de marchandifes de main d'œuvre, où le gain feroit établi fur la perte qui réfulteroit du bas prix des productions des biens-fonds. On ne confond pas ici le produit net ou le revenu pour la Nation avec le gain des commer-çans & entrepreneurs de manufactures; ce gain doit être mis au rang des frais par rapport à la Nation; il ne fuffiroit pas, par exemple, d'avoir de riches laboureurs, fi le territoire qu'ils cul-tiveroient, ne produifoit que pour eux. Il y a des Royaumes où la plûpart des manufactures ne peuvent fe foutenir que par des priviléges exclufifs, & en mettant la Nation à contribution par des prohibitions qui lui interdifent l'ufage d'autres marchandifes de main d'œuvre. Il n'en eft pas de même de l'agriculture & du commerce des productions des biens-fonds où la concurrence la plus active multiplie les richeffes des nations qui poffédent de grands territoires. Nous ne parlons pas ici du commerce de trafic qui eft le lot des petits Etats maritimes ; mais un grand Etat ne doit pas quitter la charrue pour devenir voiturier. On n'oubliera jamais qu'un miniftre du dernier fiécle ébloui du commerce des Hollandois & de l'éclat des manufactures de luxe, a jetté fa patrie dans un tel délire, que l'on ne parloit plus que commerce & argent, fans penfer au véritable emploi de l'argent, ni au véritable commerce du pays.

10. That the desertion of inhabitants who take their wealth out of the kingdom is avoided.

11. That no barriers at all are raised to external trade in raw produce; for as the market value is, so is the reproduction.

12. That the prices of produce and commodities in the kingdom are never made to fall; for then mutual foreign trade would become disadvantageous to the nation. *As the market value is, so is the revenue.*

13. That people do not believe that cheapness of produce is profitable to the lower classes; for a low price of produce causes a fall in their wages, reduces their well-being, makes less work or remunerative occupations available for them, and reduces the nation's revenue.

14. That the well-being of the lower orders is not reduced; for then they would not be able to contribute sufficiently to the consumption of the produce which can be consumed only within the country, and the reproduction and revenue of the nation would be reduced.

15. That the increase of livestock is encouraged; for it is livestock which provides the land with the manure which procures abundant crops.

16. That no encouragement at all is given to luxury in the way of ornamentation; for this is maintained only to the detriment of luxury in the way of subsistence, which sustains the market for raw produce, its proper price, and the reproduction of the nation's revenue.

17. That the Government's economic policy is concerned only with encouraging productive expenditure and external trade in raw produce, and that it refrains from interfering with sterile expenditure.[1]

18. That means to meet the extraordinary needs of the state are expected to be found only in the prosperity of the nation and not in the credit of financiers; for monetary fortunes are a clandestine form of wealth which knows neither king nor country.

19. That the state avoids contracting loans which create rentier incomes, and which bring about a trade or traffic in finance, through the medium of negotiable bills, the discount on which causes a greater and greater increase in sterile monetary fortunes, which

---

[1] The work involved in making manufactured and industrial commodities for the nation's use is simply something which costs money and not a source of revenue. It cannot yield any net profit through sale abroad, except in countries where manufacturing labour is cheap because of the low price of the produce which serves for the subsistence of the workers; a condition which is very disadvantageous so far as the product of landed property is concerned. Also, such a condition should be not found in states with a free and unobstructed external trade which maintains the sales and prices of raw produce, and which happily does away with the small net product which could be obtained from an external trade in manufactured commodities, the gain from which would be based on the loss which would result from the low prices of the products of landed property. Here the net product or revenue accruing to the nation is not confused with the gains of the merchants and manufacturing entrepreneurs; these gains, from the point of view of the nation, ought to be ranked as costs. It would not be sufficient, for example, to have rich husbandmen, if the territory which they cultivated were to produce for them alone. There are kingdoms where the greater part of the manufactures can be kept going only by means of exclusive privileges, and by laying the nation under contribution through prohibitions forbidding it to use other manufactured commodities. This is not the case with agriculture and trade in the products of landed property, where the most energetic competition results in the expansion of the wealth of nations with large territories. I am not speaking here of re-export trade, to which small maritime states are fated; but a large state should not abandon the plough in order to become a carrier. It will never be forgotten that a Minister of the last century, dazzled by the trade of the Dutch and the glitter of luxury manufactures, brought his country to such a state of frenzy that no one talked about anything but trade and money, without reflecting on the true employment of money or on a country's true trade.

vent des richeſſes néceſſaires pour l'amélioration des biens-fonds & pour la culture des terres.

20°. Qu'une Nation qui a un grand territoire à cultiver, & la facilité d'exercer un grand commerce de denrées du crû, n'étende pas trop l'emploi de l'argent & des hommes aux manufactures & au commerce de luxe, au préjudice des travaux & des dépenſes de l'agriculture ; car préférablement à tout, le Royaume doit être bien peuplé de riches laboureurs (a).

21°. Que chacun ſoit libre de cultiver dans ſon champ telles productions que ſon intérêt, ſes facultés, la nature du terrein lui ſuggerent, pour en tirer le plus grand produit qu'il lui ſoit poſſible ; car on ne doit point favoriſer le monopole dans la culture des biens-fonds, parce qu'il eſt préjudiciable au revenu général de la Nation ; le préjugé qui porte à favoriſer l'abondance des denrées de premier beſoin, préférablement à celle de moindre beſoin au préjudice de la valeur vénale des unes ou des autres, eſt inſpiré par des vues courtes qui ne s'étendent pas juſqu'aux effets du commerce extérieur réciproque qui pourvoit à tout, & qui décide du prix des denrées que chaque Nation peut cultiver avec le plus de profit. Ce ſont donc les revenus & l'impôt qui ſont de premier beſoin pour défendre les ſujets contre la diſette, & contre l'ennemi, & pour ſoutenir la gloire & la puiſſance du Monarque.

22°. Que le Gouvernement ſoit moins occupé des ſoins d'épargner, que des opérations néceſſaires pour la proſpérité du Royaume ; car de trop grandes dépenſes peuvent ceſſer d'être exceſſives par l'augmentation des richeſſes.

23°. Qu'on ſoit moins attentif à l'augmentation de la population qu'à l'accroiſſement des revenus ; car plus d'aiſances que procurent de grands revenus eſt préférable à plus de beſoins preſſans de ſubſiſtance qu'exige une population qui excede les revenus ; & il y a plus de reſſources pour les beſoins de l'Etat, quand le peuple eſt dans l'aiſance, & auſſi plus de moyens pour faire proſpérer l'agriculture (b).

Sans ces conditions, l'agriculture, qu'on ſuppoſe, dans le Tableau, produire comme en Angleterre cent pour cent, ſeroit une fiction : Mais les principes n'en ſont pas certains.

(a) On ne doit s'attacher qu'aux manufactures de marchandiſes de main d'œuvre dont on a les matieres premieres, & qu'on peut fabriquer avec moins de dépenſe que dans les autres pays : Et il faut acheter de l'étranger les marchandiſes de main d'œuvre, qu'il peut vendre à meilleur marché qu'elles ne coûteroient à la nation, ſi elle les faiſoit fabriquer chez elle. Par ces achats, on provoque le commerce réciproque : car ſi on vouloit ne rien acheter, & vendre de tout, on éteindroit le commerce extérieur, & les avantages de l'exportation des denrées du crû.

(b) L'idée dominante de la guerre dans les Nations, fait penſer que la force des Etats conſiſte dans une grande population ; or la partie militaire d'une Nation ne peut ſubſiſter que par la partie contribuable : ſuppoſeroit-on que les grandes richeſſes d'un Etat s'obtiennent par l'abondance d'hommes ; mais les hommes ne peuvent obtenir & perpétuer les richeſſes que par les richeſſes, & qu'autant qu'il y a une proportion convenable entre les hommes & les richeſſes. Une Nation croit toujours qu'elle n'a pas aſſez d'hommes, & on ne s'apperçoit pas qu'il n'y a pas aſſez de ſalaire pour ſoutenir une plus grande population, & que les hommes n'abondent dans un pays, qu'autant qu'ils y trouvent des gains aſſurés pour y ſubſiſter.

separate finance from agriculture, and which deprive the latter of the wealth necessary for the improvement of landed property and the cultivation of the land.

20. That a nation which has a large territory to cultivate, and the means of carrying on a large trade in raw produce, does not extend too far the employment of money and men in manufacturing and trading in luxury goods, to the detriment of the work and expenditure involved in agriculture; for more than anything else the kingdom ought to be well furnished with wealthy husbandmen.[1]

21. That each person is free to cultivate in his fields such products as his interests, his means, and the nature of the land suggest to him, in order that he may extract from them the greatest possible product; for monopoly in the cultivation of landed property should never be encouraged, because it is detrimental to the general revenue of the nation. The prejudice which leads to the encouragement of an abundance of produce of primary necessity, in preference to that of less necessary produce, to the detriment of the market value of one or the other, is inspired by short-sighted views which do not extend as far as the effects of mutual external trade, which makes provision for everything and determines the price of the produce which each nation can cultivate with the most profit. Thus it is revenue and taxes which are of primary necessity in order to defend subjects against scarcity and against the enemy, and to maintain the glory and power of the monarch.

22. That the Government troubles itself less with economising than with the operations necessary for the prosperity of the kingdom; for expenditure which is too high may cease to be excessive by virtue of the increase of wealth.

23. That less attention is paid to increasing the population than to increasing the revenue; for the greater well-being which a high revenue brings about is preferable to the greater pressure of subsistence needs which a population in excess of the revenue entails; and when the people are in a state of well-being there are more resources to meet the needs of the state, and more means to make agriculture prosper.[2]

Without these conditions, an agriculture producing 100 per cent, as we have assumed it to do in the *Tableau* and as it does in England, would be fictitious; but the principles displayed in the *Tableau* would be no less certain.

[1]A nation ought to devote itself only to those manufactured commodities for which it possesses the raw materials and which it can make at less expense than in other countries; and it should purchase from abroad such manufactured commodities as can be bought at a price lower than the cost which would be involved if the nation made them itself. Through these purchases mutual trade is stimulated; for if nations tried to buy nothing and sell everything, external trade and the advantages of the export of raw produce would be done away with.

[2] The predominant idea which nations have about war makes it thought that the strength of states consists in a large population; but the military part of a nation can subsist only through the tax-paying part. One would imagine that the great wealth of a state is obtained through an abundance of men; but men can obtain and perpetuate wealth only by means of wealth, and to the extent that there is a proper proportion between men and wealth. Nations always believe that they do not have enough men, and it is not understood that there are insufficient wages to support a greater population, and that men are plentiful in a country only to the extent that they find assured gains there to enable them to subsist.